Self-Agency in Psychotherapy

The Norton Series on Interpersonal Neurobiology
Allan N. Schore, PhD, Series Editor
Daniel J. Siegel, MD, Founding Editor

The field of mental health is in a tremendously exciting period of growth and conceptual reorganization. Independent findings from a variety of scientific endeavors are converging in an interdisciplinary view of the mind and mental well-being. An interpersonal neurobiology of human development enables us to understand that the structure and function of the mind and brain are shaped by experiences, especially those involving emotional relationships.

The Norton Series on Interpersonal Neurobiology will provide cutting-edge, multidisciplinary views that further our understanding of the complex neurobiology of the human mind. By drawing on a wide range of traditionally independent fields of research—such as neurobiology, genetics, memory, attachment, complex systems, anthropology, and evolutionary psychology—these texts will offer mental health professionals a review and synthesis of scientific findings often inaccessible to clinicians. These books aim to advance our understanding of human experience by finding the unity of knowledge, or consilience, that emerges with the translation of findings from numerous domains of study into a common language and conceptual framework. The series will integrate the best of modern science with the healing art of psychotherapy.

A Norton Professional Book

Self-Agency in Psychotherapy

Attachment, Autonomy, and Intimacy

Jean Knox,
PhD, MBBS, MRC Psych.

W. W. Norton & Company
New York • London

Portions of Chapters 3 and 4 reprinted from: Knox, J. (2009). Mirror neurons and embodied simulation in the development of self-agency. *Journal of Analytical Psychology* 54, 3: 307–324. Reprinted by permission of Wiley-Blackwell.

A modified version of this paper appears as Chapter 5: Knox, J. (2009). When words do not mean what they say: Self-agency and the coercive use of language. *Journal of Analytical Psychology* 54, 1: 25-41. Reprinted by permission of Wiley-Blackwell.

A modified version of this paper appears as Chapter 6: Knox, J. (2007). The fear of love: The denial of self in relationship. *Journal of Analytical Psychology* 52, 5: 543–564.

A modified version of this paper appears as Chapter 8: Knox, J. (2009). The Analytic Relationship: Integrating Jungian, attachment theory and developmental perspectives. *British Journal of Psychotherapy* 25, 1: 5–23. Reprinted by permission of Wiley-Blackwell.

Case material described in Chapter 8: Courtesy of Warren Colman.

Figure 2.1 reprinted from Petkova & Ehrsson, 2008.

Figures 3.1 (Figure AB-20 Diecephalon) and 3.2 (Figure AB-7 Forebrain/Midbrain/Hindbrain) courtesy of HOPES: Huntington's Outreach Project for Education at Stanford (http://hopes.stanford.edu).

Figure 4.1 reproduced with permission from *The Symbolic Species: The Co-evolution of Language and the Human Brain*, by Terrence Deacon, 1997, New York: Norton. Courtesy of Terrence Deacon.

For information about permission to reproduce selections from this book, write to Permissions, W. W. Norton & Company, Inc., 500 Fifth Avenue, New York, NY 10110

For information about special discounts for bulk purchases, please contact W. W. Norton Special Sales at specialsales@wwnorton.com or 800-233-4830

Manufacturing by Quad Graphics, Fairfield
Digital production: Joe Lops
Production manager: Leeann Graham

Library of Congress Cataloging-in-Publication Data

Knox, Jean, 1948–
  Self-agency in psychotherapy : attachment, autonomy, and intimacy / Jean Knox.
    p. cm.
  Includes bibliographical references and index.
  ISBN 978-0-393-70559-1 (hbk.)
  1. Self. 2. Attachment behavior. 3. Autonomy (Psychology)
  4. Intimacy (Psychology) 5. Psychotherapy. I. Title.
  BF697.K635 2011
  155.2—dc22

                                                             2010031963

ISBN: 978-0-393-70559-1

W. W. Norton & Company, Inc., 500 Fifth Avenue, New York, N.Y. 10110
www.wwnorton.com
W. W. Norton & Company Ltd., Castle House, 75/76 Wells Street, London W1T 3QT

1 2 3 4 5 6 7 8 9 0

Contents

PART I
The Relational, Developmental, and Neurobiological Foundations of Self-Agency

PART II
Clinical Aspects of Self-Agency

Acknowledgments

I AM GRATEFUL TO A NUMBER OF PEOPLE who have helped me at crucial stages in writing this book. The invitation from Allan Schore and Deborah Malmud to write a book on self-agency enabled me to see that it would fill a significant gap in the psychotherapy literature—that it is a book whose time has come. My many discussions with colleagues who are researching in related fields have been invaluable in enabling me to widen the scope of my study and to include the relevant articles from other disciplines. I would particularly like to thank James Astor, Joe Cambray, Linda Carter, Warren Colman, Sue Gerhardt, George Hogenson, Georgia Lepper, John Merchant, and Jo Tucker, who have all contributed greatly to my understanding of the theoretical issues and their clinical applications that I explore in this book. Pramila Bennett has been a very great help in preparing the book for publication. All of these have also offered constant friendship and support, for which I am always grateful. My thanks to Vani Kannan and the Norton team.

I am also grateful to Beatrice Beebe, Peter Fonagy, Raya Jones, Jaak Panksepp, Bruce Reis, Oliver Turnbull, and Vittorio Gallese for their helpful comments on some of the ideas explored in this book or on draft chapters, or for helping me to locate relevant articles. I would also like to thank Nadia Fina, Brett Kahr, Jane Ryan, Steven Flower, Massimo Giannoni, Andrew Samuels, and Caterina Vezzoli for offering me opportunities to present my ideas to clinical colleagues in seminars and conferences, occasions that provide useful feedback and opportunities to revise and refine my ideas. I am also grateful to my patients who have given their permission for the case illustrations in the book.

I am also very grateful to Helen Campbell-Hart for permission to use her print *Cityscape* for the front cover and to Susan Moxley for her help in preparing it for publication. And my thanks to John, Olivia, and Gareth for their encouragement and support.

Earlier versions of Chapter 5, "When Words Do Not Mean What They Say: Self-Agency and the Coercive Use of Language" and Chapter 6, "The Fear of Love: The Loss of Agency in Relationship" were published in the *Journal of Analytical Psychology*. An earlier version of Chapter 8, "The Analytic Relationship: Integrating Jungian, Attachment Theory, and Developmental Perspectives," was published in the *British Journal of Psychotherapy*. I am grateful to Wiley-Blackwell for permission to use these articles.

Self-Agency in Psychotherapy

Introduction:
What Does Self-Agency Mean?

THE SELF IS APPARENTLY A SIMPLE CONCEPT. Each of us has a sense of self, encompassing all the thoughts, beliefs, desires, expectations, and fantasies that reflect our own sense of a unique identity. This was the dominant Enlightenment view of "a stable, coherent, knowable self, a self that is conscious, rational, and autonomous" (Reis, 2005, p. 86). But this view began to crumble on two fronts. One, of course, was Freud's "great revelation that there were more thoughts on an individual's mind than he or she was aware of, that the ego is not master in its own house" (p. 86).

But although he has not entered public folklore in the same way, William James (1890/1983), in his *Principles of Psychology*, also began to disassemble this "folk psychology" sense of a unified identity. He made a distinction between two aspects of self, the self as subject, or the "I," and the self as object, or the "Me." James eventually concluded that there is no subject of experiences, no metaphysical I, apart from the physical being who does the thinking. Rather, he concluded that "the passing thought . . . is itself the thinker" (p. 401). The distinction James drew between the I and the Me contributes to the distinction I frequently make in this book between the sense of self (me-ness) and the sense of self-agency (I-ness), but with an important difference, namely that the concept of self-agency can be thought of as a way of reframing the Jamesian I. In this view, the body's physical experience of agency forms the core and foundation for the emotional and psychological experience of agency (I-ness), an example of Mark Johnson's (1987) view that our bodily experience directly creates symbolic meaning and conceptual thought.

An important contribution to this debate has been made by Shaun

Gallagher, who has reframed this as the distinction between the sense of agency, which he defines as the sense that the subject is the one who is causing or generating an action, "for example, the sense that I am the one who is causing something to move, or that I am the one who is generating a certain thought in my stream of consciousness" (2000, p. 14), and the sense of ownership, defined as the sense that I am the one who is undergoing an experience, "for example, the sense that my body is moving regardless of whether the movement is voluntary or involuntary" (p. 14). In the light of subsequent research, Gallagher has since suggested

> that the sense of agency was likely based on efferent signals involved in movement preparation (something present in voluntary action), while the sense of ownership was associated with proprioceptive and sensory feedback (which we have in both the case of involuntary movement and voluntary movement). (2006)

He suggests that the sense of ownership is complex and depends on multisensory comparisons between efferent (outgoing) and afferent (incoming) signals. The more integrated these signals, the clearer the sense of ownership for bodily movement.

The most recent development in this debate on what, exactly, constitutes the core or minimal sense of self has been made by Gallese and Sinigaglia, whose research on mirror neurons is discussed in Chapter 3. But the point of their latest article is that self-attribution of agency and self-ownership do not actually constitute the minimal notion of self; they argue that we have a sense of body that precedes the sense of agency and sense of ownership and on which these depend. This basic "body schema" is not of action itself, but of the "power for action"— a prereflective consciousness of the body as the intentional "source of potential actions that are owned by the body even before any explicit feeling of agency" (Gallese & Sinigaglia, 2010, p. 750).

Whatever the conceptual refinements of the I and the Me, or agency and ownership, a key question is how they develop. A theme that increasingly recurs in the study of the self in a wide range of disciplines is that the development of a sense of self is shaped throughout our lives by the interpersonal and social contexts in which we find ourselves. This relational and constructionist approach to the self is at the heart of studies of interactions between mothers and infants in developmental psychology, of interpersonal neurobiology and mirror neuron research, of relational and attachment models of psychoanalysis and psychotherapy, and of social constructionism and dialogism in the social sciences. Let me give just a few key examples from some of these disciplines.

First, attachment theory views the sense of self as essentially relational. Internal working models are an aspect of implicit memory, storing information in the form of general patterns of experience and expectation that influence us outside our conscious awareness. In other words, the unconscious sense of self is formed by internalization of a relational dynamic between self and other, from the first moments of life. In *A Secure Base*, John Bowlby spelled this out very clearly:

> The working models a child builds of his mother and her ways of communicating and behaving towards him, and a comparable model of his father, together with the complementary models of himself in interaction with each, are being built by a child during the first few years of his life, and, it is postulated, soon become established as influential cognitive structures. . . . [T]hese models of a parent and self in interaction tend to persist, and are so taken for granted that they come to operate at an unconscious level. (1988, pp. 129–130)

Second, interpersonal neurobiology and developmental studies have subsequently clarified the interpersonal and neurobiological mechanisms that underpin the formation of internal working models and the self. Allan Schore (2003b, p. 25) described a wealth of neuroscience research that shows that the infant's earliest attachment experiences specifically influence the experience-dependent maturation of early developing regulatory systems of the right brain, especially the limbic system, which is involved in the processing of emotion. It is this right-brain to right-brain interactive regulation that underpins the infant's developing capacity for self-regulation and affect regulation:

> Studies in neuroscience now report that this early maturing right hemisphere is centrally involved in "maintaining a coherent, continuous and unified sense of self" (Devinsky, 2000), and that a right frontal lobe process, one that connects "the individual to emotionally salient experiences and memories underlying self-schemas, is the glue holding together a sense of self" (Miller et al., 2001). (Schore & Schore, 2008, p. 12)

Another line of investigation has been that of Jaak Panksepp, who draws on a wealth of neurobiological research to support a strongly epigenetic approach to the development of higher mental processes. He has powerfully and convincingly argued that the evolutionary psychologists make a fundamental error when they suggest that evolution has created genetically determined specific socioemotional and cognitive modules within the human neocortex (Panksepp & Panksepp, 2000). The learning processes of the human neocortex are highly dependent on our cultural, social, and interpersonal experiences, which play a key part in the development of what Panksepp described as the "idiographic self."

A new line of enquiry in neurobiology has been emerging over the past decade—mirror neuron research—and I shall also examine the contribution that this research makes to our understanding of the relational basis for the development of self-agency. Much of this work centers on the automatic firing of the same neuronal networks in one person's brain when observing the actions of another person, which also fire when performing the action, a relational interaction at the most fundamental biological level (Rizzolatti & Sinigaglia, 2008).

Third, relational psychodynamic models include a range of schools, object relations, self-psychology, interpersonal, and relational. Greenberg and Mitchell (1983) and Perlow (1995) have detailed the complex areas of similarity and difference between these approaches, but central to them all is the view that attachments (or to use the psychoanalytic term, object relations) are primary, not "derivates of drive discharge" (Taub, 2009, p. 507). For example, this was central to the view of Henry Stack Sullivan, one of the founders of a relational model:

> The infant in Sullivan's system has no psychological existence prior to his or her embeddedness in interactions with the caretakers and discovers him- or herself as well as the "object" through a complex developmental process. (Greenberg & Mitchell, 1983, p. 95)

In the past 20 years, this relational and constructivist view of the self has been the focus of a remarkable combination of groundbreaking observational research on mothers and infants with new theoretical and clinical approaches to psychoanalytic practice. The work of Beatrice Beebe and Frank Lachmann (2002), the Boston Change Process Study Group (BCPSG, 2007), Fonagy, Gergely, Jurist, and Target (2002), Daniel

Stern (1985), Allan Schore (1994, 2003b), Ed Tronick (2007), and others has provided us with a robust, evidence-based model of the central role that the internalization of real interpersonal experience plays in the development of the sense of self and self-agency. This work is discussed in more detail in Chapter 2, and its implications for the clinical practice of psychotherapy are discussed in Part II.

Fourth, the self has been the focus of study not only in the clinical arena but also in the social sciences. The relational models of psychotherapy are linked to social constructionism, although Taub (2009) has pointed out that there are significant areas of divergence between them, partly because social constructionism itself is not a unitary discipline. Raya Jones has highlighted two main strands, one based mainly on the work of Rom Harré, who regarded the dynamics of speech as the foundation for thought and self-concepts. Jones (2003, p. 362) wrote: "The theory posits the self as a discursive production: 'selves emerge from complex bodies of knowledge that are organized like oral stories' (van Langenhove & Harré, 1993, p. 94)." In other words, selves are constructed solely in discourse. The other strand derives from the work of Gergen, who focused on

> the intersubjective construction of meaning, both at the level of society (especially the construction of knowledge in psychology) and at the level of the individual, namely how one's actions and emotions become meaningful to oneself and others. . . . Gergen's thesis views the self as emerging top-down, from the social relationship "surrounding" the individual's behaviour. (Jones, 2003, p. 360)

In contrast, the concept of construction is used rather differently in constructivist psychology, which assumes an intrapersonal mental space within which understandings of oneself are achieved. Dialogism is one development of this constructivist model of the self. Hermans and his colleagues (Hermans & Kempen, 1993; Hermans, Rijks, & Kempen, 1993) suggested that the self is a "dialogical self," a notion that has its roots in James's distinction between the I and Me, but also in Bakhtin's (1973) theory of a multiplicity of voices. Hermans claimed that each "me" has a speaking voice "to represent its point-of-view vis-à-vis other characters and their voices in the polyphonic or dialogical self." Baressi (2002) wrote:

This idea, which has its basis in Bakhtin's (1973) theory of Dostoevsky's poetics, presupposes that the self is constituted in some fashion out of a multitude of voices, each with its own quasi-independent perspective, and that these voices are in a dialogical relationship with each other. In elaborating what they mean by a "voice" and its implications for the dialogical self the authors state: "In order to become dialogical, personal meanings (e.g., an idea, a thought about something, a judgment) must be embodied. Once embodied, there is a 'voice' which creates utterances that can be meaningfully related to the utterances of another voice. It is only when an idea or thought is endowed with a voice and expressed as emanating from a personal position in relation to others that dialogical relations emerge." (2002, pp. 212–213)

In this dialogical view the self is envisaged

as a constellation of dialogically structured positions, each with their own world view and voice in relations of intersubjective exchange and dominance. The "I" moves between positions in an imaginal landscape, depending on time, place and situation, resulting in a multi-voiced self. (Georgaca, 2001, p. 224)

Shweder has taken an interactionist position on the development of the human psyche and self to the logical widest conclusion:

Cultural psychology is the study of the way cultural traditions and social practices regulate, transform, and permute the human psyche, resulting less in psychic unity for humankind than in ethnic divergences in mind, self, and emotion. Cultural psychology is the study of the ways subject and object, self and other, psyche and culture, person and context, figure and ground, practitioner and practice live together, require each other, and dynamically, dialectically and jointly make up each other. (1990, p. 1)

Self-Agency: An Experience Grounded in Intersubjectivity

Allan Schore emphasized the fact that no one discipline is sufficiently comprehensive to encompass the complexity of the human mind and brain:

> Rather, an integration of related fields is essential to the creation of a heuristic model of both developmental structures and functions that can accommodate and interpret the data of various biological and psychological disciplines and can freely shift back and forth between their different levels of analysis. (2009, p. 3)

It is a combination of relational, emergent, constructivist, and sometimes constructionist perspectives on the self that forms the framework for the exploration of self-agency in this book. Whatever their differing emphases, the disciplines I have outlined above converge in the view that new kinds of relational experience, beginning with the infant's earliest experience of key attachment figures, contribute to the construction of our sense of self. Families, social peer groups, sexual partners, parenting, working colleagues, and the wider culture in which we and our personal relationships are embedded alter and widen our sense of self-with-other, contributing to a sense of identity that can feel reasonably stable in all these different contexts. Once a relational model of the development of the self has been fully recognized, the importance of a person's experience of agency becomes more obvious.

Self-agency means the experience that we can influence our physical and relational environment, that our own actions and intentions have an effect on and produce a response from those around us, and it is this experience of action and consequence that lies at the heart of definitions of agency across disciplines. Anthropologist and linguist Gary Palmer defined agency:

> Agency is the capacity of an intentional being or social group to make choices, to perform actions that have intended consequences, to effect results, or to control situations. (2007, p. 1048)

This definition has much in common with that of a social cognitivist, Bandura, who suggested that agency is an essential aspect of our humanity: "The capacity to exercise control over the nature and quality of one's life is the essence of humanness" (2001, p. 1). He also defined agency as intentional, action-based, and related to the consequences of one's actions:

> To be an agent is to intentionally make things happen by one's actions. Agency embodies the endowments, belief systems,

self-regulatory capabilities and distributed structures and functions through which personal influence is exercised, rather than
residing as a discrete entity in a particular place. (p. 2)

Bandura went on to suggest that human agency is about psychological
action and reaction, not just physical:

Human agency is characterized by a number of core features
that operate through phenomenal and functional consciousness.
These include the temporal extension of agency through intentionality and forethought, self-regulation by self-reactive influence, and self-reflectiveness about one's capabilities, quality of
functioning, and the meaning and purpose of one's life pursuits.
Personal agency operates within a broad network of sociostruc-
tural influences. In these agentic transactions, people are produc-
ers as well as products of social systems. (p. 1)

Shaun Gallagher, professor of philosophy and cognitive sciences,
emphasized that self-agency depends on the intention that precedes
action, the sense that one is the initiator or source of the action:

Experimental research on normal subjects suggests that the sense
of agency for action is based on that which precedes action and
translates intention into action. In addition, research that correlates initial awareness of action with scalp recordings of the lateralized readiness potential in motor cortex, and with transcranial
magnetic stimulation of the supplementary motor area, strongly
indicates that one's initial awareness of a spontaneous voluntary
action is tied to the anticipatory or pre-movement motor commands relating to relevant effectors. (2000, p. 16)

But in relationships, agency is not just physical but social, as Bandura
suggested, and so we experience it through the impact or influence we
have on other human beings. Of course, a crucial issue is how we determine that a response relates to our own intention and action, and this
may mean very different things at different points in a person's development. For example, Tronick (2007, p. 11) pointed out that the dominant
view has been that the mother-infant interaction is ideally highly synchronized and attuned. But his own empirical studies did not support

this model, and he suggested that it romanticizes the mother-infant relationship. What his research showed, also found in the studies by Beatrice Beebe and colleagues (Beebe et al., 2010; Jaffe, Beebe, Feldstein, Crown, & Jasnow, 2001) and the Boston Change Process Study Group (2002), was that there is a frequent lack of coordination in all infant-adult relationships and that a crucial part of their interactions lies in re-achieving a matching from a mismatching state, a mutually regulated reparatory process. It is the infant's capacity to repair disruption that allows him or her to experience a sense of agency by playing a part in cocreating a more harmonious interaction.

So self-agency is always at the heart of psychological growth and development, and it follows a developmental trajectory that I examine in detail in Chapters 1 to 4, from the realm of bodily action and reaction in the first few months of life, through social, teleological, and intentional levels of agency to the mature expression of agency in language. I offer a brief summary of these stages here:

Self as Agent

1. Physical agency, 0–6 months: Awareness that actions produce changes in the physical environment (perfect contingency).
2. Social agency, 3–9 months: Actions produce behavioral and emotional mirroring (imperfectly contingent) responses in other people—action at a distance.
3. Teleological agency, 9–24 months: Sense of purpose—actions seen as goal directed. Capacity to choose action to bring about desired outcome. Intention not yet recognized as separate from action.
4. Intentional agency, 2 years: Recognition of intentions as distinct from action. Actions are seen as caused by prior intentions and desires. Actions can change mental states.
5. Representational agency, 3–4 years: Actions seen as caused by intentions, which are also recognized as mental processes. Mind is represented to itself, so intentions are not just means to an end but mental states in themselves.
6. Autobiographical self: Organization of memories as personally experienced—linked to self-representations and awareness of personal history. (Fonagy et al., 2002, pp. 204–207)

So what are the specific mechanisms that help infants along the developmental trajectory toward a mature representational level of a sense of self and of self-agency? The research evidence comes from a number of different disciplines that converge on the progression of self-agency from the infant's initial relational experience in bodily action and reaction, to psychic maturity, where mind and emotion can be related to, processed, reflected on, and contained internally, without the need to express them in direct bodily action. This evidence is described in Chapters 2–4.

The Importance of Turn-Taking in the Development of Self-Agency

Bodily action is the foundation on which all subsequent human interaction and communication (including conversation) is constructed. This process starts from birth, as the newborn infant begins to imitate the actions of others, as Meltzoff and Gopnik (1993) have shown. Specifically, the interactional process that has been repeatedly demonstrated to play a crucial role in human communication at all levels is turn-taking. Turn-taking is a pattern of action and reaction exchanges between people, whether seen in the behavioral patterns of the exchanges between mother and baby (Beebe et al., 2010; Cohn & Tronick, 1988; Jaffe et al., 2001; Tronick, 2007) or in the complex verbal exchanges of an analytic therapy session (Lepper, 2009a). In any interaction, one person's action produces a turn-taking response in the other, and so turn-taking plays a fundamental role in the development of self-agency, which has been defined as finding oneself through action and reaction in relationship. This turn-taking behavior starts from the earliest moments of life, manifesting itself in a burst-pause-burst pattern in feeding that is unique to human infants (Kaye, 1982). Horst Hendriks-Jansen regarded turn-taking as

> an emergent phenomenon that itself serves as the scaffolding or dynamic context for more advanced patterns of behavior. It may be thought of as the cradle of meaning. . . . Turn-taking is initiated by burst-pause-burst in sucking, but it depends for its emergence on the mother's folk-psychological stance. (1996, p. 277, emphasis added)

The work of Beatrice Beebe and colleagues has shown that patterns of turn-taking between mothers and their 4-month-old infants can predict specific forms of attachment that those infants demonstrate at 1 year and the forms of disturbance of turn-taking are linked to specific forms of insecure attachment at 1 year (Beebe et al., 2010; Jaffe et al., 2001).

So the central role that this turn-taking plays in the infant's development of self-agency also means that this developmental process is highly vulnerable to the influence of the social and relational environment that the child experiences. Beatrice Beebe described the catastrophic effects that serious maternal misattunement can have on the psychological and emotional development of her baby, including the development of self-agency. It is the affect regulation and reflective function of the parent that form the foundations and scaffolding for a solid sense of identity and agency. The absence of this parental attunement is devastating, leading to lifelong states of mind in which people feel that they do not really exist, that they have a kind of psychic black hole at their very core, and to endless painful attempts to achieve a sense of reality and emotional depth by imitating others who seem to have such experiences (Deutsch, 1942; Ledermann, 1991; Seligman, 1982; Solomon, 2004). In this state, people do not experience themselves as having any sense of agency and in later sections of this book I describe some of the clinical consequences of this lack of a sense of self and of self-agency.

The Effect of Adverse Experience on Self-Agency

The continuing dependence of the human psyche on our interpersonal, social, and cultural context makes a stable sense of self-agency more fragile than we often realize—it can easily be distorted and damaged by changes in interpersonal and social circumstances, particularly by adversity, even for adults who have had secure childhood experiences and who are confident of their sense of agency in the world. Those who suddenly lose their jobs or homes or whose families break up become highly vulnerable to a loss of identity if they no longer feel that they have an emotional impact on their loved ones or have their former part to play in their community. Durkheim (1897/1951) described this state of alienation as "anomie" and as one of the causes of suicide. Al Alvarez explained:

> Anomic suicide . . . is the result of a change in a man's social position so sudden that he is unable to cope with his new situation. Great, unexpected wealth or great, unexpected poverty . . .

a searing divorce or even a death in the family can thrust a man
into a world where his old habits are no longer adequate, his old
needs no longer satisfied. . . . He kills himself because, for better
or worse, his accustomed world has been destroyed and he is lost.
(1971, p. 82)

Tragic and traumatic events can cruelly expose us as powerless pawns
in an indifferent world and shatter our comfortable illusions that we
are agents in control of our own lives. Depression, alcoholism, self-
harm, and suicide are the evil spirits that often accompany the loss of
self-agency that is the consequence of this kind of economic and social
upheaval, even more so when there has been severe trauma or abuse.
Indeed, one of the most distressing aspects of many forms of psychological illness is the experience of not being oneself, that one's mind and
emotions have become to varying degrees alien and frightening, an experience of alienation that is beautifully captured in Joanne Greenberg's
(1964) autobiographical novel *I Never Promised You a Rose Garden.*

This powerful account of the author's own experience of dissociated
identities is in accord with the research of van der Hart, Nijenhuis, and
Steele (2006), who suggested that a conscious sense of self-agency can be
fragmented as part of structural dissociations in the personality, so that
different subpersonalities may each have a sense of agency. At its most
extreme, in dissociative identity disorder, alternative and dissociated
personalities temporarily take over the person's identity and self-agency,
with the core personality often having no recollection of what an alternative personality said or did when in control (Mollon, 1999; Sinason,
2002; van der Hart et al., 2006). Even more ordinary experiences may
activate differing experiences of self-agency, depending on the relational
context. There are times when even the most securely attached people
can find themselves catapulted back into a childhood state of self-doubt
and insecurity, triggered by some current event that has activated an
internal working model in which a sense of powerlessness and a lack of
self-agency predominate. Meares (1998) has described this as a "traumatic memory system."

In addition, if the child has to internalize aspects of the parent's
attitude and behavior that bear no relation to the child's own experience, these cannot then be integrated and come to feel like an alien self
(Fonagy et al., 2002). As Fraiberg, Adelson, and Shapiro (1975) so evocatively wrote: "in every nursery there are ghosts. These are the visitors

from the unremembered past of the parents, the uninvited guests at the christening." A less poetic term to describe the mechanism by which the parental ghosts are incorporated into the infant's unconscious is transgenerational transmission. This projection of unconscious parental psychic contents into the child's unconscious may give rise to massive defenses against what is experienced as an alien intrusion, if the parental unconscious is very threatening. Alicia Lieberman has explored the ways in which the child may become "the carrier of the parents' unconscious fears, impulses and other repressed or disowned parts of themselves" and the fact that "these negative attributions become an integral part of the child's sense of self" (1999, p. 737). Fonagy et al. (2002) also suggested that projective identification is the main defense against an intolerable experience of hostile caregiving. The alien unassimilated parts can only be dealt with by forcing them into others.

Under these circumstances, the child's own development of agency becomes profoundly inhibited. In Chapter 6, "The Fear of Love," I describe the devastating impact it has on a child, when the parent cannot tolerate the child's growing autonomy and agency and seeks to destroy it by dominating, undermining, or more subtly disapproving of the child's independent exploration of the world. Instead of encouraging the child's agency, this kind of parent needs to impose his or her own, needing the child to remain a passive object whose only role is to reflect the parent's identity.

A Relational Model of Self-Agency and of the Unconscious

A relational and constructivist model of the self has implications for the concept of the unconscious that are highly relevant for our understanding of self-agency. I will briefly highlight these.

1. There is no clear-cut distinction between conscious and unconscious states of mind. There are many unconscious senses of self, revealed through a wealth of evidence from attachment, developmental, and neuroscientific research. We can often be conscious of an immediate state of mind in the here and now, but we may be entirely unable to reflect on that experience or make any meaningful sense of it. For example, the flashbacks suffered in PTSD are encoded as sensory fragments rather than as verbally accessible memories and are triggered without warning by sights, sounds,

or smells, often without the sufferer having any idea when or why they will occur (Brewin, Dalgleish, & Joseph, 1996; van der Kolk & Fisler (1995). A patient with a form of brain damage known as split-brain syndrome confabulates, that is to say, produces "a plausible story to square the behavior of his left and right hemispheres and, when attention is drawn to the inconsistencies in his story, instantly produces yet another plausible story" (Hendriks-Jansen, 1996, p. 122). An attachment theory or relational view of the unconscious is very different from Freud's model of a clear repression barrier between the conscious and unconscious mind.

2. The unconscious is not unified as Freud suggested but consists of multiple implicit self-with-other schemas. In attachment theory, the unconscious and the self are not unitary but are divided into clusters of self-with-other experiences. One of the most important implications of this model for the sense of self is that we can have as many different experiences of self as we have significant relationships. There is evidence that the internal working models that develop in the context of the relationship with one parent can be different from those developed with the other parent; for example, the degree of security or the type of insecure pattern can be markedly different with each parent (Steele, Steele, & Fonagy, 1996). As we grow and relate to other significant people such as teachers, grandparents, or siblings, we have an increasing range of self-other experience and an increasingly complex unconscious sense of self as we internalize more relational patterns of self-with-other. This attachment theory perspective is echoed in the narrative and dialogical models of the self, where there is no unifying center of consciousness or unconsciousness, but multiple selves, each of which may take center stage depending on the context.

For some people, whose experiences fluctuate wildly and include profound or persistent trauma, there is often no consistent or coherent pattern of internal working models and therefore no single consistent sense of self-agency (Bretherton, 1995; Fonagy et al., 2002, p. 239; Slade, 1999, p. 802); each internalized self-other relationship carries a different sense of agency. Indeed in dissociative identity disorder, self-agency may be disconnected from the core self and attributed to one or more alternative dissociated personalities, as Joanne Greenberg (1964) so dramatically described.

3. There are no innate (in the sense of inherited) unconscious

contents. The third consequence of a relational and context-dependent view of the self is the challenge this model poses to a key feature of psychoanalytic theory, that predetermined, innate unconscious contents in the human unconscious, directly derived from instinctual drives, determine the course of each person's mental and emotional development regardless of their interpersonal, social, and cultural environment. I have argued elsewhere (Knox, 2003) and in Chapter 1 of this book that the innatist theories of psychoanalysis and analytical psychology need radical revision in the light of these new relational, developmental, and emergent models of the human psyche; for example, the Jungian concept of archetypes can be reframed, not as innate modules but as early developmental achievements, equating to embodied image schemas.

These three challenges to classical psychoanalysis are brought together in attachment theory, which offers a much-needed alternative model of unconscious processes and of the self to those of psychoanalysis, with the concept of internal working models, unconscious schemas of self-other relationships in which cognition and emotion are inextricably intertwined (Bowlby, 1988). It is this model, linked with contemporary developmental and neurobiological research on intersubjectivity, that provides the framework for the exploration of self-agency in this book.

Clinical Relevance of Self-Agency

So how is this kind of detailed research evidence about the vital role of affect regulation and contingency in early infancy relevant to our clinical work with adult patients? How does the development of self-agency relate to our clinical work as psychotherapists and analysts? I discuss this in more detail in later chapters, in which I explore the ways in which specific aspects of self-agency come alive in the consulting room. But here I offer some pointers to that later discussion.

A regression to earlier and more action-based levels of functioning of the sense of self often lies at the heart of a range of clinical phenomena, such as the malignant regression identified by Balint (1968) and psychotic states in which symbolic capacity is lost. For example, Hannah Segal's famous description of a patient who could not play his violin because he regarded it as masturbation in public would seem to arise from a belief that the pleasure he derived from playing was not symbolically sexual but was an actual sexual action, performed in public (Segal, 1986, p. 49). This demonstrates the operation of the sense of self-agency at the physical and teleological levels; in the teleological mode, because sexual actions bring pleasure, if playing the violin is pleasurable it must derive from an actual sexual act. In Chapter 5, I look at the ways in which even language can become a tool for more primitive levels of self-agency, so that words become actions to coerce and control the responses of the other rather than the means to an open dialogue between two minds; this is a coercive level of communication that is powerfully portrayed in Harold Pinter's plays.

But the developmental trajectory of self-agency is not all one way. The achievement of later stages does not eliminate earlier ones. Sandler and Joffe (1967) suggested that regression can be understood as the reemployment of previous structures that have been inhibited in the course of development. The activation of more primitive, action-based developmental stages of self-agency is an example of this kind of regression, which can become the basis for a powerful defensive system, in which constant shifting from one dissociated state of self-agency to another prevents any integration or any psychic development. This is part of the clinical picture in borderline personality disorder (BPD). Fonagy and Luyten suggested that BPD patients' propensity for vicious interpersonal cycles and their high levels of affect dysregulation and impulsivity reflect impairments in different facets of mentalization, each related to impairments in relatively distinct neural circuits:

> BPD is primarily associated with a low threshold for the activation of the attachment system and deactivation of controlled mentalization, linked to impairments in the ability to differentiate mental states of self and other, which lead to hypersensitivity and increased susceptibility to contagion by other people's mental states, and poor integration of cognitive and affective aspects of mentalization. (2009, p. 1355)

In essence, this combination of easily aroused attachment anxiety with a loss of the capacity for reflective awareness leads to a loss of an ability to differentiate self from other, a key part of the picture at the teleological and intentional levels of self-agency. In this kind of clinical picture, a more primitive level of self-agency may emerge and dominate psychic functioning, only to be temporarily replaced by the more mature and partially established level of the reflective and autobiographical level of self-agency.

If this is the case, then the level of self-agency that unconsciously predominates will also profoundly influence the effectiveness of the analyst's approach. If a person's sense of self-agency is functioning at the teleological level, in which he only feels real when he is controlling the actions or feelings of another person, then interpretations which rely on that person's reflective function will be doomed to failure. This is frequently the case with borderline patients. At the intentional level, forbidden desires or wishes may feel dangerously powerful, able to create wishes and desires in the other—for example, the analyst; in this case, interpretations of incestuous wishes may be vehemently resisted because the patient's unconscious belief is that if the analyst knows about those wishes, he or she may be seduced by them.

These few examples are given to illustrate the need for a truly developmental approach to analysis itself—the recognition that as a person's implicit unconscious moves between developmental levels, the analyst's use of technique and overall analytic stance needs to mirror those fluctuations and use the method most suited to the current unconscious developmental level of self-agency. It is this developmental approach to self-agency that has been largely neglected by psychoanalysts. Even Jungian analysts who focus on the role of the self in guiding deintegration and reintegration do not discuss the changing experience of self-agency at different developmental stages. Self-psychologists might seem to focus on self-development but actually view the analytic process as one that "leads to the transmuting internalization of the selfobject analyst and his functions and thus to the acquisition of psychic structure" (Kohut, 1984, p. 172). In other words, for Kohut, change comes about through the processes of introjection and identification, not coconstruction.

In contrast, a truly developmental model views the analysis as creating the conditions that allow the patient's own internal developmental processes to be mobilized and so become the context in which the inhibited development of self-agency can be overcome; a mature and stable autobiographical and reflective self can gradually develop, replacing a pattern in which teleological and intentional levels dominate the patient's unconscious psychic functioning and so her conscious relationships, both with the analyst and in the outside world. An increasingly complex and fully psychic self-agency can emerge, in which the sense of self does not depend on the direct physical or emotional impact one has on another person, but on the capacity for self-reflection and awareness of the mental and emotional separateness of self and other. Differing analytic techniques are all ways of assisting the emergence of the patient's capacity to symbolize, that is, to separate thought from action, to hold in mind and reflect on self and other as mental and emotional subjects, not just physical objects.

The importance of problems of self-agency in the creation of psychopathology and the implications for the practice of psychotherapy are discussed in Part II. But before I explore the clinical aspects of self-agency in more detail, I want to expand on some of the implications of the relational-constructivist-epigenetic paradigm of human psychic development that I have outlined here and the relevance of this approach for the development of self-agency. In Chapter 1, I examine the implications of contemporary biological models of human psychological development and draw out their implications for psychoanalytic theories.

PART I
The Relational, Developmental, and Neurobiological Foundations of Self-Agency

1

The Challenges to Psychoanalytic Theories From Developmental Research

OVER THE PAST TWO OR THREE DECADES, contemporary attachment theory and intersubjective and relational models of psychotherapy have increasingly challenged the original paradigms of the human mind offered by Freud, Jung, and Klein. All three argued that unconscious contents are derived from innate structures in the mind, that the human mind has preprogrammed drives (libido) or structures (archetypes) that lead inevitably to certain mental processes or "phantasies" (Spillius, 2001; Stevens, 2002). This belief in innate unconscious mental content appears in a number of different guises across the spectrum of the early psychodynamic models of human development and the human mind. Although this way of understanding the mind takes a number of different forms, they all have in common the assumption that humans are born with, as it were, packages of inherited information that are activated during development and so structure our learning and experience of the world as we grow and mature.

Biological Determinism: The Belief in Innate Unconscious Contents, Structures, and Processes

Freud was adamant that libido is a biological, sexual force or drive that shapes our mental experience, giving rise to unconscious "phantasy." Freud's detailed account of his longest analysis, that of the "Wolf-Man," was written to refute Jung's view that neurosis arises from a desire to avoid current realities by regression to infantile states of mind (Freud, 1918). But, in addition to using the case history to demonstrate the causative role of infantile neurosis, Freud also used it to argue that

these scenes of observing parental intercourse, of being seduced
in childhood, and of being threatened with castration are unques-
tionably an inherited endowment, a phylogenetic inheritance. A
child catches hold of this phylogenetic experience where his own
experience fails him. He fills in the gaps in individual truth with
prehistoric truth. (1918, p. 578)

Freud went on to make a rare statement of agreement with Jung about
the existence of this "phylogenetic inheritance" even though he then
argued that it is a "methodological error to seize upon a phylogenetic
explanation before the ontogenic possibilities have been exhausted" (p.
578).

But in this chapter I explore evidence from contemporary biology
and neuroscience that the contents of the human mind are not under
genetic control in this way, but are formed from real-life experiences.
One of the most remarkable and, to my mind, frustrating aspects of the
Wolf Man case history is Freud's emphasis on an inherited knowledge
of the primal scene, which undervalues the childhood traumas that the
Wolf Man suffered, which were entirely sufficient to lay the foundations
for both his childhood and adult neuroses. In fact, many aspects of the
case history beautifully demonstrate the causal significance of meaning,
the way in which early experiences impact on a child's psychic development and powerfully influence the formation of object relations and the
direction of sexual interests.

Indeed, most of the basic tenets of attachment theory emerge in his
discussion of the factors contributing to the Wolf Man's later problems.
The dream itself (that his bedroom window flew open to reveal several
white wolves sitting silently on the branches of a big walnut tree outside
the window) supports contemporary perspectives on trauma. Van der
Kolk and McFarlane (1996, p. 8) suggested that "in PTSD, the past is
relived with an immediate sensory and emotional intensity that makes
victims feel as if the event were occurring all over again" and this is
indeed how the Wolf Man felt as he woke up from the wolf nightmare
in a state of terror that he was about to be eaten by the wolves.

There is no doubt that the Wolf Man was a traumatized child.
Freud's own detailed case study and an extensive subsequent psychoanalytic literature describe numerous childhood traumatic experiences
that probably contributed to the Wolf Man's neurosis both in childhood and in later life. Indeed, Harold Blum (1980) has suggested that

the Wolf Man suffered from multiple chronic traumas and was a borderline personality. It certainly seems as though his nurse, his governess, his sister, and his parents were either intrusive, sexually abusive and seductive, deeply inconsistent, or depressed and emotionally unavailable. There are too many examples in the case history to detail here. From an attachment theory perspective, we simply do not need the phylogenetic part of Freud's explanation, the view that some innate knowledge of the primal scene is genetically inherited. The extensive failures of reflective function and affect regulation shown by all his key attachment figures are entirely sufficient to explain both his childhood and adult symptomatology.

However, Freud insisted that the case material demonstrated the Wolf Man's "wish for sexual satisfaction which he was at that time longing to obtain from his father" (1918, p. 506), and that, although the form his infantile sexual desires took was distorted by actual events, behind both his infantile neurosis and his adult psychopathology lay the hereditary schema, the inherited knowledge of the primal scene. Victoria Hamilton (1996) has pointed out that this danger is inherent in psychoanalysis, that Freud's own idea of instinctual drive decrees that innate physiological processes and their associated drives determine the symbolism of the mind.

Jung also came to assert that there is innate knowledge in the human mind—a phylogenetic inheritance of ancestral experience. For Freud, it was the inheritance of the primal scene and for Jung it was the inheritance of archetypes. Jung initially suggested that mental symbolism is not predetermined by biology, epitomized in the distinction he drew between a symbol and a sign:

> The symbol is not a sign that disguises something generally known—a disguise, that is, for the basic drive or elementary intention. Its meaning resides in the fact that it is an attempt to elucidate, by a more or less apt analogy, something that is still entirely unknown or still in the process of formation. (1967, para. 492)

But although Jung initially took this subjective hermeneutic approach, I think he was also fatally drawn back into a more deterministic reductionist model with his theory of archetypes, underlying mental structures that he thought had evolved by natural selection. This is also a model in which brain and body are thought not only to act as the necessary raw materials for the construction of human psychic life but also to determine its content and its motivation. This formed the basis for his model of a collective unconscious, which he described as "all psychic contents that belong not to one individual but to many, i.e., to a society, a people or to mankind in general" (Jung, 1971, para. 692). So for a while, Jung rejected the deterministic view that the human psyche comes into existence with preformed mental content, but got caught up in it again with his own variant of this kind of determinism, with his model of archetypes and the collective unconscious.

So the concept of the archetype seems to create a similar problem in Jungian theory, in terms of psychic innateness, that instinctual drive does in psychoanalysis. Archetypes are often thought of as preformed, innate packets of imagery and fantasy waiting to pop out like butterflies from a chrysalis given the right environmental trigger, a model which suggests that something other than mind itself has created these mental contents. Jung struggled to avoid this trap, with his later division of the concept of archetype into the archetype-as-such and the archetypal image, but I have argued elsewhere that this was not entirely successful in extricating him from this fundamental misunderstanding of the nature and limits of genetic inheritance where mental process and content are concerned (Knox, 2003).

So the apparent gulf between psychoanalytic and Jungian groups of therapists in terms of the psychic forces that shape unconscious mental content should not blind us to the fact that the psychoanalytic concept of unconscious "phantasy," and the Jungian concept of the archetype share a view that we inherit unconscious content—whether it is described as imagery, ideas, or fantasy. It does seem as though the very ideas that Freud and Jung thought most differentiated each from the other were actually those where they showed the most similarity.

In this sense, both psychoanalysis and analytical psychology, which have prided themselves on their intense and sophisticated study of subjective experience, can actually therefore be seen to be reductionistic, insofar as psychic life is reduced and objectified by attempts to explain its functioning in terms of innately determined psychic structures. The psychoanalytic view that instinctual drive creates specific unconscious "phantasy," and the Jungian view that archetypes are inherited organizing structures in the collective human psyche are models that are both based on an implicit assumption that a ground plan or blueprint of the human psyche is inherited in our genes and that this blueprint contains specific desires, such as the infant's incestuous wishes, or the potential for specific types of imagery, such as the archetypes of the collective unconscious.

This kind of "innatism," a view that the human brain has inherited modules of information, is a misunderstanding of the emergent nature of the development of the human mind and brain that is by no means unique to psychodynamic theory. Evolutionary psychologists argue that, through the process of natural selection, the human mind has developed domain-specific, content-rich programs specialized for solving ancestral problems (Barkow, Cosmides & Tooby, 1992; Pinker, 1994, 1997; Tooby & Cosmides, 2005). The essence of this argument is this:

> The programs that comprise the human brain were sculpted over evolutionary time by the ancestral environments and selection pressures experienced by the hunter-gatherers from whom we are descended. These unlearned programs are a part of the brain by virtue of being part of its evolved architecture. They are programs that reliably develop across the ancestrally normal range of human environments. (Tooby & Cosmides, 2005, p. 27)

So evolutionary psychologists seem to fall into the same innatist trap as Freud and Jung, with their view of a universal and uniform human psyche, even if they describe it in different terms and ascribe different contents to these innate domains. In the next section, I summarize the evidence that demonstrates the fatal flaws inherent in this approach to the development of the human mind.

An Integrated Biological, Developmental, and Relational Model of Psychotherapy

In recent years, the debates within the psychotherapy world have increasingly reflected the impact of relational and social constructionist models of the self. That does not mean that these ideas are universally accepted—there remains a significant number of psychotherapists, whether Freudian, Kleinian, or Jungian, who believe that innate drives or structures in the human mind determine the nature and content of unconscious mental life. But there is also an increasingly influential developmental, emergent paradigm, drawing on the empirical studies

I mentioned in the introduction, which demonstrates the crucial role played by intimate relationships in the development of the human psyche. In the United States, there is also a strong representation of relational models in clinical training institutes and in the clinical and academic publications from relational analysts such as Stolorow and Atwood, Lewis Aron, Beatrice Beebe, Jessica Benjamin, Adrienne Harris, Joseph Lichtenberg, Stephen Mitchell, Bruce Reis, and many others. Interpersonal psychoanalysis has its own training institute in New York, the William Alanson White Institute.

But in most psychotherapy training (at least in Britain) there is often an uneasy mix of these approaches with the innatist models I have described above, partly because psychotherapy clinicians are not necessarily familiar with the scientific evidence that can help us to make an informed judgment about the validity (or otherwise) of psychodynamic theories relating to the developmental processes in the human mind and brain. These new fields of study suggest that, rather than biology determining psychic development, it is interpersonal experiences and what these mean to us that shape the development of mind. To assert that our desires are predetermined by our genetic makeup, by our hormones, or by any other biological forces fails to reflect the ontogeny of information in development—the fact that both physical and psychological end products (bodies and minds) emerge out of developmental processes that are both self-organizing and highly dependent on the environment and relationships (Oyama, 2000). An emergent model of development has at its core the view that a stream of current experience constantly reshapes and guides the development of the human mind and brain, continuously switching some genetic pathways on and others off in a highly interactive way (Deacon, 1997; Karmiloff-Smith, 1992; Panksepp & Panksepp, 2000). Tronick succinctly summarized this view, that experience changes genes and brain—that the influence is not just one way. Genes and brains are not static entities but change throughout development:

> It is necessary to recognize that experience, genes, and brain, as well as the structures and processes of all three, are not only fundamentally different at different ages, but their constant interplay is also different and makes for qualitative differences in the totality of the biopsychological organization of the individual in each moment of the lifespan. Attempting to understand how things change must be a constant consideration because change affects

what is happening now, and what is happening now affects the future. (Tronick, 2007, p. 6)

The problem is that psychotherapists want a model that is biologically grounded, reflecting our acceptance that the human mind depends on a human brain and that our theories must accurately reflect contemporary evidence about how the brain actually works. But we also want a model that reflects our awareness of the cultural embeddedness of human minds and brains and their development. Is it possible to reconcile social constructionism or constructivist psychology with biological models of human psychic development? A number of authors have examined this question but have not directly analyzed the underlying aspects of the biological models that render this kind of integrationist approach problematic. They deal with it by simply stating that we are social by nature (Taub, 2009, p. 515). For example, Stephen Mitchell, the founder of relational psychoanalysis in the United States, stated that social relations "are themselves biologically rooted, genetically encoded, fundamental motivational processes" (1988, p. 18) and, as Taub pointed out, argued that we cannot ignore the fact that we do have biological bodies, which are, at least in part, outside the role of social construction (Taub, 2009, p. 516).

But defining attachment as the fundamental biological instinct still perpetuates the view that a specific emotional and psychological process is innate, that "culture is wired into our very bodies" (Mitchell, 2002, p. 70; Taub, 2009, p. 517). This simply shifts innatism from Freud's instincts and Jung's archetypes to Bowlby's attachment needs. The question I am posing here is: What does it actually mean to state that "we have a biological need for human relationships"? (Schwartz, 1999, p. 143). This integration of biology with a relational constructivist perspective stands or falls on the question, "What exactly is hard-wired into our genetic code?" An emotional experience of a "need for relationship" cannot be encoded in genes, any more than archetypes or incestuous desires can be. A core emotion may be programmed into our limbic systems, such as the SEEKING system that Panksepp (1998) proposed, but not the specific subjective experience of the desire for closeness to another person, which requires a capacity for conceptual thought and self-awareness that only emerge through the developmental and learning processes involved in actual experience of real relationships. The principles on which this argument is founded can be found in the extensive literature of scientists such as Susan Oyama (2000), Annette

Karmiloff-Smith (1992), Horst Hendriks-Jansen (1996), Richard
Lewontin (2000), Stephen Gould (2001, pp. 269–286), Jaak Panksepp
(1998), and others. Robert Neimeyer has recently clearly spelled out
that an integration of biological with a constructivist view of the self
absolutely requires a biology based on epigenetic principles

> that views human meaning and action as the emergent outcome
> of a series of hierarchically embedded systems and subsystems.
> . . . [I]n biology, epigenesis stands in contrast to theories that
> view an organism's structures, behaviors or capacities as either
> essential and inborn or as the simple and predictable result of
> maturational unfolding. Instead, new structures are seen as
> emerging through the interaction of a multi-leveled organism-
> environment system, in which the functioning of each constitu-
> ent feature (e.g., chromosomes) is shaped through transactions
> of more basic levels (e.g., genes) and higher order ones (e.g., cell
> matrices). As applied to human functioning, epigenesis implies
> that meaning and action emerge from a similarly multi-layered
> system of systems, which include bio-genetic, personal-agentic,
> dyadic-relational and cultural-linguistic levels. (2009, p. 23)

Niemeyer concluded that "in this integrative model, all psychologically
significant structures and symptoms emerge from the complex interaction of all levels of this comprehensive system, rather than from a given
level considered in isolation" (p. 23).

Panksepp and Panksepp (2000) offered a detailed analysis of what
they rather poetically described as "the seven sins of evolutionary psychology." They highlighted one of the most important errors that is
central to evolutionary psychology, the view that the human neocortex
has "genetically pre-ordained 'modules' that generate specific types of
psychological strategies" (2000, p. 108). Panksepp and Panksepp argued
that there is a fundamental confusion in this model between the functions of the more recently evolved human neocortex and the much older
subcortex that we share with other mammals. Their view is that the
human neocortex evolved as a very general and flexible form of intelligence dedicated to general-purpose symbolic processing and that "evolutionary psychologists appear to be seeking specific socio-emotional
modules among higher brain functions where the predominant functions may only be general-purpose cognitive/thinking mechanisms"

(p. 111). Evolutionary psychology is a discipline that, I have pointed out, has many conceptual similarities to the innatism inherent in both Freud's and Jung's models of the mind (Knox, 2003).

It is not in the human neocortex but in the subcortical systems of the brain, the basal ganglia and the limbic system, that anatomical, neuro-chemical, and functional features common to all mammals have evolved (Maclean, 1990; Panksepp, 1998). It is within these subcortical areas that special-purpose emotion-processing operating neural systems can be found:

> Many of the apparent special-purpose functions in the higher regions of adult brains may only emerge as a result of specific types of life experiences. In contrast, there are many special-purpose, genetically-dedicated circuits for various emotions and motivations in subcortical regions shared by all mammals. (Panksepp & Panksepp, 2000, p. 108)

Panksepp has offered a wealth of research to support his view that these core motivational and emotional systems are those of SEEKING, RAGE, LUST, CARE, PANIC, and PLAY (Panksepp, 1998). These are capitalized to mark the fact that they refer, not to conscious emotional states of mind, but to specific neurobiological circuits in the subcortical systems of all mammalian brains. Panksepp's conclusion is:

> In short, we believe that all too many "stories" of evolutionary psychology may be scientifically explained by the interaction between basic emotional systems and the unique general-purpose abilities that human beings possess. If so, the foundations of "human nature" will boil down to an "animal nature" that was solidified in evolution long before the Pleistoscene. (Panksepp & Panksepp, 2000, p. 113)

An argument along similar lines that I would highlight is that made by Hendriks-Jansen that we may be born with innate patterns, but only of physical activity, not conceptual meaning, and these patterns of activity are the foundation on which learning takes place:

> These patterns have no meaning to the infant; they are not pro-duced as tentative solutions to some problem. It is only through

interaction with the mother and the physical environment that they gain any definition or meaning at all. . . . But natural selection has already ensured that the right material is at hand in the forms of patterns of activity that are naturally recognized as "meaningful" by the mother and are easily shaped through interaction with the cultural environment. (1996, p. 133)

Or, as Hogenson (2009) put it, the mother bootstraps the infant into the world of adult meaning. The implications of this emergent model of mind for psychotherapy have been particularly studied in analytical psychology by Cambray and Carter (2004), Hogenson (2004, 2009), Knox (2003), and Merchant (2009) and in psychoanalysis by Atwood and Stolorow (1984), Beebe and Lachmann (2002), BCPSG (2007), Benjamin (1995), Fosshage (2002), Lichtenberg, Lachmann, and Fosshage (2002), Mitchell (1988), Modell (1984), Reis (2005, 2009), Schore (2003b), Stern (1985), and Tronick (2007), among many others.

So, to summarize, we can inherit basic emotional and motivational systems through our mammalian subcortical circuits. We can also inherit patterns of behavior—of action and interaction that are uniquely human. But both of these are nonconceptual and depend on the cognitive information-processing functions of the human neocortex to acquire conceptual and symbolic meaning. And the meanings we construct and attribute to our own (and other people's) actions and experience are highly dependent initially on the meaning they are given by our primary caregivers in our infancy. I discuss the way the caregiver's "folk-psychological" stance acts as scaffolding for the infant's development of self-agency in more detail in Chapter 4. But in addition, throughout life, new relationships provide opportunities for new patterns of meaningful experience to emerge; the past influences the present but does not completely determine it.

Self-Agency as Central to an Interpersonal Model of Psychotherapy

The traditional analytic models, in which innate forces somehow determine the nature of unconscious processes and psychic reality, tend to downplay the real relationship and the role of self-agency in that context. This is why contemporary relational and attachment-based approaches to psychotherapy are attracting such interest within the community of practicing psychotherapists and counselors. Once a constructivist model of the development of the self has been fully recognized, the importance of the infant's experience of agency in relationships becomes more obvious. Infants discover themselves by exploring the reactions that they create in others in response to their own actions. Broucek suggested, "This sense of efficacy and the pleasure associated with it are in my opinion the foundation of self feeling" (1979, p. 312).

Of particular interest to the infant seems to be the closeness, or degree of contingency, of the action and response (Bahrick & Watson, 1985; Papousek & Papousek, 1974). Gergely and Watson (1996) suggested that initially a very close or perfectly contingent response seems to be of most interest, but the infant's attention shifts toward exploring lesser degrees of contingency as the development of self-agency progresses. Beatrice Beebe and Joseph Jaffe's research suggests that for infants of 4 months, a midrange of contingency of vocal rhythms is optimal for secure attachment (Jaffe et al., 2001). The developmental model offered by Fonagy and his colleagues helps to clarify this shift in the focus of the infant's exploration of agency. The trajectory of contingency is inherent in the five developmental stages of agency, which I described in the introduction and which are outlined again here:

Self as Agent

1 Physical agency, 0–6 months: Awareness that actions produce changes in the physical environment (perfect contingency).
2. Social agency, 3–9 months: Actions produce behavioral and emotional mirroring (imperfectly contingent) responses in other people—action at a distance.
3. Teleological agency, 9–24 months: Sense of purpose—actions seen as goal directed. Capacity to choose action to bring about desired outcome. Intention not yet recognized as separate from action.[1]
4. Intentional agency, 2 years: Recognition of intentions as distinct from action. Actions are seen as caused by prior intentions and desires. Actions can change mental states.

---

1 The word *teleological* means something rather different from the way Jungians understand the term, although they both refer to a purposive state. In Csibra and Gergely's (1998) model, teleological is a state of mind that represents others' actions in terms of their concrete and visible outcomes.

5. Representational agency, 3–4 years: Actions seen as caused by intentions, which are also recognized as mental processes. Mind is represented to itself, so intentions are not just means to an end but mental states in themselves.
6. Autobiographical self: Organization of memories as personally experienced—linked to self-representations and awareness of personal history. (Fonagy et al., 2002, pp. 204–207)

In discussing this model, I want to draw out the implications of the issues of contingency in the relational dynamics between infant and caregiver. Of course, in the first days, weeks, and months of life, any such experience would not be conscious, but nevertheless, the infant can still experience agency initially at a motor action level and later at an emotional and intentional, if still unconscious, level (BCPSG, 2007; Decety & Meyer, 2009; Panksepp, 1998).

In the first few months of life, the infant's developing sense of self as a physical and social agent depends on a perfectly contingent response from the physical environment. This attention bias toward perfect contingency has been identified by Watson (1994, 1995) as a mechanism for self-detection and so serves

> an evolutionary function of developing a primary representation of the bodily self as a distinct object in the environment by identifying those stimuli that are the necessary sensory consequences of the body's motor actions and over which the infant exercises perfect control. (Fonagy et al., 2002, p. 167)

So, for example, the perfectly contingent response of the infant's own hands as he or she moves them enables the infant to distinguish self from the external world and to develop a sense of the physical self as a distinct object that "can initiate action and exert causal influence on its environment" (Fonagy et al., 2002, p. 208).

At the social level of self-agency, the infant explores the impact he or she has on the other's behavioral responses. Gergely and Watson (1996) suggested that, at about 3 months, infants move from a preference for perfect contingency, which reflects the exploration of physical agency, to high but imperfect contingency, where the caregiver's response mirrors the infant's actions to a considerable degree but where some element of surprise and unpredictability in the nature of that social response is enjoyed and even actively sought by the infant. The mechanism they proposed by which infants can be aware of this may be the "contingency detection module." But this idea of a module has recently been questioned by mirror neuron researchers (Gallese, Rochat, Cossu, & Sinigaglia, 2009) who suggested that the perception-action neuronal pathways provide the basis for this contingency behavior, without the need to postulate any cognitive module. These ideas are explored further in Chapter 2.

An additional point to be made is that this body of research on contingency, for example by Bahrick and Watson (1985), does not explore contingency directly in the face-to-face exchanges between infant and caregiver, but by means of an experimental model in which infants observed their own movements on a live monitor that directly reflected their own behavior or on a monitor that showed them a previously recorded image of their own movements. More recent research by Gergely and Watson (1996) and Koos and Gergely (2001) used an indirect "mirror interaction situation" in which mother and infant were seated next to each other, with their direct view of each other prevented by a barrier, but they could see each other and interact in a mirror in which both were visible. A very different line of research (Jaffe et al., 2001; Beebe et al., 2010) explores the issue of contingency directly in the face-to-face interaction between infant and caregiver, and I discuss this in more detail in Chapter 2.

At the teleological level, the focus is on the impact of the subject's action, in terms of bringing about a desired goal; consequence (not cause) takes center stage because the infant's focus is on a range of possible outcomes. The infant explores choice and preference, in terms of choosing from a range of possible actions, in order to bring about a desired effect, but still at a behavioral level (Csibra & Gergely, 1998, 2007). Once again, mirror neuron research questions the notion that this level of agency is based on a cognitive rational process—that infants use reason to infer what is the most efficient means to achieve a goal. Gallese et al. (2009, p. 107) suggested instead that infants can understand another's intentions on the basis of their own motor knowledge; in other words, an infant can understand others' action goals only when the infant can already perform the action herself.

The sense of self as intentional agent requires an appropriate emotional response from the caregiver, which allows the infant to learn that his or her desires have been communicated to another mind that has understood them, processed them, and responded in a way that reflects both the infant's and the caregiver's intentionality. The infant thus experiences a sense of agency, but also finds that the response contains new and unfamiliar aspects which reflect the intentions and agency of the other person. Intention is experienced in its own right and as separate from action, from about 2 years of age onward (Fonagy et al., 2002, pp. 237–241).

At the representational level, the capacity to reflect on one's own and others' intentions develops. The self as agent only becomes conscious at the level of the representational self, a stage in which mind can be used both to affect the world and also to reflect on its own processes. The capacity for reflective function depends on the ability to hold onto a representation of oneself and others as mental and emotional beings. For this capacity to develop, the infant has to internalize the parent as someone with a mental image of the infant as a person with a mind and emotions. In this way infants gradually acquire the awareness of their own mind with its feelings and thoughts and a sense of mind as an agent of change, through the attuned responses from caregivers to their intentions and emotions.

These stages of self-agency are levels of psychic organization in the implicit unconscious, structuring experience while themselves remaining outside awareness. But the achievement of the representational level is insecure and may break down under pressure; when this happens, we unconsciously begin to function from a more primitive and behavioral level of self-agency in which thoughts, beliefs, desires, intentions, and fantasies are not communications from one mind to another or from one part of one's own mind to another (unconscious to conscious, for example) but are experienced more as controlling behaviors, bringing about actions because they reflect the earlier levels of self-agency, at which mind and intention have not yet been decoupled from behavior and action.

In the next two chapters, I describe the evidence that supports the view of a developmental trajectory of self-agency from physical, social, and teleological levels, expressed through action, to psychological and representational levels experienced in self-awareness, mentalization, and language; for example, I discuss the challenge that mirror neurons offer to the apparently commonsense idea that agency and intentionality are essentially conscious (Borg, 2007). One of the foremost mirror neuron researchers, Corrado Sinigaglia (2008), pointed out that much intentionality is encoded entirely unconsciously, in sequences of "motor action chains." He argued that action understanding is certainly not the same as mind reading, the intentional attributions concerning mental states, such as beliefs, desires, and intentions—the conscious reason for performing an action. Sinigaglia pointed out the fact that "mirror neurons cannot capture reasons, beliefs, desires, and intentions . . . is not, however an argument against the possibility of their having a role in intentional attribution" (2008, p. 89).

A number of other clinicians and researchers discuss self-agency from a more clinical perspective, but all share the view that our sense of self-agency is often far from being under our conscious control. Van der Hart et al. (2006) suggested that a conscious sense of self-agency can be fragmented as part of structural dissociations in the personality, so that different subpersonalities may each have a sense of agency. At its most extreme, dissociative identity disorder is a terrifying experience of having several different selves, any one of which can take over and dominate the whole personality for a while (Mollon, 1999; Sinason, 2002).

Stage, Phase, Template, State, or Process? Differing Models of Development and Their Relevance for Self-Agency

Although developmental researchers would agree that the sense of self and self-agency initially develop entirely unconsciously, there are significant differences in their accounts of these developmental processes, and I want to briefly outline some of the key issues here. In relation to the developmental levels of self-agency described above, are they most accurately seen as developmental *stages, phases, states, templates,* or *processes?*

One of the major challenges that contemporary developmental biologists have posed confronts the idea that development in any modality passes through specific and static developmental stages, whose form and timing are predetermined by genetic instructions or an environmental trigger. Johnson and Morton suggested that this static stage model is inadequate to account for the dynamic processes of change in development, the shift from one organizational level to another. They agreed with Oyama's view that the emergence of new developmental capacities depends on the information contained in the preceding developmental level of phenotypical organization, rather than in preexisting genetic or environmental instructions (Johnson & Morton, 1991, p. 9).

Hendriks-Jansen also argued that Piaget's stage model of

development was too rigid and inadequate to describe observed developmental processes:

> Individual activity patterns had their own developmental profiles, and though their onsets and peaks might tend to occur at roughly the same ages for all children in a particular culture, this could not be ascribed to a rigid sequence of overall, unifying, internal equilibria. Some children follow idiosyncratic paths, and each mother-infant pair builds up its own repertoire of interactive patterns, substantially different from those of other mothers and infants. (1996, p. 253)

Karmiloff-Smith also rejected a stage model and its roots in "a static genetic blueprint for maturation" (1992, p. 10). She suggested that this is a fatal flaw both in Piaget's stage view of development (in which there is no domain-specific knowledge but age-specific and stage-dependent fundamental changes across the entire cognitive system) and in the contrasting modular view of development of those such as Fodor and Chomsky (although Fodor, 2000, has more recently offered his own critique of an excessively modular approach):

> The exclusive focus of nativists like Fodor and Chomsky on biologically specified modules leaves little room for rich epigenetic-constructivist processes. Moreover, Fodor's concentration on input systems. . . . Doesn't help us to understand the way in which children turn out to be active participants in the construction of their own knowledge. (Karmiloff-Smith, 1992, p. 10)

She suggested instead a *phase* model of development, in which recognizable phase changes recur at different times in each developmental domain (e.g., language, physics, or numeracy). These changes include the process of "representational redescription," by which "implicit information *in* the mind subsequently becomes explicit information *to* the mind, first within a domain and then sometimes across domains" (1992, p. 18). The contrast with a stage model is that, in a phase model, this process of reencoding of implicit information into an increasingly explicit format does not involve a simultaneous change, at a predetermined stage, across domains but occurs recurrently "within microdomains throughout development, as well as in adulthood for some kinds of new learning" (Karmiloff-Smith, 1992, p. 18). Self-agency is a domain of development and Karmiloff-Smith's domain-specific phase model, involving a progression from implicit to increasingly explicit levels of organization, exactly reflects the developmental trajectory of self-agency, from the physical, through the implicit levels of social, teleological, and intentional levels of agency to the explicit representational level.

Another way of framing developmental processes is to speak of a *state*, a term defined by Tronick as "the semistable organization of the organism as a whole at a given moment" (2007, p. 423). These states include everything from basic physiological needs, such as hunger, to complex, meaningful interpersonal interactions, and they are highly dependent on mutual regulation between infant and caregiver. Hendriks-Jansen (1996, p. 263) is critical of the concept, at least if applied to an infant's emotional expression as expressing specific internal states, rather than as dynamic activity patterns. But Tronick uses the term to mean a temporary state of stability in a constantly shifting and evolving dynamic system of interaction between mother and infant. This mutual regulation process is itself a form of dyadic state that is internalized by the infant, and the repeated sequenced experiences give rise to expectancies about how relationships are patterned. These expectancies can be seen as a form of *template*, structuring the infant's future interactions in a dynamic way, one that is highly dependent on the kind of experience and its timing and so is unique for each child:

> An infant experiencing the toxic stress of abuse for the first time is affected differently than a toddler, and the toddler who chronically experienced stress as an infant experiences it differently than the toddler who did not experience undue stress. These differences are not only differences in the context of the past, they are also constitutive, embodied and embedded in the actual operation of the processes that generate the toddler's sense of place in the world. (Tronick, 2007, p. 6)

This description does not use the term template, but it is implied here, I think, and is used to describe developmental levels of organization within any particular domain; it was the way Bowlby thought of internal working models. Fonagy et al. (2002, p. 7) questioned the idea that early patterns of relationship are internalized as a permanent template or pattern but instead suggested that early experience acts as a regulator that controls developmental processes. So in their view, "healthy" experience facilitates optimal development across the spectrum of psychic trajectories, including that of self-agency; on the other hand, adverse early experience inhibits progression through these developmental stages.

But is this view of the regulating role of early experience really incompatible with the template model initially proposed by Bowlby? Clinicians often rediscover how powerfully a past pattern, template, or experience can seem to erupt into a present relationship, so that the patient relates to the present relationship as though it were the past. One brief clinical example illustrates the point:

> A patient described how, when she was 10 years old, she was returning to her home after school and had witnessed her mother commit suicide by jumping out of a window. This patient would always arrive for her sessions a few minutes early, even after her therapist raised this for discussion. Eventually it became apparent that she was unconsciously doing so on the basis of an unconscious belief that she might prevent her therapist from committing suicide in the same way; if she arrived a few minutes early she might not be too late this time.

I suggest that the logic of a developmental model of self-agency combines features both of a template model and also of early relational experience as a regulator of subsequent development. It is the level of self-agency of early relational experience that is internalized as a pattern of expectation about relationships in general. For example, if a parent is functioning at the teleological level of self-agency, she will interpret the relationship with her baby in terms of her and her baby's actions rather than attribute it to their respective affective states because her own thoughts and feelings are not decoupled from action. Alicia Lieberman gave a particularly striking example:

> One mother, for example, perceived her 3-month-old baby daughter as so "cunning" that, according to the mother, the baby jumped from her crib to the adjacent parental bed to sneak a feeding at the breast while the mother was asleep and then jumped back to her crib. This was the only explanation the mother could

find for her breasts feeling rather empty of milk when she woke
up in the morning. (1999, p. 739)

Lieberman revealed that the mother was unable to relate to her own
inner feelings of emptiness, rooted in her own childhood deprivation,
and to her fear of not having enough to give her daughter. Instead, she
experienced her emotional emptiness in a concrete and behavioral way,
as breasts empty of milk, and decided that the baby's actions must be
the cause, even though such behavior would clearly be impossible for a
3-month-old baby.

This kind of concrete, behavioral relational experience does seem to
be mostly accurately described as a template, a pattern of relationship
that the baby internalizes and that regularly resurfaces in later relationships. In this case, the mother's own childhood experience of emotional
emptiness and deprivation, that her needs were not held in mind, acted
as a relational template for her experience with her own daughter, whose
needs she could not empathize with nor hold in mind, but could only
experience as persecuting behavior—she could only experience relationship at the teleological level.

But this is also a developmental inhibiting factor, because the child's
capacity to develop a sense of self-agency at a mental and emotional
level, decoupled from action, can only emerge through a relationship with a caregiver who can experience her own self-agency through
mind and emotion, not just action. If she cannot do this, she cannot
coconstruct a relational experience with the infant, in which thoughts,
feelings, and intentions have agency in themselves, without having to
be expressed in physical action. Without such a relational template to
internalize, the infant's self-agency cannot move along a developmental
trajectory to the intentional and representational levels of agency but
remains stuck at the same action-based teleological level as that of the
primary caregiver.

So it seems that the use of the terms *phase, state, template, and process*
all capture some aspects of the constantly shifting interactive patterns
of activity and experience between mother and infant, but none of them
is sufficient to capture the whole picture. For example, a mother and
infant may achieve a semistable *state* of turn-taking in their interaction,
a pattern of experience that if reliably and regularly repeated becomes
a pattern of expectancy, or a *template* for future relationships. Perhaps
then, some new element is introduced; perhaps a new game is started

by the mother. The infant changes state, becomes alert and excited, and enters a *phase* of new learning, perhaps a phase involving representational redescription of the new information he or she has just received. This interaction is a developmental *process* and it may take place in a steady way or in bursts of activity that eventually lead to the achievement of a new semistable state.

It is always the interactive patterns between infant and caregiver that play a fundamental role in these shifting dynamics and in the next chapter I describe the developmental evidence for them in more detail.

2

Developmental Research on the Embodied and Relational Roots of Self-Agency

RECENT RESEARCH DEMONSTRATES WITH GREAT FORCE how easily our sense of self, seeing ourselves through our own eyes, can be fooled. Petkova and Ehrsonn (2008), from the Karolinska Institute in Stockholm, have shown that people can actually be convinced that they inhabit a different body from their own, by wiring the goggles worn by a volunteer to a camera mounted in the eye area on a mannequin. When the volunteers looked down, the camera moved down as well, giving the volunteers the image of the mannequin's torso, which they experienced as their own. When the experimenter threatened to attack the mannequin with a knife, the volunteers showed physiological fear responses. Even more disturbing is the fact that when the experimenter wore the camera instead of the mannequin and shook hands with a volunteer, the volunteer became convinced that he was shaking hands with himself, not with another person (Figure 2.1).

This experiment highlights the crucial role that the body plays in our sense of identity. Bodily action, whether carried out or simulated, is the first step in our discovery of our agency—it is through bodily action that we first explore the world around us and find out both the impact it has on us and the impact we have on the world. Gergely and Watson (1996) pointed out infants' preference for perfect contingency during the first 3 months of life, reflecting infants' focus on their physical agency, the direct impact their actions have on the objects around them.

From these beginnings, infants gradually discover and explore their inner world of intention, desire, and agency, through increasingly social

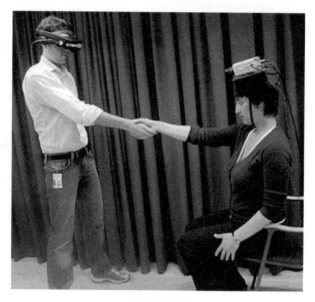

FIGURE 2.1
Experiment to illustrate the perceptual illusion of body-swapping. Reproduced by permission from "If I Were You: Perceptual Illusion of Body Swapping," by V. I. Petkova and H. H. Ehrsson, 2008, *PloS One*, *3*(12), e3832

and psychological interchanges with caregivers, leading to a growing understanding that both self and others are mental and emotional beings with desires, beliefs, thoughts, intentions, and emotions of their own. I describe the developmental and neurobiological basis for this trajectory of self-agency in Chapter 4. But what Petkova and Ehrsson (2008) have shown is how fragile these later developments are—creating an illusion for the research subjects that they inhabit a different body makes them become literally uncertain of who they are at the most basic physical level.

Developmental Studies of Self-Agency in Infancy

To exist as a self is to experience ourselves as subjects, with a sense of agency, even though this is initially unconscious. A number of studies demonstrate that, from birth, infants have a sense of physical agency, exploring the effect their actions have on the world around them. They also discover the social sense of agency through turn-taking interactions with the primary caregiver; this experience of agency in relationships gradually becomes reencoded as implicit relational knowing, and finally as mentalization and the explicit capacity to relate to and communicate with others who are recognized as separate from self, as described in Chapter 1. This is not, of course, a conscious process but an implicit agentive stance (Bahrick & Watson, 1985; Decety & Chaminade 2003; Fonagy et al., 2002; Gergely & Watson, 1996; Lewis, Allesandri, & Sullivan, 1990).

So the foundations for this developmental process in infancy are crucial and they repeatedly show how vulnerable the infant's development of agency is to the responses of the primary caregiver. I shall start by describing some of the earlier research by Daniel Stern and colleagues on the relational roots of the self and then link this with related but separate research, first by Ed Tronick, second by Beatrice Beebe, and finally by Peter Fonagy.

The Boston Change Process Study Group and Implicit Relational Knowledge

Daniel Stern (1985) was probably the first developmental researcher to capture the imagination of psychotherapy clinicians with his book *The Interpersonal World of the Infant.* He described the development of the sense of self in a series of stages, each of which depends upon relational experience with the primary and other caregivers. Since then, the Boston Change Process Study Group (BCPSG) has provided a wealth of evidence about psychological and emotional development in infancy. A number of important theoretical and clinical developments have emerged from the work of this group. For example, they have redefined the concepts of surface and deep unconscious, arguing that developmental research overwhelmingly suggests that "throughout the lifespan relational meaning continues to be conveyed primarily through the apprehension of relational acts." It is through implicit relational interaction with caregivers that the small child learns the rules of emotional engagement: "what forms of affective relatedness can be expressed openly in the relationship and what forms need to be expressed only in 'defensive' ways, that is, in distorted or displaced forms" (BCPSG, 2007, p. 851).

One of the most crucial of these relational patterns is the child's expression of agency and the nature of the response that this evokes from the caregiver. The BCPSG authors gave an example of a mother who cannot bear her infant's affectionate touch and so repeatedly interrupts or overrides her infant's attempts to exercise initiative. This relational interaction is internalized by the infant, which leads him to "inhibit his own initiatives around physical contact with her" (BCPSG, 2007, p. 846). But the authors argued that it is not the mother's mental content (her hateful thoughts) that the infant internalizes and defends against, but the much more fundamental relational and behavioral dynamic, in which infant approach causes maternal withdrawal, that becomes part of the infant's implicit unconscious, so that he becomes inhibited in open expression of affection and of agency, in later life. This is also what Fairbairn described in his account of the schizoid personality (1952c), which I describe in more detail in Chapter 6.

Another example comes from the work of Louis Sander, who beautifully described and demonstrated how the infant's psychological and emotional development is utterly dependent on the interpersonal relationship with the primary caregivers. He conducted a simple but remarkable experiment in which one group of newborn babies were fed on demand, compared with another group who were fed every 4 hours regardless of their emotional state. Within a few days, the demand-fed sample began to show the emergence of one or two longer sleep periods in each 24 hours and after a few more days, these longer sleep periods began to occur more frequently at night. In other words, their sleep rhythms began to synchronize with the diurnal 24-hour day of the caregiver. The babies fed on a strict 4-hour routine showed no such change. Sander explicitly linked these findings to the babies' experience of their agency in the relationship with the mother:

> We now refer to the initiation of self-organizing, self-regulating, self-correcting moves as reflecting the agency of the individual. Achieving a coherent sense of "self-as-agent"—differentiated, valid, and competent within one's context of life support—brings us to a key goal of both the developmental and the therapeutic processes. I suggest that the process of achieving a coherent sense of self-as-agent is an example of the way "principles of process in living systems" can be applied to the task of integrating biological, developmental, and therapeutic levels we have been assigned. (2002, p. 16)

These examples highlight the theme that is central to this book, namely that it is bodily action and reaction in relationship that are internalized to create the implicit unconscious, and this is why the extent to which the infancy's agency is facilitated by the caregiver at these very early stages is so fundamental to the later psychological experience of agency.

Ed Tronick and the Mutual Regulation Model

Ed Tronick has worked closely with the BCPSG but has also developed his own models of parent-infant interaction. He highlighted the importance of the infant's agency in relationship, proposing that mutual regulation is fundamental to the child's developing sense of agency or, in his words, "effectance":

> The ability of the partner and infant to mutually regulate the quality of the interaction has a fundamental effect on how the infant feels about himself—that is, on the child's feeling of effectance: the sense of what he can or cannot accomplish. (Tronick, 2007, p. 206)

The observational study of mothers and infants by developmental researchers was revolutionized by the use of video recording, which allowed a second-by-second analysis of their fleeting interactions that vividly demonstrated each partner's interpersonal agency. These recordings show so much more clearly than normal observation how vulnerable the infant's development of agency is to the responses of the primary caregiver. The turn-taking "conversation" between caregiver and infant includes the burst-pause-burst pattern of feeding that I described in the introduction, but Ed Tronick emphasized that there are communicative goals and rules governing their interactions and that these goals and rules "generate the communicative behavior of each participant and predictions about the other's communicative behavior" (2007, p. 250). Mother and infant collaborate to communicate with each other and coordinate the timing of their respective contributions. The regulation of joint activity depends on "a shared lexicon of communicative acts, shared interactive rules and shared time." This is true of all interpersonal communication (see the discussion of Levinson's concept of the human interaction engine in Chapter 4) and mother-infant interaction is simply a special case of this pattern, in that the infant and mother are at very different developmental levels. But they are nevertheless both participants in a dyadic regulatory system that functions "to scaffold an infant's limited regulatory capacities" (Tronick, 2007, p. 9). This is achieved through a communicative system in which

> infants had to have organized communicative displays related to their internal state and to their external intentions and goals, and caregivers had to have capacities to apprehend and respond to the meaning of these messages. (p. 10)

If the mother does not take part in the rules of the mutual regulation conversation, the consequences are highly disturbing to the infant, even in the short term. It is as though the infant's experience is "if I can't affect you, then I don't exist." The evidence that this is how the infant feels comes from the "still face" experiments (Tronick, 2007). The mother's lack of emotional responsiveness, even for 3 minutes, creates a response of bewilderment, anxiety, shame, and depression in the infant, which has been shown to linger for several minutes afterward. If the failure of reciprocity continues in the long term it may be devastating. A key issue is the development of the child's ability to manage and overcome stress and the child's sense of agency in overcoming a negative interaction. Tronick pointed out that we often romanticize the mother-infant interaction, expecting that it should always be harmonious. But in fact, a degree of disharmony or disruption in mother-infant interactions actually serves a useful purpose in providing the infant with an opportunity to renegotiate the exchanges and so to experience agency through directly affecting the nature of the caregiver's response. Ed Tronick suggested that when the goals of intersubjective dialogue are met between mother and infant, "a confirmation of self takes place" (2007, p. 261). In other words, the infant experiences self-agency.

Of course this can go badly wrong when the child's efforts to affect the parent have no effect or regularly evoke an adverse reaction. A depressed parent responds to the child's positive displays with negative reactions of withdrawal, anger, or despair, so that the child comes to experience his or her own agency as the cause of these negative reactions and may well conclude that any expression of agency is destructive (Tronick, 2007, p. 217). Tronick suggested that in general, when caregivers do not follow the rules of reciprocity, infants learn helplessness—however hard they try to elicit a normal reaction, they eventually learn that their actions have no effect and that the goals of mutuality must be given up. Tronick concluded that "the infant develops a pattern of behavior that precludes human interchange, and in such withdrawal a denial of the child's self is produced" (2007, p. 261). It is precisely the long-term relational consequences of this kind of withdrawal that I describe in Chapter 6, "The Fear of Love."

Beatrice Beebe and Colleagues and the Coconstruction of Relational Patterns

Beatrice Beebe's work with a number of collaborators is closely related to that of the BCPSG and also that of Ed Tronick, but is of particular interest in being the most recent research to correlate specific patterns of mother-infant interactions in very early infancy with later attachment styles and provide overwhelming evidence of the interpersonal basis for the development of self-agency. Their work offers detailed second-by-second analysis of videos of mother-infant interactions. Such a micro-analytic look was advocated by Peck (2003), who argued that more fine-grained and precise investigation might elucidate the process of attachment transmission.

Beebe and Lachmann (1994, 2002) questioned the usual psychoanalytic model of internalization, preferring the concept of coconstruction because it attributes more agency, a more active part in shaping the interaction, to the infant. They argued that what is internalized is the interpersonal patterns of mutual regulation of all behaviors (e.g., attention, orientation, and touch, as well as affect) by a mother and her baby, which happens almost entirely nonconsciously, a point also strongly emphasized by the BCPSG group. An important point to emphasize here is that all patterns of interaction are internalized, not just those where the mother and baby are closely attuned to each other. In their analysis, Beebe et al. (2007, 2010) translated the concept of regulation into that of contingency, a concept that is neutral (with respect to positive or negative connotation) in their hands. Interactive contingency measures the degree to which one partner's behavior is predictable from that of the other. Self-contingency measures the degree of stability (predictability) within an individual's behavioral rhythms. Self-contingency addresses only one aspect of what is more generally defined as self-regulation (Beebe, 2010, personal communication). Beebe et al. highlighted the importance of the degree of self- and interactive contingency, writing:

> Our central hypothesis in predicting 12-month attachment from
> 4-month self- and interactive contingency is that insecurity biases

the system toward contingency which is both heightened (in some modalities) and lowered (in others), compared to values of secure dyads. This hypothesis stands in contrast to the usual position of the infant literature which typically postulates that "more" contingency is "better." (2010, p. 10)

Beebe et al. concluded from their review of the literature and from their own microanalytic studies that:

A number of macro- and micro-analytic studies now converge on an "optimum midrange model" of interactive contingency for attachment and social outcomes, in which both higher and lower degrees of contingent coordination are problematic. Maternal overstimulation, intrusiveness, inconsistency, and particularly high or low levels of maternal stimulation and/or infant and mother responsiveness are associated with insecure outcomes. (2010, p. 23)

It is precisely this midrange experience of interactive contingency that is optimal for the infant's experience of agency—the experience of making an impact on the mother, eliciting a response that reflects the infant's agency but does not overwhelm it. In Beebe et al.'s (2010) most recent studies, they observed 4-month-old infants and their mothers and identified a number of interaction patterns. One of their most striking findings is that 4-month-old infants who later develop disorganized attachment patterns have mothers who are unable to allow themselves to be emotionally affected by their infants' distress; they shut down emotionally, closing their faces (maintaining an overly stable facial expression, akin to a momentary still-face), looking away from the infant's face and failing to coordinate with the infant's emotional state, in a pattern that may be a self-protective dissociation:

Mothers of future D infants may, out of awareness, be afraid of the facial and visual intimacy that would come from more gazing at the infant's face, more coordination with the infant's facial-visual shifts, and more "joining" the infant's distressed moments. These findings confirm and extend Lyons-Ruth's (2008; Lyons-Ruth et al., 1999) proposals that mothers of disorganized infants engage in disrupted and contradictory forms of affective communication, especially around the infant's need for comfort when distressed. (Beebe et al., 2010, p. 99)

Beebe et al. went on to hypothesize:

> If her procedural experience could be put into words, we imag-
> ine that the mother of the future D infant might feel, "I can't
> let myself be too affected by you. I'm not going to let myself be
> controlled by you and dragged down by your bad moods (Karlen
> Lyons-Ruth, personal communication, October 17, 2008). I
> refuse to be helpless. I'm going to be upbeat and laugh off your
> silly fussing." She might feel, "I can't bear to know about your
> distress. Don't be like that. Come on, no fussing. I just need you
> to love me. I won't hear of anything else. You should be very
> happy." And she might feel, "Your distress frightens me. I feel
> that I am a bad mother when you cry." . . . Or she might feel,
> "Your distress threatens me. I resent it. I just have to shut down."
> (2010, p. 100)

Beebe et al. conjectured that these 4-month-old infants, who are later classified as having disorganized attachment at 1 year, may experience:

> the combination of maternal withdrawal of engagement coor-
> dination and "too-steady" faces as a kind of affective "wall."
> Maternal positive faces specifically at moments of infant distress
> further connote a "stone-walling" of infant distress: an active
> maternal emotional refusal to "go with" the infant, a refusal to
> join infant distress, disturbing the infant's ability to feel sensed.
> "We infer that future D infants come to expect that their moth-
> ers will not 'join' their distress with acknowledgments such as
> maternal 'woe face,' an empathic form of maternal facial mirror-
> ing. Instead they come to expect that their mothers are happy,
> surprised, or 'closed' when they are distressed." (2010, p. 100)

For infants, this kind of discordance between their own emotional distress and the maternal denial or refusal that follows is a profound assault on their experience of agency in the relationship. Such an implicit relational pattern leaves the infant with the experience that distressed emotional states meet with a noncontingent, aversive response from the parent. Even though Beebe's research demonstrates that there are many modalities of communication in which the mother's contingency coordination remains intact in dyads where infants are classified D at 1 year, the mothers of these future D infants (mothers who are preoccupied with their own unresolved abuse or trauma) cannot bear to engage with their infants' distress. Essentially, the mother is unable to regulate her own distress when faced with her infant's distress and so cannot regulate that of her baby, let alone mentalize about the baby's experience. My own view is that the baby comes to learn that his distress frightens or overwhelms her and that this implicit relational dynamic could become a pattern of expectation for all subsequent relationships. In the second section, I describe some adult patients who seem to have this belief at the core of their relational experience.

Another older observational study (Goldberg, Blokland, Cayetano, & Benoit, 1998) provided some evidence that also supports the view that the mother's capacity to accurately identify and relate to her infant's negative emotions is crucial. When shown videotapes of their infants expressing a range of emotions, dismissing mothers seemed least interested in or responsive to the infant's affect, while preoccupied mothers were inappropriately responsive. It was the secure-autonomous mothers who showed real empathy, being able to mirror the videotaped infant's negative expressions with negative expressions of their own. They were also more able to recognize fearful expressions, whereas the dismissing mothers tended to misidentify this as interest. This research highlights the importance of the mother's ability to recognize and relate to the infant's emotions, especially negative emotions.

The key point here is one that is powerfully made by Beebe and Lachmann (1994, 2002)—that the infant and caregiver coconstruct a relational dynamic, governed by three organizing principles: (1) ongoing regulation, (2) disruption and repair, and (3) heightened affective moments, all of which contribute to regulation in relation to mutual attention, affect, spatial orientation, and touch.

But the experience of agency also depends on a capacity to draw on our own emotions in a reasonably controlled and purposeful way without being overwhelmed by them. So the capacity for affect regulation also plays a vital part in the development of self-agency, and once again we see that the research evidence convincingly supports the view that the baby's earliest relationships play a fundamental role in the development of affect regulation. Beatrice Beebe's studies of mother-infant interactions show how vital it is for infants' sense of agency to feel able to manage their own emotions and bodily experiences. Their research suggests that 4-month-old infants whose relational experience creates later disorganized attachment suffer from a profound disturbance in the experience of agency in regard to their own states and are more prone to feel helpless to use their emotional and bodily states to organize their own behavior:

> We propose that the future D infant will have difficulty know-
> ing himself (a) in his moments of discrepant affect, for example
> as he smiles and whimpers in the same second; (b) as his own
> engagement self-contingency is lowered, making it more difficult
> to sense his own facial-visual action tendencies from moment-to-
> moment, more difficult to develop a coherent expectation of his
> own body; (c) as he has difficulty touching (self, object, mother),
> and specifically difficulty touching his own skin; and as he gets
> "stuck" in states of "no touch"; all of which disturb his visceral
> feedback through touch, and disturb his own agency in regulating
> distress through touch. (Beebe et al., 2010, p. 104)

The difficulty these infants have in self-comforting through touch and the confusion about what they are feeling contribute to the lack of coherence of self-experience.

Peter Fonagy and the Role of the Caregiver's Capacity to Mentalize

The process of the development of self-agency has three essential characteristics—it is relational, developmental, and also largely unconscious, at least at the earliest levels of self-agency. Fonagy et al. underlined all three of these points, emphasizing the relational basis of self-agency, writing that "we see the self as originally an extension of the experience of the other" (2002, p. 8), and that "the self as agent arises out of the infant's perception of his presumed intentionality in the mind of the caregiver" (p. 11) and "out of inter-personal experience, particularly primary object relationships" (p. 4). They drew on the developmental studies of Gergely, Csibra, and Watson to highlight the developmental and unconscious aspects of self-agency, challenging the essentially Cartesian view, widely held across disciplines from philosophy to developmental psychology, that we "have direct and infallible access to intentional mental states, rather than seeing this as a hard-won developmental acquisition" (2002, p. 3). They suggested that conscious access to the complexity of a range of intentional mental states "may be at best partial and could be totally absent" (2002, p. 4). In other words, in infancy we are acting as agents long before we can be conscious of our agency. This echoes William James's view that bodily sensation precedes reflection:

> Common-sense says, we lose our fortune, are sorry and weep; we meet a bear, are frightened and run; we are insulted by a rival, are angry and strike. The hypothesis here to be defended says that this order of sequence is incorrect . . . that we feel sorry because we cry, angry because we strike, afraid because we tremble. (1890/1983, pp. 1065–1066)

The parent's capacity to mentalize acts as a powerful relational stimulus for the child's developmental trajectory of self-agency, from bodily action to thought and feeling. Fonagy et al. (2002) highlighted the relational basis for this process, suggesting that the parent's attuned reactions reflect back to the infant his own behavior but in a different, more explicit format—the use of facial expression, tone of voice, and simple language—which facilitate the infant's own reencoding of his behavioral experience into implicit and then explicit knowledge. A developmental and emergent view of the self proposes that we become fully human, aware of ourselves and others as psychological and emotional beings and capable of empathy and identification with each other, only when others consistently relate to us as fully human from the earliest moments of infancy. In other words, the parents' perception of their baby as a human being with a self, long before the infant has any such sense of self, is precisely what allows the self to develop. The parent attributes a mind and emotion to the infant before the infant has any capacity for complex thought or feeling or for any degree of self-reflection or moral awareness. This is an example of the scaffolding process (which I describe in more detail in Chapter 4), by which caregivers facilitate infant development by relating to children as though they were at a slightly more advanced developmental stage in any domain (e.g., self-agency) than they actually are.

Although Fonagy and his colleagues placed relationship at the heart of the development of the self, they also emphasized the importance of cognition in the development of self-agency, in the form of mentalization and reflective function. This led them to question the traditional concept of the internal working model, arguing that early experiences are not laid down as an enduring unconscious template but that adverse early experience disrupts later life by inhibiting the development of the capacity to mentalize, specifically in states of high affective arousal. This model suggests that developmental deficits in cognitive capacities and affect regulation, rather than the enduring influence of past emotional patterns of relationship, are the fundamental issue in clinical problems such as borderline personality, in which self-agency is often expressed through physical or emotional coercion (Fonagy et al., 2002, p. 7). Fonagy et al.'s view is that the implication of such developmental failures is that the focus of therapy needs to shift from "the internalization of the containing object to the internalization of the thinking self from within the containing object" (2002, p. 288). In more recent work, Fonagy and Luyten (2009) offered a more developed model of borderline personality disorder, suggesting that the core features reflect impairments in four different facets of mentalization, each related to impairments in relatively distinct neural circuits underlying these facets:

1. A low threshold for the activation of the attachment system and deactivation of controlled mentalization, linked to
2. impairments in the ability to differentiate mental states of self and other, which lead to
3. hypersensitivity and increased susceptibility to contagion by other people's mental states, and
4. poor integration of cognitive and affective aspects of mentalization.

Fonagy and Luyten do acknowledge the central role played by maternal mirroring in the development of affect regulation in their infants. But they focus on one specific maternal response, "marking," in which the mother's response to her infant's communication is exaggerated, to enable to infant to recognize that her response reflects the infant's emotions, not her own.

The Long-Term Impact of Early Relational Experience

The suggestion by Gergely and Watson (1996), and others, that maternal marking plays a central role in the infant's developing sense of self perhaps does not fully take into account the research on implicit turn-taking behaviors, which can only be observed in microanalytic studies and which form an interpersonal behavioral unconscious, as researchers such as Daniel Stern, Allan Schore, Ed Tronick, and Beatrice Beebe have shown. These authors have offered detailed evidence to support their view that it is the patterns of embodied affective interaction with early key attachment figures that form the template for later relational experience; what is internalized is a relational self-other dynamic, not static aspects of the other. This becomes an expected pattern for all subsequent relationships. These goals involve a quite complex range of social exchanges, some of which involve the caregiver apparently disrupting the interaction, but which the infant is then able to repair. A model in which marking is the key process for facilitating the infant's development of affect regulation and mentalization does not include the complex coconstruction of interactions revealed in this other research.

It is these dynamic interpersonal processes that create a template of unconscious expectations that persists into adult life. Broussard and Cassidy (2010) assessed the attitude of mothers to their newborn babies, using the Neonatal Perception Inventory (NPI), which measures the mother's perception of her baby compared with her view of an average baby. Previous research (Broussard, 1976) showed that a mother's positive perception of her infant, as "better" than average, correlates with low risk for subsequent psychosocial problems, while her view that her infant is not better than average correlates with higher risk. In this latest research, Broussard and Cassidy demonstrated that this negative effect continues right into adult life:

> The experience of having been viewed negatively by one's mother as a newborn, as assessed with the NPI, substantially increased the risk of insecure adult attachment. The odds of having an insecure AAI for adults whose mothers had held a negative perception of them at 1 month old were 18 times greater than for adults whose mothers had perceived them positively. (2010, p. 165)

This research coincides with the clinical experience of most therapists, who are constantly confronted with the reality of the powerful unconscious hold that the past can have over our perception of the present, so that we relate to the present as though it were the past, as the clinical examples I give in the next paragraph demonstrate. Indeed, the concept of the transference itself is a description of the experience that the past comes alive in the consulting room, and the work of the BCPSG (2007) offers a more relational and less cognitive account than that of Gergely and Watson for the nature of the infant's experience of the relationship with the mother and of defenses, one in which the infant plays a more active role in creating the maternal response.

In the introduction, I highlighted a theme that runs throughout this book, that embodied relational patterns and implicit affective interactions structure the intrapsychic development and organization of the human mind and brain. This is what internalization really means, not that some thought or fantasy is somehow passed to and taken in by one person's mind from another's (Beebe & Lachmann, 2002; Tronick, 2007). Internalization is a metaphor for the fact that the relational environment—the nature of the embodied and affective experience the infant has with the caregivers—facilitates the development of some patterns of thought, feeling, and relationship, but may inhibit others. The neurobiological basis for this process is described in detail by Schore (2001), and I describe his model more fully in Chapter 3.

So relational interpersonal experience creates an emotional environment that functions in the same Darwinian way as the physical environment—the family patterns of relationship that a child grows up in act as the child's particular interpersonal environment, selecting some relational and emotional patterns of development over others. Two clinical examples illustrate the reality of the power that past experience and the associated affective scripts have to influence the way we interpret present events and relationships and often re-create past interpersonal patterns in our current relationships.

Clinical Illustration 1

A male patient started a session by saying that he was quite worried by the irritation he felt toward his wife over the past week in relation to a facial grimace she had started to make when she was tired and under stress. She was a social worker and had been under enormous pressure at work recently because her case load was so heavy, with very complex and difficult cases. He did not know why he found her facial grimace so annoying, but he found himself surreptitiously watching her, becoming anxious that she might do it again in front of other people.

I remembered that he had recently been very conscious of his mother's mental and emotional frailty. She had a long history of psychiatric illness, with a number of hospital admissions when he was a child. I commented to my patient that as a child, he must have surreptitiously watched for signs in her behavior that might indicate that she was becoming ill again. He remembered that she also developed a similar movement of her head and face under stress, which was often a prelude to the onset of her illness. He remembered the feelings of anxiety and anger that he felt when he saw her facial grimaces.

He was quite shocked to recognize that his own anxiety and anger about the past pattern of his mother's behavior were so similar to his feelings toward his wife and then realized that when his wife was ill, for example, with a heavy cold, he often anxiously checked with her to make sure that she was eating enough. He realized that this was what he also did with his mother, because she neglected to eat when she was ill.

I think this is an example of the activation of an unconscious pattern of the client's childhood relationship with his mother, characterized by his constant vigilance for signs of a decline in her state of mind and his anxiety and anger over her mental and emotional frailty. This did seem to be operating as a template in relation to his relationship with his wife—he was unconsciously expecting her to deteriorate as his mother had done and was experiencing the same feelings that he had had as a child.

Clinical Illustration 2

Another example demonstrates how easily relationships can be sabotaged when two people each bring their own childhood templates into their relationship with each other. Judith Pickering has called this the "interlocking traumatic scene" and gave one vivid example.

The couple were on their honeymoon, on the Great Barrier Reef. The wife, Mimi, said, "Well, we went on this wonderful boat trip, but when it came to jumping in the water, he got cold feet! I said: 'For goodness sake, we came all this way, just get in.'" As they reflected on this in therapy, Mimi remembered that when she was a child, her mother was always nagging her to get in the water in swimming lessons. She clapped her hand to her mouth and said, "Oh my God, I must have seemed just like my mother!"

Pickering went on to describe the ways in which each partner enacted their own and their partner's traumatic childhood experiences:

> Two totally different scenes were thus simultaneously enacted with manifold roles for each player. Steven identified with and played out both Mimi and himself as a child. Mimi incarnated

both her nagging mother and his domineering father. Steven wore the mask of Mimi's preoccupied father staring into space, then enacted her father's demeaning retorts, concurrently switching from the intimidated boy to his autocratic father . . . and so it went on, and back. (2006, p. 261)

Both of these examples illustrate the powerful hold that unconscious templates of early relational patterns can have on a person's perception of a current relationship and the ways in which they feel able to express a sense of agency within that relationship.

Objective empirical evidence for these interpersonal schemas comes from a recent study (Siegel & Demorest, 2010). They are conceived of as affective scripts: sequences of behaviors that regulate emotion in interpersonal relationships (Hoelzer & Dahl, 1996; Siegel, Sammons, & Dahl, 2002). A representative sample of transcripts of a long-term psychotherapy were assessed by independent raters using FRAMES, and this consistently identified core maladaptive scripts in hundreds of narratives, which also emerged in enactments with the therapist.

But the powerful hold that this kind of early interpersonal experience can have on the infant's development is not immutable. Even brief relational experience can modify entrenched patterns in early infancy. Van den Boom (1995) demonstrated the power of the relational environment to modify emotional development from the earliest days of life, in a simple experiment in which she selected 100 infants whose postnatal personalities were highly irritable immediately after birth and so much harder for their mothers to cope with than more placid babies. If the care a parent offers makes no difference to such an emotional trait, then the initial irritability should translate into insecurity a year later, whereas if the baby's relational experience does have an effect, then this should lead to greater security of attachment. When the babies were aged 6 to 9 months, 50 of the mothers received counseling sessions to increase their responsiveness and sensitivity to their babies. Prior to the help, these mothers tended to ignore their babies. Van den Boom taught techniques for soothing the baby, encouraged play, and helped the mother to respond more sensitively to her baby. In contrast, the other 50 mothers and their irritable babies received no extra help.

When the level of emotional security of the two groups were tested at 1 year old, the contrast in the outcomes was clear. In the group who had had no help, 72% of the children were insecure, whereas in the assisted group, only 32% were. Van den Boom concluded, "enhancing maternal sensitive responsiveness results in a secure attachment relationship, and this secure bond then mediates the positive effects discerned later in development" (1995, p. 1813). The only difference was the counseling sessions, so the implication was that even the most difficult babies can become more settled and secure given consistently sensitive and attuned mothering. Other studies have demonstrated similar results.

There is an equally true reverse side to this picture of the mutual influence that a child's unconscious internal expectations and external relationships have on each other. Once a particular pattern of agency and communication has become established in infancy, it affects the responses of all subsequent relationships and so the emotional environment in which the child grows. For example, this has been demonstrated with the different attachment patterns of schoolchildren; schoolteachers who knew nothing of the child's attachment classification nevertheless reacted in quite specific and different ways to avoidant, ambivalent, and secure children:

> They tended to treat securely attached children in warm, matter-of-fact, age-appropriate ways; to indulge, excuse, and infantilize the clingier, more scattered ambivalent children; and to be controlling and angry with the avoidant children, despite the fact that they were equally needy. (Karen, 1998, p. 188)

Karen thus highlighted that the children's differing expectations about how people will respond to them often act as self-fulfilling prophecies, creating a cycle that another author described:

> The parent's early influence may sufficiently launch the infant on a path toward a particular state of attachment organization (or disorganization) so that, in a kind of feed forward model, the infant comes to participate in the formation of its own attachment, simultaneously shaping—and in some cases altering—the degree and type of parental responsiveness that can thereafter be observed. (Hesse, 1999, p. 411)

This interactive view, that interpersonal experience and intrapsychic development mutually influence each other, is at the core of what is meant by the concept of emergence in psychological development. It brings me back to the two related issues reiterated by a number of scientists such as Jack Panksepp (2008), Terrence Deacon (1997), Horst Hendriks-Jansen (1996), and Susan Oyama (2000): Not only is there no preexperiential information—no genetic blueprint guiding development, an issue that I summarized in Chapter 1—but emergence also means that as mind develops it shapes the brain itself, the neuronal pathways that are created and strengthened by repeated patterns of interpersonal experience. This point is repeatedly emphasized not only by neurobiology researchers such as Allan Schore (1994, 2003a) and Daniel Siegel (1999), but also by clinicians who increasingly question the view that there are innate determinants of psychic life, as psychoanalysis and analytical psychology both propose (Hogenson, 2004; Knox, 2003). In the next chapter I focus on some recent research on the neurobiology relating to these interactive patterns and explore some of its implications for the development of self-agency.

3

The Neurobiology of the Self
and of Self-Agency

THE RESEARCH ON THE NEUROSCIENCE OF THE SELF has already created a
vast literature and it quickly becomes apparent that there are a number
of different fields of specialist research, which are not easy to integrate
into a coherent picture. Each of these explores a particular area of neural
circuitry in the human brain and the role that the chosen networks play
in the sense of self and of self-agency. As yet, only a few researchers
are exploring how these different developmental strands of self-experience and their underlying neurobiology can be integrated to begin
to offer a more coherent overview. In one such review article, Uddin,
Iacoboni, Lange, and Keenan (2007) described the differing neural networks that are involved in creating, supporting, and maintaining the self.
They argued that the research evidence suggests that there are two main
networks:

- A network composed of cortical midline structures (CMS), which
  includes the medial prefrontal cortex, the anterior cingulate cortex, and the precuneus. This network has been linked to self-processing and social cognition and overlaps with areas that comprise
  the "default network." One of the defining characteristics of the
  default network is that the constituent areas show decreased activity during goal-related tasks but high metabolic activity when the
  mind is at rest or engaged in nonfocused activity such as autobiographical reminiscences, self-referential thought, or inner
  dialogue.
- A right-lateralized frontoparietal network that overlaps with mir-
  ror-neuron areas and that seems to be involved in self-recognition,

self-awareness, and social understanding. This mirror neuron system (MNS) is active during goal-oriented actions and is central to the sense of embodied self, bridging the gap between the physical self and others through motor simulation mechanisms.

Uddin et al. (2007) highlighted the difficulties involved in teasing apart the relative contributions of the CMS and MNS to self- and other-representation and proposed a unifying model that integrates the bodily-based sense of self that develops through mirror neuron activity, with the more social and psychological aspects of the mental self that depend on CMS activity. (I discuss these integrative processes more fully later in this chapter.)

But this model does not fully spell out the fact that the CMS also depends on the subcortical midline systems described by Jaak Panksepp (1998), which, he suggested, underpin the basic sense of a core self. So the relationship between the CMS and this more fundamental subcortical aspect of midline activity also needs to be described.

In relation to the right-lateralized frontoparietal network, there are also two separate strands of research that need to be distinguished, one on the MNS and the other on aspects of the right orbitofrontal cortex described by Allan Schore and others. These different areas of research can be combined under three headings:

1. Mirror neuron research and the development of an embodied motor-intentional self
2. The research on cortical and subcortical midline structures and the development of a core emotional self
3. The right hemisphere and the development of a relational embodied self

It will be obvious from the wording of these three strands of research that there is considerable overlap between the aspects of the self that they explore, specifically the fact that embodied interpersonal interaction is the foundation of our sense of self and of self-agency. But Uddin et al. (2007), in their description of the differing functions of two main neural networks, suggested that the MNS is restricted to involvement in the earlier physical and social levels of agency, centering on motor simulation and imitation, including imitation of the facial movements involved in the expression of emotion (Carr, Iacoboni, Dubeau,

Mazziotta, & Lenzi, 2003; Sinigaglia, 2008; Wicker et al., 2003). This seems to accord with the views of mirror neuron researchers such as Gallese who suggested that "the shift from motor goals to intentions and abstract rules is beyond the functional properties of the MNS" (Gallese et al., 2009, p. 105). In contrast, the CMS and the right brain (especially the orbitofrontal cortex) seem to have a wider range of function, in that they are involved both in basic, embodied, emotional, and relational self-experience and, at higher cortical levels, with the higher intentional and representational levels of self and self-agency, which are expressed in words, not actions.

Mirror Neuron Research

Bodily imitation has been extensively explored by developmental researchers such as Andrew Meltzoff (2005) as the mechanism for recognizing the intentionality of others and using it to discover our own. The discovery of mirror neurons offers a firm neuroscientific foundation for the view that an infant's self-agency is explored through physical action and through the direct physical mirroring of another's motor intentionality. The crucial characteristic that defines mirror neurons is that the same neurons fire both when carrying out an action and when observing another performing an action.

Mirror neurons have different degrees of specificity, but they work together as a system to encode not just the observed actions per se, but the intention to perform those actions. So when mirror neurons fire, we know what we ourselves would intend if we performed that action and we therefore attribute the same intention to the person we observe. But Sinigaglia (2008) argued that the automatic mirror neuron understanding of the intention of an observed action is certainly not the same as mind reading, the intentional attributions concerning mental states, such as beliefs, desires, and intentions—the conscious reason for performing an action. Mirror neuron activity provides a direct matching of the others' observed behavior to our own motor repertoire, a neurological mirroring process that functions automatically and does not require any conscious concept or inference. Sinigaglia pointed out the fact that

> mirror-based understanding specifically involves the immedi-
> ate recognition of the goal-relatedness of the observed motor

acts and this recognition depends on the fact that those acts are mapped onto the vocabulary of the observer's own motor acts. (2008, p. 77)

He suggested, "The fact that mirror neurons cannot capture reasons, beliefs, desires, and intentions . . . is not, however an argument against the possibility of their having a role in intentional attribution" (2008, p. 89). Mirror neurons are the means for action understanding, not mind understanding. In case any confusion remains in the mind of the reader, Rizzolatti and Sinigaglia spelled this out even more clearly:

> In humans as in monkeys, the sight of acts performed by others produces an immediate activation of the motor areas deputed to the organization and execution of these acts, and through this activation it is possible to decipher the meaning of the "motor events" observed, i.e. to understand them in terms of goal-centred movements. This understanding is completely devoid of any reflexive, conceptual and/or linguistic mediation as it is based exclusively on the vocabulary of acts and the motor knowledge on which our capacity to act depends. (2008, p. 125)

A philosopher, Emma Borg (2007), has questioned this view of mirror neurons, suggesting that maybe what the mirror neurons do is activate intentionality itself rather than the specific form it takes. She argued that mirror neurons do not read the other person's specific intention but merely identify that the other person was acting purposefully. In her view of mirror neurons, "if all they do is help determine which actions in the world count as intentional this still leaves it entirely open how one proceeds to attribute specific intentions to these actions" (Borg, 2007, p. 10). As Borg argued, picking up a cup can then lead to a number of subsequent actions, from lifting it to the mouth to drink to clearing it away.

However, Sinigaglia effectively questioned the underlying premises of Borg's argument, showing that she has not understood the highly specific function of mirror neurons; he suggested that Borg seemed to be using the term *intention* to mean conscious motivation, the beliefs and desires from which the actions of adult humans do indeed largely originate. But the word *intention* can cover a spectrum, from the completely mindless automatic motor intentionality of an amoeba engulfing food to the conscious highly symbolic expression of desire in romantic poetry. It is this confusion around the exact nature of intention that seems to give rise to some of the disagreements about the role of mirror neurons in intentionality.

Borg seemed to assume that human intentionality is always conscious. But many behaviors that appear to have conscious purposive intent are actually entirely nonconscious automatic action sequences, such as the dam building of beavers—but clearly still intentional in a motor sense. Daniel Dennett highlighted this distinction in his book *Darwin's Dangerous Idea,* in which he suggested that highly complex animal behavior results from a "something as mindless and mechanical as an algorithm. . . a set of individually mindless steps succeeding each other without the help of any intelligent supervision" (1995, p. 59). However, the problem with Dennett's model is the suggestion that these subroutines are hard-wired into each species' brain as an algorithm, a set of instructions or a computational module in the animal's mind, which has evolved through natural selection. This computational model implies some kind of centralized controlling module of information or set of instructions in the animal's brain or central nervous system, but in Chapter 1, I have described the arguments given by Oyama, Hendriks-Jansen, Panksepp, and others that demonstrate the biological inconsistencies in that model.

Mirror neuron researchers do not propose a central set of instructions in the brain, but describe these motor action sequences as "intentional chains in which each motor act is facilitated by the previously executed one" (Fogassi et al., 2005, p. 665) and propose that these chains also provide the building blocks upon which the intentional understanding of another's actions can be constructed given the appropriate contextual cues (Sinigaglia, 2008, p. 83). Rizzolatti and Sinigaglia expanded on this to explain that there are species-specific preferred action chains. For example, the action chains for grasping are more strongly linked in monkeys to putting food in the mouth than placing it elsewhere. They suggest that this bias in favor of certain action chains is genetically hard-wired in a species-specific way.

However, I would suggest that these biases are not necessarily hard-wired but are emergent, early developmental products of the infant's interaction with caregivers and with the world around them. The infants of all species learn from a very young age that putting food into one's mouth is far more enjoyable than placing it somewhere else. This view of mirror neuron phenomena as epigenetic, not innate, is also that of Jaak Panksepp, whose work I discuss in the next section (Panksepp & Northoff, 2008). These behaviors emerge from the interaction of instinctual, genetically programmed affective neural networks in the subcortex (the core-SELF described in the next section) with the stimulus provided by the species-typical environment, which together build the chain of automatic motor action sequences that is characteristic of each species, such as dam building in beavers.

Automatic behavior patterns in animals can therefore be under significant genetic influence through the influence of subcortical affective neural networks. But mental imagery and thought are the result of much more complex interactions between brain, mind, and environment and in which genetic hardwiring plays virtually no part. These higher mental processes reflect the general information-processing activity of the human neocortex, as I discussed in Chapter 1.

There is one experiment conducted by Meltzoff (2005) that does at first sight seem to undermine this argument that mirror neurons are the basis for motor or action understanding, not for understanding the conscious intention of the other person. In Meltzoff's experiment, there is a toy with a loop and another part with a hook. The infant observes the researcher, who moves as though to hang the loop on the hook, but drops it beside the hook instead, as though by mistake. Borg's objection is that infants could not understand the intention of the adult if they had never seen the toy in use before and so could not have an understanding of what constitutes typical behavior with such objects. "Why would hanging the loop on the hook in this context count as 'what's most likely to come next'?" (Borg 2007, pp. 13–14). At first sight it does indeed look as though infants, when they hang the loop on the hook, have read the researcher's mind, in that they do not copy the researcher's action but appear to read the observer's apparent conscious intention. Borg used this evidence in support of her argument that infants could not possibly read the specific intention of the adult but could identify that there is conscious intentionality behind the action.

But Sinigaglia suggested that the infant's action of hanging the loop on the hook "depends on the selection of those action chains that are most compatible with the observed situation" (2008, p. 131). But why would hanging the loop on the hook be the preferred action sequence for the infant? Would, for example, the observation that one object frequently goes into another, such as food into a mouth, be sufficiently similar to an action of hanging a loop on a hook to trigger the action chain? It seems to me that this is more compatible with the role of mirror neurons, whose activation is the mechanism by which the young of a species acquire a series of goal-directed action sequences, for example, by observing their parents' action sequences; this observation then activates the mirror neurons that are involved in the infant's own similar sequence of intention-action chains. Part of the species-typical environment is the behavior of the parent animal that stimulates and molds these automatic action sequences.

Gallese et al. extended this developmental approach to suggest that the infant's capacity to respond to a novel stimulus (such as the loop and hook) may have its origins in antenatal development, for example:

> During pre-natal development specific connections may develop between the motor centers controlling mouth and hand goal-directed behaviors and brain regions that will become the recipients of visual input after birth. . . . Such connectivity could provide functional templates (e.g., specific spatiotemporal patterns of neural firing) to areas of the brain, that once reached by visual information, would be ready to specifically respond to the biological motion like hand or face gestures. (2009, p. 106)

For the infant who hangs the loop on the hook, the completion of the act has become structured in the secondary prefrontal and parietal areas of the infant's cortex as a relational motor dynamic, probably activated by the embodied similarity with previous satisfying actions of linking— such as clasping hands together, putting thumb in mouth, and other actions by which one object is connected with another, or one part of the body with another.

Mirror neuron researchers have found that there is another category of neurons in the premotor cortex, canonical neurons, which have properties linked to, but with some differences from those of mirror neurons. Gallese and Umilta suggested that canonical neurons in the ventral premotor cortex of monkeys fired

> when the monkey, in the absence of any active movement, observed objects whose intrinsic features, such as size and shape, were strictly related to the type of action that the very same neurons motorically encoded. (2002, p. 37)

They suggested that these canonical neurons contribute to the relational basis for our understanding of objects in the world around, in that

> the objects whose observation triggers the neurons' response are analyzed in relational terms. Object observation . . . determines the activation of the motor programme that would be required, were the observer actively interacting with the object. Looking at objects means to unconsciously "simulate" a potential action. The object-representation is transiently integrated with the action-simulation (the ongoing simulation of the potential action). (Gallese & Umilta, 2002, p. 37)

Gallese and Umilta concluded that:

> Objects are not merely identified and recognized by virtue of their physical "appearance" but in relation with the effects of the interaction with an agent. . . . [T]he object acquires a meaningful value by means of its dynamic relation with the agent of this action. (2002, p. 37)

In other words, they suggest that our meaningful experience of the world around us is rooted in the kinds of physical interactions we have with it and so with the experience of agency at the physical level. The key question, of course, is whether this action-based experience of agency can form the foundation for agency at the psychological level, through symbolism and abstract thought. I discuss this in the next chapter, but here I would highlight the role of mirror neurons in empathy. Gallese points out that there is a tight link between embodied simulation and our perception of the emotions of others, shown by their facial expressions. "When people observe pictures of emotional facial expressions, they show spontaneous unconscious and rapid electromyographic responses in the same facial muscles involved in the person's facial expression" (Gallese, 2007, p. 149). He indicates that this rapid and automatic activation of facial muscles is probably triggered by activation of the MNS. Gallese concludes:

> Furthermore in an fMRI study, Carr, Iacoboni, Dubeau, Mazziotta and Lenzi (2003) showed that both observation and imitation of the facial expression of emotions activate the same

restricted group of brain structures, including the ventral premotor cortex, the insula and the amygdala. The perception and production of emotion-related facial expressions both impinge upon
common neural structures whose function could be characterized
as that of a mirror matching mechanism. (Gallese, 2007, p. 149)

empathy

This kind of automatic empathy, based on the activation of shared facial
expression, plays a crucial role in the experience of agency in social relationships, from infancy onwards.

The Research on Subcortical Midline Structures and the Development of a Core Emotional Self

The model I shall draw on most extensively is that of Jaak Panksepp,
whose groundbreaking book *Affective Neuroscience* was published in
1998. There and in subsequent publications (Panksepp, 2008; Panksepp
& Northoff, 2009; Panksepp & Panksepp, 2000), he takes a biological
epigenetic approach in which higher functions are identified as emergent properties of the interaction of low-level core neural networks with
higher cognitive abilities. Panksepp repeatedly warned of the error of
assuming that genetic control determines the nature of the conscious
human mind. He stated: "Evolutionary psychologists have yet to reveal
a single higher human mind function that has clearly been molded by
genetic inheritance, not even the famous 'language instinct'" (2008,
p. 414). His view accords with the epigenetic models of the developmental biologists and psychologists, such as Susan Oyama and Annette
Karmiloff-Smith, that I described in Chapter 1.

But this does not mean that Panksepp in any way underestimates
the importance of biology in the development of the self. The key issue
is the neurological and developmental level at which genetic influence
predominates. Panksepp suggested that the most basic form of self is
biological and transspecies, consisting of genetically ingrained neural
networks that allow an organism to selectively and adaptively relate to
its environment. This proto-SELF consists of integrative processing and
sensitivity to an organism's own internal bodily states and functions,
motor activity, and environmental stimuli and is present not just in
humans but in other mammals and even in early vertebrates. Damasio
also used the term *proto-self* to define "a coherent collection of neural
patterns which maps, moment by moment, the state of the physical

structure of the organism in its many dimensions" (1999, p. 154). But Panksepp capitalizes SELF to make clear that he is referring to evolutionarily determined specific midbrain neural networks, rather than to a concept or conscious experience of self. The networks for the proto-SELF are those of the midbrain, such as the periaqueductal gray and the deep layers of the superior colliculi. This subcortical midline system (SCMS) is in effect an autonomic-affective body schema, which activates "coherent action patterns with all the bodily and affective accompaniments of normal emotions" (Panksepp & Northoff, 2009, p. 199). Panksepp pointed out that the deep layers of the superior colliculi may well be the first evolutionary site for a bodily representation of the self, in that they contain multimodal sensory systems and motor control functions that can control simple orientation responses, such as the eye movements an animal needs for rapid orientation during pursuit (1998, p. 77). He also highlighted the role of the midbrain locomotor region (Figure 3.1), which integrates neural networks that are essential for setting up coherent action patterns (1998, p. 312). Panksepp's view is that these motor functions are more central to the SELF than are somatosensory processes. It is action and motor coherence that allow an organism to function in its environment. I would suggest that the proto-SELF can therefore be considered as the neural network underpinning the most fundamental motor expression of agency.

The proto-SELF provides the evolutionary substrate for the emergence of the core-SELF, which includes specific and clearly defined core emotional circuits concentrated in the medial mesencephalic and diencephalic deep subcortical regions and shared by all mammals (Figure 3.2). (The mesencephalon is the midbrain, including the areas described in the previous paragraph. The diencephalon is the posterior part of the forebrain that connects the midbrain with the cerebral hemispheres, encloses the third ventricle, and contains the thalamus and hypothalamus.)

Panksepp has offered a wealth of research to support his view that these motivational and emotional systems of the core-SELF are those of SEEKING, RAGE, LUST, CARE, PANIC, and PLAY (Panksepp, 1998; Panksepp & Panksepp, 2000). These are capitalized to mark the fact that they refer, not to conscious emotional states of mind, but to specific neurobiological circuits in the subcortical systems of all mammalian brains. The core-SELF is the level at which primary-process consciousness is possible, once the proto-SELF is linked to these

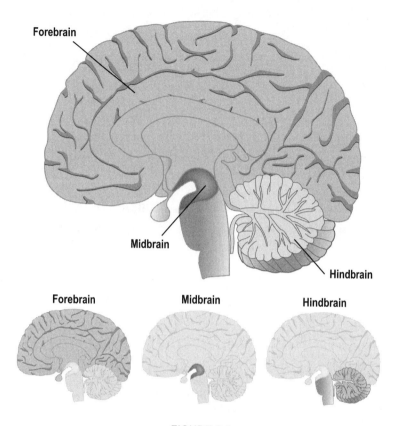

FIGURE 3.1

Diagram of the midbrain. From *A Dictionary of Biology*. 2004, Encyclopedia. com, accessed March 8, 2010.

affective networks. This "affective consciousness" is the "relation of one's body to the incentives in the environment as well as internally generated emotional arousals" (Panksepp & Northoff, 2009, p. 196), in other words, a primitive form of consciousness, which at this level is essentially affective.

The proto-SELF and the core-SELF together constitute the nomothetic SELF, the word *nomothetic* being used to make it clear that this is a universal neural substrate, shared across mammalian species, and not an individual subjective experience of self (the idiographic self, which I shall describe in a moment). Panksepp and Northoff highlighted the importance of agency in this nomothetic mammalian level of self:

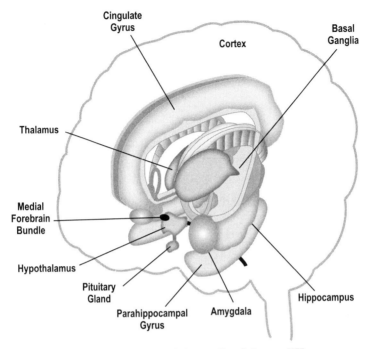

Cingulate
Gyrus

Cortex

Basal
Ganglia

Thalamus

Medial
Forebrain
Bundle

Hypothalamus

Pituitary
Gland

Parahippocampal
Gyrus

Amygdala

Hippocampus

Diencephalon = Thalamus + Hypothalamus + MFB

FIGURE 3.2

Diagram of diencephalous.

Such a basic level of self may allow organisms to become spon-
taneously active organisms, able to relate intimately to the environment soon after birth. We envision the core-SELF to allow
organisms to be active agents, as opposed to simply passive information-processing machines. (2009, p. 194)

One of the emotional/motivational systems of the core-SELF is that of
the SEEKING system, which generates the seeking of resources essential to survival:

A system that provides a goad with no fixed goal for exploratory/
investigatory activity. This system is capable of helping construct
goal-directed behavior patterns based on the confluence of bodily

need states, environmentally accessible reward objects, and contextual contingencies. (Panksepp & Panksepp, 2000, p. 119)

This system of the core-SELF could therefore be regarded as the emotional and motivational foundation of self-agency, a system that provides the drives and urges that direct an organism's motor activity and by which it seeks to meet its needs.

The nomothetic SELF emerges not only from the activity of SCMS, but also from that of higher medial cortical levels, which facilitate affective cognitive integration, so yielding a fully developed nomothetic SELF. This process of integration is described by Panksepp as "self-related processing" (SRP), which allows stimuli from the environment to be related and linked to organismic needs by processing within SCMS. Panksepp and Northoff postulated that:

> Core SRP operates automatically, is deeply affective, and is developmentally and epigenetically connected to sensory-motor and higher cognitive abilities. This core-SELF is mediated by SCMS, embedded in visceral and instinctual representations of the body that are well integrated with basic attentional, emotional and motivational functions that are apparently shared between humans, non-human mammals and, perhaps in a proto-SELF form, with other vertebrates. (2009, p. 194)

Self-related processing is thus an important part of the emotional experience of agency, because it allows external events to be linked to the organism's felt emotional and motivational urges (Northoff & Panksepp, 2008).

The core-SELF and SRP provide the biological platform for the emergence of environmentally constructed subjective or idiographic selves, "the reflective or cognitive self, which permits *awareness* as opposed to *raw experience* of phenomenal-affective contents" (Northoff & Panksepp, 2008, p. 195). It is these higher forms of self that are species-specific, require higher cognitive brain regions in the neocortex, and are probably largely confined to humans and some other animals (higher primates, elephants, and cetaceans). The idiographic self in humans allows self-reflection and narrative processes and so underpins the sense of self-agency at the intentional and representational levels, which I discuss in more detail in Chapter 4. The idiographic self emerges through individualized learning processes that result from each person's unique developmental-epigenetic-cultural experiences. SRP provides the foundation for epigenetic emergence of these higher idiographic forms of selfhood, integrating the core-SELF regions of the medial brain stem and medial frontal lobes with higher associative, more strictly cognitive regions of the brain such as lateral frontal and parietal cortices. Panksepp and Northoff (2009) pointed out that, once the idiographic, reflective self has become established, it can modulate the core-SELF, so that there is a two-way influence between higher and lower forms of selfhood. This is an important consideration in relation to the possible neurobiological processes by which psychotherapy may help to establish and consolidate a patient's secure sense of self and of self-agency.

The Right Hemisphere and the Development of a Relational Embodied Self

One of the strongest themes to emerge from studies of mother-infant relationships is that the infant's earliest relational experiences directly affect the development of the brain; a healthy emotional environment allows key neuronal connections to flourish, while an adverse experience of relationships means that the growth of these pathways is stunted or inhibited to varying degrees.

In Chapter 2, I highlighted the fact that this interactive view, that interpersonal experience and intrapsychic development mutually influence each other, is at the core of what is meant by the concept of emergence in psychological development. Repeated patterns of interpersonal experience create and strengthen new neuronal pathways, enabling new mental, emotional, and relational capacities to emerge. These, in turn, stimulate new responses from the caregiver, which in turn stimulate the infant's mind and brain. This point has been repeatedly emphasized not only by neurobiology researchers such as Allan Schore (1994, 2003a) and Daniel Siegel (1999), but also by clinicians who increasingly question the view that there are innate determinants of psychic life, as both psychoanalysis and analytical psychology propose. (Hogenson, 2004; Knox, 2003). There is no genetic blueprint guiding development, an issue that I summarized in the first chapter and a view supported by researchers such as Panksepp & Panksepp (2000), Deacon (1997), Hendriks-Jansen (1996), and Oyama (2000).

Allan Schore has explored the relational basis for the development of the brain, particularly the neuronal pathways involved in interpersonal experience and emotional regulation. His book *Affect Regulation and the Development of the Self* (Schore, 1994) was the first to pinpoint the role of right-brain interaction between mother and infant in facilitating affect regulation and a stable and secure sense of self. He suggested that the core of the self lies in patterns of affect regulation that integrate a sense of self across state transitions, thereby allowing for a continuity of inner experience. This highlights the importance of affect regulation in contributing to self-agency, our sense of being able to draw on and manage our own emotions for our own purposes and to express our conscious intentions, rather than being flooded by emotions that feel alien and out of control.

In recent articles, Schore argued that attachment theory has now moved from being primarily a theory of behavioral interaction between mother and infant to become one centered on affect and self-regulation, a view strongly supported by the observational studies of Beatrice Beebe and colleagues (discussed in Chapter 2). This shifts the focus of theory from external observed behavior to the internal world of felt experience, emotion, and relationship, the implicit relational knowledge the infant acquires from the first moments of life. Schore's research shows that the self-other relationship is embedded in infant-caregiver, right hemisphere to right hemisphere, affective, attachment communications (Schore, 1994, 2001 2003a, 2003b, 2005, 2009). He pointed out that the emotion-processing human limbic system myelinates in the first year and a half (Kinney, Brody, Kloman, & Gilles, 1988) and the early maturing right hemisphere, which is deeply connected into the limbic system, is undergoing a growth spurt at this time, so attachment experiences specifically impact on limbic and cortical areas of the developing right cerebral hemisphere (Cozolino, 2002; Henry, 1993; Schore, 1994; Siegel, 1999).

These findings have important implications for our understanding of the development of self-agency and the crucial part that empathic maternal mirroring plays in this process. Neurobiological research on the mother-infant intersubjective dialogue indicates:

> A number of functions located within the right hemisphere work together to aid monitoring of a baby. As well as emotion and face processing the right hemisphere is also specialized in auditory

perception, the perception of intonation, attention, and tactile information. (Bourne & Todd, 2004, pp. 22–23)

So from infancy through all later stages of the life span, the right hemisphere is dominant for the development of our implicit relational knowing, the "nonconscious reception, expression, and communication of emotion and the cognitive and physiological components of emotional processing" (Schore, 2009, p. 6). In the previous chapter I described the research that shows that it is the turn-taking interactions and the experience of agency in the earliest relationships that form the foundation for this implicit relational knowing and for the subsequent development of self-agency.

Decety and Chaminade supported Schore's view of the central role of the right hemisphere in relationship, writing that "self-awareness, empathy, identification with others, and more generally intersubjective processes, are largely dependent upon the right hemisphere resources, which are the first to develop" (2003, p. 591). More recently, Decety and Meyer stated:

> Shared neural circuits, self-awareness, mental flexibility, and emotion regulation constitute the basic macrocomponents of empathy; these are mediated by specific neural systems, including aspects of the pre-frontal cortex, the anterior insula and fronto-parietal networks. (2009, p. 14)

Decety and Meyer extended this exploration of the role of the right hemisphere to suggest that it not only underpins empathy but also the infant's gradual discovery of his or her agency, and that the capacity to experience agency is also critical for empathy:

> In a completely empathic experience, affective sharing must be modulated and monitored by the sense of whose feelings belong to whom (Decety & Jackson, 2004). Furthermore, self-awareness generally and agency in particular are crucial aspects in promoting a selfless regard for another, rather than a selfish desire to escape aversive arousal. (2009, p. 149)

So the mothers so poignantly described in the research by Beebe et al. (2010), discussed in Chapter 2, who could not bear their babies' distress because it aroused too much distress of their own, exactly reflect the situation described by Schore, Decety, and others. They were unable to show a selfless regard, to use their right brains to empathize with or mentalize about their babies. Their inability to relate empathically would, in turn, inhibit the infant's developing right brain and so that child would also grow up with a diminished capacity for both empathy and agency, unless the parent is lucky enough to benefit from the kind of intervention so effectively offered to mothers by van den Boom (described in Chapter 2).

So what areas of the right brain are involved in the experience and attribution of agency? Decety and Meyer (2009) drew on neuroimaging studies to propose that the junction of the right inferior parietal cortex with the posterior temporal cortex (the temporoparietal junction) plays a critical role in the distinction between self-produced actions and actions generated by others. The temporoparietal junction is an association cortex that

> integrates input from the lateral and posterior thalamus, as well as visual, auditory, somesthetic and limbic areas. It has reciprocal connections to the prefrontal cortex and to the temporal lobes. Because of these anatomical characteristics, this region is a key neural locus for self-processing: it is involved in multisensory body-related information processing as well as in the processing of phenomenological and cognitive aspects of the self. (Decety & Meyer, 2009, p. 149)

Awareness of agency—that an action is self-generated—seems to depend on activation of the anterior insula bilaterally, whereas attributing an action to another person activates the right inferior parietal cortex, as shown by Farrer and Frith (2002), who conducted experiments in which participants were asked to use a joystick to drive a circle along a specific path. In one case, they knew they controlled the movement of the circle, so attributed the action to themselves, and the anterior insula was activated; in another case, they knew that the experimenter was actually in control, even though they themselves performed the same action with the joystick, and so they did not attribute the action to themselves. In this case the right inferior parietal cortex was activated. Interestingly, another experiment (Modinos, Ormel, & Aleman 2009) that involved reflecting on oneself or on another person seemed to activate the left insula. But this experiment did not involve any action on the part of the participants, but only a process of conscious reflection on self and other. So this may not have activated the neural circuits directly concerned with the experience of agency, but rather those concerned with self-awareness; so the distinction between a sense of self (the Jamesian Me) and self-agency (the Jamesian I) may be reflected in these neurobiological findings.

But the experience of agency depends not only on the impact one has on the other, but also on the capacity to self-regulate one's own emotional and bodily states. The psychological regulatory structures described by self psychology originate in the right hemispheric specialization in regulating stress and emotion-related processes (Sullivan & Dufresne, 2006). Indeed, the brain's major self-regulatory systems are located in the orbital prefrontal areas of the right hemisphere (Bradshaw & Schore, 2007). Schore (1994) marshalled a wealth of evidence to support the view that the experience-dependent maturation of this affect regulatory system is thus directly related to the origin of the self and that the right hemisphere is specialized for generating self-awareness and self-recognition, and for the processing of "self-related material" (Miller et al., 2001).

Can These Three Models Be Integrated Into a Coherent Neurobiological Account of the Development of Self-Agency?

Each of these areas of research investigates a different aspect of self and of self-agency. Mirror neuron researchers study the role of motor simulation as the basis for a sense of embodied self. Panksepp and his colleagues examined the midline subcortical and cortical systems that create an emotional core SELF, while Allan Schore and colleagues placed the development of the right brain at the heart of the relational self from the first moments of life.

This brings me to the key question: To what extent do these networks become integrated during development, to contribute to a sense of self and of self-agency? There are, as yet, few articles that offer such integrative models, but there are some references to the issue of integration in some of the research I have already cited. For example, Biven and Panksepp (2007, p. 142) took up the point that I emphasized earlier in this chapter, that the mirror neuron-based intentional action chains, described by Fogassi et al. (2005), may not be hardwired (genetically determined) but may be developmentally programmed by the midline subcortical systems—the SCMS described by Panksepp—that control attentional and emotional arousal. This would be in keeping with the epigenetic and emergent view of psychological development, for which I described the detailed and overwhelming evidence in Chapter 1.

Once a connection between midline and mirror neuron networks has been established by such developmental processes, there is the possibility for the influence to be reciprocal. So not only can the SCMS entrain mirror neuron intentional chains, the mirror neuron system can directly affect the CMS that activate the core-SELF emotional networks. The fact that there are direct neural connections between these two systems is also described by Carr et al. (2003), whose research showed that both observation and imitation of the facial expression of emotions activated ventral premotor cortex (part of the MNS) and also the insula and the amygdala (part of the limbic system). So the superior temporal and inferior frontal cortices, which are critical areas for action representation, are connected to the limbic system via the insula. Thus, the insula may be a critical relay from the mirror neuron system to the SCMS, and so from action representation to emotion.

Modinos et al. (2009) also highlighted the importance of the insula in self-reflection and generally in self-referential processing, including interoceptive awareness, and awareness of subjective feeling and bodily arousal states. They suggested that insular activity could actually be related to an emotional component that might be inherent to self-processing; in other words, to the self being an emotional entity per se, since emotion almost always involves consciously or unconsciously evaluating an event as relevant to a person's concerns or goals:

> Taken together, this evidence supports the notion that the insula is a supramodal structure, involved in a myriad of processes closely related to facilitating a sense of self. Disturbances in insula activity may result in social and emotional impairments commonly observed in psychopathology, as recently suggested by a study showing differential insula involvement in the failure to maintain adequate social interactions by people with Borderline Personality Disorder. (Modinos et al., 2009, e4618)

These social and psychological aspects of the development of agency may also depend on the activity of cortical midline and right brain structures, such as the anterior cingulate and the orbitofrontal cortex. Allan Schore (2001), in particular, has described in detail how early relational experience with an empathic attuned caregiver allows the regulatory functions of the orbitofrontal cortex to impact on the limbic and subcortical midline systems that govern the experience of emotion. Schore regards the links between cortex, especially the right orbitofrontal cortex, and subcortical systems as crucial:

> In its critical period the orbitofrontal areas are synaptically connecting with other areas of the cerebral cortex, but they are also forging contacts with subcortical areas. And so the orbitofrontal cortex is a "convergence zone" where cortex and subcortex meet. (2001, p. 224)

He highlights how vulnerable this system is to adverse relational experiences, in that early trauma or neglect induces excessive pruning of cortical-subcortical limbic-autonomic circuits. This severe growth impairment creates a developmental structural defect in limbic system organization. This has significant implications not only in terms of damage to the individual's maturing stress coping systems, but also for the development of self-agency, because, as I have indicated, self-agency develops out of an active process of exploration, through processes such as turn-taking, in relationship. At a neurobiological level, self-agency can be thought of as an aspect of the SEEKING system of the core-SELF and SCMS that Panksepp described. So if the cortical-subcortical connections are severely impaired, relationships can no longer stimulate the primordial motive systems to attach, which are located in subcortical components of the limbic system.

> These brainstem neuromodulatory and hypothalamic neuroendocrine systems that regulate the HPA axis are in a critical period of growth pre- and postnatally, and they regulate the maturation of the later developing cerebral cortex. . . . Severe attachment problems with the caregiver negatively impact the postnatal development of these biogenic amine systems. (Schore, 2001, p. 207)

It is precisely this kind of damage to the attachment and SEEKING neural systems that may underpin some of the clinical phenomena, which center on a profound inhibition of self-agency in relationships and which I describe in Part II.

The orbitofrontal cortex is not only where the cortex and subcortex meet, but also a convergence zone where the external and internal worlds meet, primarily through the relationship with the primary caregiver in infancy. So the role of the right brain and the development of the relational self is another central component of the integration of the three perspectives on the self that I am focusing on in this chapter. Schore emphasized that caregiver-induced trauma is qualitatively and quantitatively more potentially psychopathogenic than any other social or physical stressor because the immature infant's brain is utterly dependent on the primary caregiver for stress regulation:

> The stress regulating systems that integrate mind and body are a product of developing limbic-autonomic circuits (Rinaman, Levitt, & Card, 2000), and because their maturation is experience dependent, during their critical period of organization they are vulnerable to relational trauma. (2001, p. 207)

When the caregiver fails to regulate the infant's distress, this leads to a blunting of the stress response in the right (and not left) prefrontal cortex, and these interruptions of early cortical development specifically affect limbic association areas and social behavior (Talamini, Koch, Luiten, Koolhaas, & Korf, 1999). So, in human infancy, relational trauma interferes with the experience-dependent maturation of the brain's coping systems, and therefore has a long-enduring negative impact on the trajectory of developmental processes, including that of self-agency. Clinical descriptions of the long-term impact of relational trauma on the development of self-agency follow in Part II.

In a comprehensive overview of the links between the three neural networks, in the article I cited at the start of this chapter, Uddin et al. (2007) proposed a unifying model that links the right brain, the MNS, and the CMS in representing the self. They supported Schore's view of the importance of the right hemisphere for a sense of self, emphasizing "that a network of right frontoparietal structures is vital for generating self-awareness" (2007, p. 153), but also pointed out that these frontoparietal areas involved in self-recognition significantly overlap with areas that contain mirror neurons. They went on to review evidence that suggests that:

A right lateralized MNS is involved in understanding the multimodal embodied self (e.g. its face and its voice) whereas CMS seem to represent a less bodily grounded self as shaped by its social relationships. Interactions between these two systems are likely to be crucial to social functioning. (Uddin et al., 2007, p. 153)

Uddin et al. went on to amplify this account of the CMS, by describing its role in maintaining social and psychological aspects of the self, which involve evaluative processes, such as self-referential judgments and self-appraisal. These CMS areas are also involved in other social tasks, such as processing social relationships, which require an understanding of others' mental states, so, in effect, acting as a constant monitor of the self in a social context, a form of evaluative simulation comparable to the motor simulation of the MNS.

They pointed out that the existence of direct connections between the precuneus, which is a major node in the CMS, and the inferior parietal lobe, part of the MNS, suggests that this is one pathway by which the two networks may interact and coordinate their activity. There are also connections between the mesial frontal areas and the inferior frontal gyrus (Rizzolatti & Luppino, 2001). Uddin et al. concluded:

Although the exact nature of the interactions between these two networks is unknown, it is likely that the direct connections between them facilitate integration of information that is necessary for maintaining self-other representations across multiple domains. One intermediate representational domain in which both neural systems might cooperate is the domain of imagination. (2007, p. 156)

I discuss imagination more fully in Chapter 4, examining the part it plays in the developmental trajectory of self-agency from bodily action to emotional and mental expression. But to understand why imagination is so important from a neuroscientific and developmental perspective, I first need to introduce a fairly recent discovery in neuroscience, the default network, which Uddin et al. regarded as critically important to the processes by which the brain integrates memories, emotions, and self-experience.

The Default Network

The default network is a network of brain areas comprising the posterior cingulate and precuneus, anterior cingulate and medial-prefrontal cortex, and temporoparietal junctions, which show more metabolic activity when the brain is at rest than during attention-demanding and goal-directed tasks, consuming 30% more calories for its weight than any other area of the brain (Raichle et al., 2001).

Buckner, Andrews-Hanna, and Schacter describe the multiple functions of the default network:

> The default network is active when individuals are engaged in internally focused tasks including autobiographical memory retrieval, envisioning the future, and conceiving the perspectives of others. Probing the functional anatomy of the network in detail reveals that it is best understood as multiple interacting

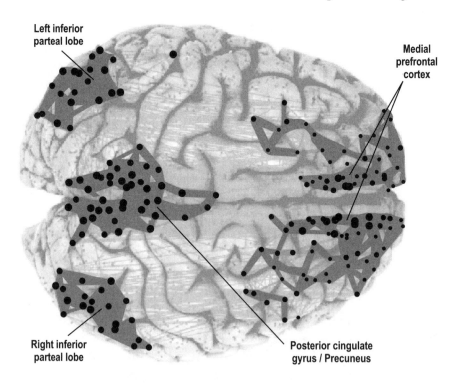

FIGURE 3.3
The default network

subsystems. The medial temporal lobe subsystem provides information from prior experiences in the form of memories and associations that are the building blocks of mental simulation. The
medial prefrontal subsystem facilitates the flexible use of this
information during the construction of self-relevant mental simulations. These two subsystems converge on important nodes of
integration including the posterior cingulate cortex. (2008, p. 1)

Put together, these suggest that the default network might provide the
brain with an inner rehearsal for considering future actions and choices.
At first this was considered to be the mechanism for daydreaming but, in
2003, Michael Greicius found that there are resting state fluctuations in
the default network—slow waves of neural activity that ripple through in
a coordinated fashion, linking its component brain areas into a coherent
unit. The waves were up to 100 times slower than typical EEG brain-
waves. These synchronized waves were found in both sedated humans
and in early sleep, thus refuting the idea that they are only involved in
conscious daydreaming (Greicius et al., 2008). Researchers now believe
that the default network is central to the process of selectively storing
and updating memories based on their importance from a personal perspective and their emotional quality. To prevent a backlog of unstored
memories building up, the network is constantly communicating with
the hippocampus and returns to its sorting process whenever the brain is
not engaged in an active task.

Northoff and Panksepp also emphasized the importance of the
default network in self-related processing (SRP), suggesting that high
degrees of self-relatedness and emotional processing correspond to high
resting-state neuronal activity, particularly in the subcortical and cortical midline regions, which are part of the default network:

The resting state is characterized by a predominance of interoceptive and affective processing with exteroceptive input remaining almost absent so that only the former, but not the latter, is
related to current goal-orientation in self-related processing during the resting state. (2008, p. 262)

In the article referred to earlier, Uddin et al. (2007, p. 155) also pointed
out that the CMS forms part of the default network and that it is likely
that one function of the default network is to act as a constant monitor of

the self and its social relationships. Imagination is attracting increasing attention from neuroscience researchers and it is the activity of imagining that seems to integrate the different neural networks that contribute to the psychological expression of self-agency.

In the next chapter I examine the developmental and neurobiological processes that contribute to the developmental trajectory of self-agency, from its earliest expression through action to the mature experience of agency in mental processes such as imagination and symbolic thought.

4

From Action and Imitation to
Empathy and Mentalization

IN CHAPTER 3, ONE OF THE AREAS OF RESEARCH I described was the role that mirror neurons play in action understanding. In essence, it is through our own physical experience of agency that we intuitively understand the actions of other people, even though this understanding is not at all under conscious control. It might be called a kind of procedural knowledge, based on an instantaneous and automatic mapping of the other person's actions onto our own motor action sequences, which are activated when we see the other person's actions. This kind of direct mirroring also applies to emotional experiences, in that another person's facial expression of an emotion has been shown to activate the same neuronal pathways as those that fire when we experience the emotion directly ourselves (Rizzolatti & Sinigaglia, 2008; Wicker et al., 2003). So this kind of direct neuronal mirroring of another's action or emotion seems to be one of the key neurobiological processes that underpins the experience of self-agency at the physical level, which depends on the highly contingent and unconscious, automatic response our own actions (including facial expressions) produce from the other person, right from the earliest moments of life (Meltzoff & Gopnik, 1993).

But human relationships are based on much more than automatic imitation and action understanding, or even the direct mirroring of emotional experience. Decety and Meyer have carefully differentiated imitation from empathy and have summarized the neuroscience of both of these, showing that both play an important role in the development of agency. They suggested that imitation is not a simple matching mechanism, but a complex construct involving a number of different processes, such as "perception-action coupling, visual attention, short-term memory, body schema, mental state attribution and agency" (Decety & Meyer, 2009, p. 143) and that these are orchestrated by distributed neural network connectivity. So even imitation is a continuum, ranging from automatic unconscious mimicry to conscious intentional reproduction. Decety and Meyer argued that the mirror neuron mechanism underpinning direct perception-action coupling, which I described in Chapter 3, is the basic neural mechanism unifying this variety of phenomena and that while it provides a key foundation for the building of imitative and mind-reading competencies, other mechanisms are needed for their full maturation. The other mechanisms that probably fulfill this role are those of the cortical midline structures, limbic system, and right orbitofrontal cortex (described in Chapter 3).

Empathy is much more than imitation; it involves the capacity to relate to and use our imagination to identify with another person's feeling and experience, even when these are different from our own. It requires emotion sharing, an ability to put ourselves in the other person's shoes, not just to map his or her experience onto our own. Indeed, there is nothing more alienating for a person in distress than when someone says to them, "I know just how you feel," and then proceeds to tell a story about his or her own experience that bears no relation to the person's distress and shows that he or she has not understood it at all.

The capacity for real empathy depends on the recognition of the other person as separate, with a mind and emotions of his or her own. Imitation may play an initial role in emotion sharing, as Sinigaglia (2008) and Gallese (2007) suggested, but empathy requires one person to be able to recognize the difference between self and other and to adopt a focus on the emotions and intentionality of the other. So Decety and Meyer went on to emphasize strongly that empathy is not only more than imitation, it is also more than emotion sharing, because it also depends on cognitive processes of perspective taking and executive control, "which allow individuals to be aware of their intentions and feelings and to maintain separate perspectives on self and other" (2009, p. 144). A representational sense of agency, and the ability to mentalize, therefore play an important role in empathy as they facilitate the differentiation of self-executive from observed behaviors: "knowing whose action (including emotions) belong to whom preserves individuals from overidentifying with the observed target, which would otherwise lead to empathic distress" (p. 144). In other words, without a mental and emotional awareness of the separate agency of self and other, there can be no real empathy.

I would like to move on to explore this developing ability to differentiate self from other, which is so fundamental to the capacity for real empathy. I have suggested in the previous chapters that the development of this sense of agency begins in the rhythm of the turn-taking behaviors between mother and infant—the interpersonal interactions that constitute the baby's earliest recognition of the social world into which he or she has been born. The complexity and reciprocity of mother-infant communication has been amply demonstrated by a number of researchers (Beebe et al., 2010; Jaffe et al., 2001; Marvin, Cooper, Hoffman, & Powell, 2002; Schore, 1994, 2003a & b; Stern, 1985; Trevarthen, 1993; Tronick, 2007). The core of these interactions is facial and vocal affective attunement and mirroring, fine-tuned behavioral exchanges that function at the implicit level, the implicit relational knowing described and documented by these authors and others, as described in Chapter 2. Gergely and Watson have suggested that, up to about 3 months, infants prefer perfect contingency between action and reaction with the caregiver, while other researchers, such as Beebe and Tronick, have shown that from about 4 months, infants prefer a midrange of contingency, marked by regular small episodes of disruption and repair in the attunement between mother and infant, in which the infant experiences agency at the social level, the active role he or she plays in these social exchanges.

This is then followed by the increasing awareness of the capacity to influence the emotions and mental state of other people, the teleological and intentional levels. These are the interactions that first explore psychological agency but are dominated by the sense of coercion toward and by others, for example the infant's imperative pointing, which uses the adult as a tool to obtain a desired object, directing the adult's behavior without an awareness of the adult's mind or intentionality (Lizkowski, 2006, p. 157). Finally, the most mature level of agency, the representational level, emerges, in which there is a recognition of self and other each as separate and independent agents, able to communicate and affect each other without coercion.

So the infant does experience and express agency before the capacity for theory of mind develops at around 3 years of age. This later-developing capacity for mentalization is still rooted in the subtle, fleeting, unconscious, behavioral, and emotional interactions between mother and baby from the earliest moments of the baby's life, that provide the relational basis for the infant's emotional and relational development, as I described in Chapter 2. It is this implicit level of communication and response to each other's body movements, facial expression, tone of voice, and intonation that determines the development of affect regulation, the baby's increasing ability to experience the world in a manageable way and to regulate his or her emotional states. It is also the basis for the infant's developing sense of agency—the baby's initial experience of a mother whose affective responses (the playful exaggeration of facial expression and tone of voice) show that she is empathizing with her baby's feelings, seeing things from her baby's perspective, but also that she is not totally identified with and overwhelmed by her infant's distress but can hold on to her own sense of self (Beebe et al., 2010; Gergely & Watson, 1996). The parent's ability to mentalize also allows a child to develop the same capacity, to experience psychological agency, because he or she finds that feelings can be understood, responded to, and given meaning by an empathic parent, who finds a language that fits the baby's experience. Mentalization moves the experience of agency from coercion in the teleological stage to communication at the intentional and representational levels.

From Action Patterns to Symbolization and Reflection

The accumulation of research evidence over the past two decades overwhelmingly supports the view that the emotional aspects of the development of self-agency, those centered on affect regulation, are rooted in embodied and affective relational experience (Schore, 1994, 2003a). This implicit, embodied, and affective level of relating is not superseded by mentalization but continues to operate throughout life, as Levinson's studies on adult human interaction and Lepper's analysis of psychotherapy transcripts, described below, suggest.

But the same relational and emergent approach is also needed for us to fully understand the aspects of cognitive development that are crucial to the mature development of self-agency—the capacity to relate to our own and others' mental processes, evident in the ability to mentalize and to relate to, understand, and use symbol and metaphor and so to express agency in words rather than actions.

A powerful case has been made by Gallese and Lakoff that the move from action understanding to the capacity for symbolization depends on the decoupling of secondary motor areas of the brain from the primary motor cortex. I referred to their work in Chapter 3 and discuss this aspect of their argument in more detail later in this chapter. They suggest that the formation of embodied "image schemas" (a nonconscious form of cognitive organization, developing out of our bodily interactions, which establishes patterns of understanding and reasoning) is the first step in this process in that they are the first concepts to emerge through this decoupling process; they provide the implicit procedural foundations for the subsequent development of the complex and rich symbolism of the human mind (Gallese & Lakoff, 2005; Lakoff & Johnson, 1980).

Annette Karmiloff-Smith and colleagues have offered a detailed analysis of the way in which embodied implicit procedural knowledge, including that of embodied image schemas, is gradually transformed and reencoded into conscious explicit knowledge; she calls this process representational redescription and argues that it is a process that drives the move from implicit procedural to explicit conscious knowledge in each domain of knowledge, such as language, number understanding of the physical world, and psychological awareness. Representational redescription consists of a series of stages from an implicit format (Level I) in which representations are in the form of automatic procedures for analyzing and responding to stimuli, through a level of nonconscious generalized schematic knowledge (Level E-1). Karmiloff-Smith gave the example of the concept of a striped animal; the concept "striped" allows a recognition of this pattern generally, such as on a zebra and on a zebra crossing (1992, p. 21). Levels E-2 and E-3 are available to consciousness, but only E-3 is capable of expression verbally. This view holds that cognitive development proceeds by a process of "recoding information that is stored in one representational format or code into a different one. Thus a spatial representation might be recoded into linguistic format, or a proprioceptive representation into spatial format" (Karmiloff-Smith, 1992, p. 23). This model offers a comprehensive information-processing account of the process that underpins the developmental trajectory of self-agency from embodied procedural experience to conscious reflective knowledge. Fonagy et al. explicitly acknowledged that, in relation to self-agency, there is a process of establishing secondary representations of primary procedural states and that "this hypothesized secondary representation-building process can be conceived of as a special case of what Annette Karmiloff-Smith (1992) has called 'representational redescription'" (2002, p. 185).

An important aspect of the development of a psychological sense of agency is the part the primary caregiver plays in facilitating this process. To understand the mechanisms that underpin this relational process, whereby the caregiver attributes meaning and intentionality to the infant's actions before any such meaning or intentionality exists reflectively in the infant's own mind, a number of researchers draw on Vygotsky's (1978) concepts of scaffolding and of the "zone of proximal development." This refers to the distance between the child's independent problem-solving ability and her potential with assistance from more knowledgeable adults. They suggest that mothers intuitively work within the zone of proximal development to scaffold children's understanding of mind through their talk at a level more advanced than the child's independent ability level, but not so advanced as to be too distant from the child's experience.

Taumoepeau and Ruffman (2008) have refined this relational model of psychological development, suggesting that mothers provide a systematic scaffolding process in their choice of language, unconsciously structuring their communications to match the infant's current cognitive and emotional abilities and level of understanding. So mothers first talk to their children about the child's own desires, because the child has direct internal experience of those as bodily states, such as hunger or thirst. By describing these states in language, they help their child to connect these bodily experiences to mental states. Only later do mothers begin to focus on abstract concepts, such as thoughts and knowledge, because desire talk fits better into younger children's zone of proximal development—young children understand about desire before thoughts and knowledge. For children to receive maximum benefit, mother talk must be appropriately timed to fit with the child's existing understanding. Only talk of this nature can help to make explicit a child's underlying implicit understanding of mental states.

Fonagy et al. (2002) described another aspect of this process of Vygotskian scaffolding, suggesting that mothers do not just facilitate a preprogrammed development of mind understanding but play a more active role in the construction of mind understanding in their infants by attributing intentionality to behavior, before children have any sense of intentionality for themselves. So the meaning that children attribute to their actions is not really their own but reflects the meaning given to them by their mothers:

> The caregiver produces intentionality through complex linguistic and interactional processes, primarily through behaving towards the baby and child in such a way that it leads him eventually to

postulate that his own behavior may best be understood in terms of ideas and beliefs, feelings and wishes that determine his actions and the reactions of others to him. Unconsciously and pervasively, with her behavior the caregiver ascribes a mental state to the child that is ultimately perceived by the child and internalized, permitting the development of a core sense of mental selfhood. (Fonagy et al., 2002, p. 286)

A Vygotskian model is also evident in the approach of Astington (2002), who argued for the developmental interdependence of theory of mind and language. Astington emphasized the point that I have also extensively highlighted so far in this book, that action both precedes and drives the move to reflection and understanding, and that the action referred to is the patterns of interpersonal interactions that mother and baby mutually engage in from birth. In taking a mentalistic stance in our conversations with children, we embed theory of mind in our very speech, so that as children acquire language they also acquire theory of mind (Astington, 2002, p. 182). So the development of mentalization and of the accompanying mature experience of self-agency through verbal communication is highly dependent on the cultural and linguistic context that the child experiences as he or she grows. Astington also used Karmiloff-Smith's model of representational redescription to underpin her view that the social world plays a crucial part for children's development of theory of mind. "What they are acquiring in developing ToM is an understanding of patterns of actions in which they are already participants" (2002, p. 198). This view is very much in accord with that of the BCPSG and of Tronick and Beebe.

For example, Tronick makes a very similar point to that made by Astington, Hendriks-Jansen, and Fonagy et al., namely that the caregiver is central to the process of attributing meaning and intentionality to patterns of infant activity that do not, as yet, reflect any such symbolic or intentional mental state on the part of the infant. Tronick emphasized the logical consequence of this, that the infant's social and cultural environment is crucial in shaping the core patterns of communication between mother and infant:

Culture tailors the phylogenetically based aspects of caregiver investment strategies to the locally specific, relatively stable, social and physical features of the environment. Most important,

> culture helps define those features of the child's behavior and
> communication that require attention and response, as well as the
> culturally appropriate form of that response. (2007, p. 99)

Although at first sight there might appear to be a contradiction between
the argument that there are core and universal patterns and rules of
human interaction, such as the turn-taking discussed in previous chapters, and the view that these are socially determined by culturally specific meanings, the authors quoted above all concur in the view that the
cultural influence is reflected in and channeled to the infant through the
particular meaning that the caregiver attributes to these universal patterns of action and interaction between infant and caregiver and between
any other human dyad.

The view that human communication both reveals universal patterns
and principles of interaction and is also culturally influenced is therefore
central to research on adult conversational interaction, such as that of
anthropologist and linguist Stephen Levinson (2002), who developed the
concept of the human interaction engine. His work brings us back to the
centrality of turn-taking. He proposes that turn-taking is one of a small
number of empirically observable practices (e.g., attribution of intention,
cooperation, reciprocity, question-answer sequences, and repairs of interactional errors) that appear to be universal across different cultures, but
with cultural variation in the rules and principles governing these universal patterns, for example, in the length of the pause considered acceptable
between turns. He takes this argument further to suggest, along lines
similar to Hendriks-Jansen, that these interactions preexist, underpin,
and make possible the development of language: "language did not make
interactional intelligence possible, it is interactional intelligence that
made language possible as a means of communication" (2002, p. 42).

The interdependence of language and brain development and the
process that leads to the emergence of the fully symbolic communication
of human language from more primitive forms of action-based pointing
found in animal communication (indexical communication) has also been
explored by Terrence Deacon (Figure 4.1). He argued that "it should be
remembered that a large fraction of a species' communicative repertoire
may have evolved for manipulative purposes," ensuring that one animal's
alarm call creates the same emotional state, in this case alarm, in all the
other members of the same species nearby (Deacon, 1997, p. 426).

In evolutionary terms, this has great survival value in the animal

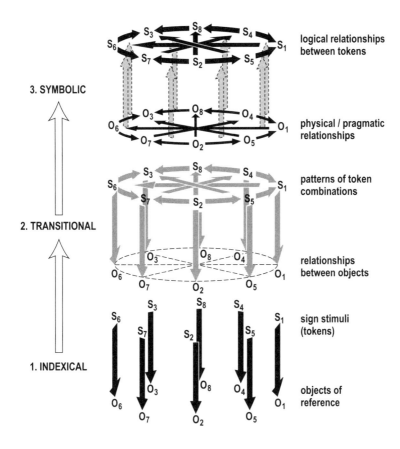

FIGURE 4.1
From signs to symbols.

world, in that a single alarm call from one animal in the group ensures that they all flee the approaching predator. It is a form of communication that functions automatically and has no place for any kind of choice about how to respond; in that sense it is controlling and coercive in evoking a specific emotional response in other animals. Deacon described this as indexical communication (1997, p. 235). It is a pattern of relating in which any communication has only one possible meaning—like the animal's alarm call—and its function is to evoke a specific behavioral or emotional response from the other person, without giving any space to reflect on that response or choose an alternative. It is a primitive form of communication that may be drawn on when survival is felt to be at risk.

This is the progression from the coercive forms of relating to the capacity to tolerate and relate to other people as separate, with minds of their own (mentalization) and has been extensively studied in this context (Bateman & Fonagy, 2004; Gabbard, 2003; Morgan, 2008). But it is also the trajectory that leads to the mature expression of self-agency and merits further exploration in that context. Indeed, it is at the level of the autobiographical self that self-agency combines with mentalization to provide a sense of self rooted in reflection, memory, and desire rather than the imperatives of action and immediate gratification. Once again, this model resonates with the process of representational redescription delineated by Karmiloff-Smith and described earlier in this chapter.

This Vygotskian model also applies to the relational interactions that take place in psychotherapy. Gotthold and Sorter (2006) explored the relevance of the BCPSG's research for adult psychotherapy. The ongoing implicit relational sequences between therapist and patient are described as "moving along," gradually increasing the patient's sense of agency so that a sense of self "becomes increasingly validated and coherent through a series of mutual regulated sequences" (2006, p. 2). They emphasized that a therapist's interpretation needs to be made from within this relational context, in the same way that a mother's talk to her baby needs to be an accurate reflection of the baby's current experience of their interaction. If the therapist fails to link his or her interpretations to the patient's experience, it may produce an aversive response in the patient that may be fatal to the therapy.

Georgia Lepper (2009a) used the method of conversation analysis (CA), a branch of pragmatics, to identify more precisely the fine details of therapist-patient interactions, in a way that parallels the second-by-second study of videos of mothers with their infants. Both methods highlight the turn-by-turn interactions of each partner in the dyad. In adult therapy, the interactions take the form of the conversational responses of patient and therapist to each other, as they try to achieve an understanding of the meaning of the patient's symptoms. In this approach, turn-taking is seen as fundamental to the coconstruction of meaning between therapist and patient, rather than the meaning being determined by the therapist's interpretations:

> In the study of conversations, it is the response of the hearer to the previous turn, and the production of the next turn in the conversation, rather than the interpretations of the investigator,

which provide the evidence for what meaningfulness is. CA concerns itself with the "procedural infrastructure of interaction,"
where a procedure is a tool for "achieving a joint understanding
of what is going on." (Lepper, 2009a, p. 1078)

The study of the form, not just the content, of conversation is at
the heart of the conversational method of psychotherapy, developed by
Hobson and Meares, based on research in which they used audiotapes to
study the "minute particulars" of the therapeutic conversation (Hobson
1985, Meares 2004). They argued that fluctuations in the state of self as
displayed in shifts in its various characteristics are manifest in the language of the therapeutic conversation:

> The study of language refers here not simply to the content of
> language. Conversation is not merely the vehicle for the trans-
> mission of pieces of information conceived as necessary to the
> therapeutic process. Of central import is the form of language,
> the way that words are used. This usage includes the tone of
> voice. Language consists of phonology, lexicon and syntax.
> (Meares 2004, p. 54)

In Part II, I explore some of the implications for the clinical practice
of psychotherapy of the central role of turn-taking and conversation in
the coconstruction of meaning and the changes in our clinical practice
that inevitably follow from a greater focus on the development of the
patient's self-agency. But first I want to discuss some specific aspects
of the neurobiological processes that I described in Chapter 3, those
that contribute to the emergence of a fully psychological sense of self-
agency, which is so closely linked to the capacity to mentalize and therefore the capacity to experience real empathy with another person, whose
experience is recognized as different from one's own.

Neurobiological Perspectives on the Development
of the Psychological, Representational,
and Symbolic Levels of Self-Agency

The developmental studies outlined above demonstrate that interpersonal interactions such as parent-infant turn-taking, patterns of self- and
other-contingency, and parental scaffolding and meaning attribution

stimulate and facilitate the infant's intrapsychic developmental processes
such as representational redescription and mentalization, which underpin the move from action-based intentionality and agency to symbolism,
language, and the representational level of agency.

But what are the neurobiological processes that underpin this development of agency into the psychological and symbolic realms? Rather
than attempt to allocate specific aspects of this process to the three networks I have described, I shall highlight two main issues:

- The development of imagination and symbolic thought, in which
  potential physical and psychological actions are simulated or
  rehearsed in the mind, rather than expressed in direct physical
  action.
- The development of the capacity to mentalize, to relate with
  empathy to the minds and emotions of others.

Imagination and Symbolic Thought

In Chapter 3, I highlighted the fact that there is universal agreement
among researchers that bodily action (including facial expression) is
the foundation of our experience of agency. Thirty years ago, Mark
Johnson (1987) anticipated the fundamental role of bodily experience
in the development of mind and concept formation; in his remarkable
book *The Body in the Mind: The Bodily Basis of Meaning, Imagination, and
Reason*, he examined how our physical sense impressions become mental experiences. His answer was that the two become connected in a
"schema," which "is a structure of a schematizing activity of imagination in time" (1987, p. 153). So Johnson placed imagination at the heart
of mind, stating that "there can be no meaningful experience without
imagination" (1987, p. 152). His view of imagination is that:

> It supplies all of the connections by means of which we achieve
> coherent, unified, and meaningful experience and understanding.
> . . . [O]ur ordered world, and the possibility of understanding any
> part of it, depends on the existence of this synthesizing activity.
> (1987, p. 151)

He proposed that the earliest stage of concept formation is image
schemas, simple embodied spatial gestalts that capture the patterns
of our physical experience of the world around us and the processes

by which objects and bodies relate to each other. The idea of image schemas was taken up by Jean Mandler, who suggested that they are the means whereby "spatial structure is mapped into conceptual structure" and so form the basis for the earliest forms of meaning in the development of the infant mind (1992, p. 591). She argued that there is a process of active recoding of this spatial information into ever more explicit meanings, which constitute an explicit knowledge system. This recoding process abstracts the key features of the relational interaction into a meaningful concept, and Mandler equates this recoding to the representational redescription model offered by Karmiloff-Smith.

In the article by Gallese and Lakoff cited in Chapter 3, they examined the evidence from contemporary neuroscience that supports this view that the human mind's understanding and use of concepts, symbols, and metaphor derive from our experience of bodily action. They suggest that "the same circuitry that can move the body and structure perceptions, also structures abstract thought" (Gallese & Lakoff, 2005, p. 17) and that "there are no dedicated and specialized brain circuits for concepts in general or for abstract concepts in particular . . . that concepts of a wide variety make direct use of the sensory-motor circuitry of the brain (pp. 18, 19). For example, they suggest that the latest research supports this hypothesis:

> In the case of the concept of grasping, one would expect the parietal-premotor circuits that form functional clusters for grasping to be active not only when actually grasping, but also when understanding sentences involving the concept of grasping. (Gallese & Lakoff, 2005, p. 18)

When their article was published, they were in the process of conducting further fMRI scans to test whether the same circuits would fire not only with literal sentences but also with the corresponding metaphorical sentences. Thus the sentence "He grasped the idea" should activate the sensory-motor grasping-related regions of the brain. Research by Buccino et al. (2005) supports this hypothesis. The heart of their argument is that rational thought and imagination are simulated actions: "typical human cognitive activities such as visual and motor imagery, far from being of a disembodied, modality-free, and symbolic nature, make use of the activation of sensory-motor brain regions" (Gallese & Lakoff,

2005, p. 10) and "the sensory-motor system can characterize action concepts and in simulation, characterize conceptual inferences" (p. 16).

Gallese and Lakoff's model could offer an explanation for the development of self-agency from motor activity to abstract thought. In actions, the premotor cortex is neurally connected to the motor cortex, cheoreographing simple movements into complex actions. But these premotor-to-motor connections can be inhibited and the premotor areas are then "capable of carrying out imaginative simulations. Furthermore these imaginative simulations can carry out abstract conceptual reasoning as well as actions and perceptions. The result is a neural theory of metaphor" (2005, p. 15). Gallese and Lakoff specifically link these ideas to image schemas as abstract generalizations in which the core pattern of the embodied metaphor is expressed (2005, p. 16). Abstract concepts and metaphor are neural simulations in secondary areas, with the connections to the primary areas (which carry out an actual action) inhibited. Gallese suggested that there is "a 'structuring' computational circuit within the pre-motor system that can function in two modes of operation" (Gallese, 2007, p. 666). In the first mode, this area is linked to action execution and action perception. In the second mode, the same structuring system is "de-coupled from its action execution/perception function and can offer its structuring computations to non-sensory-motor parts of the brain" and is applied to abstract domains, yielding abstract inferences. Gallese et al. extended this model to propose that:

> The development of the MNS can be conceptualized as a process whereby the child learns to refrain from acting out the automatic matching mechanism that links action perception and execution. Such development could be viewed as a process leading from mandatory reenactment to a covert simulation of the observed motor acts, most likely *through the maturation of pre-frontal inhibiting mechanisms*. (2009, p. 106, emphasis added)

So this disconnection, of secondary premotor areas from those primary areas that directly control action, offers a possible neuroscientific explanation for the move from motor activity to the most primitive concepts (image schemas) and to more complex conceptual and symbolic representation. The abstract concepts—symbols—have become disconnected from their motor actions, although still embedded in and derived through them. Gallese and Lakoff suggested that the development of concepts, imagination, and metaphor is based on "structuring circuits in the sensory-motor system . . . whose neural connections to specific details can be inhibited, allowing them to provide inferential structure to 'abstract' concepts" (2005, p. 19). The generalization process involved in abstract thought is not the result of new mental structures, but the result of the inhibition of the connections between secondary and primary areas—what is new is the development of the inhibitory connections.

This decoupling process of secondary from primary motor areas might also play a part in the development of self-agency. It seems to me that the developmental stages of self-agency, based on a range of infant observation research, can be understood as a specific application of the theory offered by Gallese and Lakoff, that concepts are derived from perception-action neural circuitry, but are neurally simulated in a secondary area with an inhibition (decoupling) of the connections to the primary motor area. Their theory seems to offer a neuroscientific model to support the suggestion that the most mature forms of self-agency are linked with and expressed through processes such as mentalization and noncoercive communication—through symbolic expression in which the meaning of the communication is not expressed by any actual or potential physical action. More primitive forms of self-agency are still directly connected to action as in the indexical (teleological) level of communication, which persists in many adults.

In other words, the development of the intentional level of self-agency indicates the point at which intentionality can be held in mind by the infant; the infant can experience and relate to his or her desires and intentions as mental and emotional events, without turning them directly into an action. So, at the intentional and representational levels, the sense of self-agency becomes an experiential concept in the infant's mind, resulting from, but not directly linked to, physical action. Agency and intentionality can be represented symbolically and can be expressed through the language of desire; they do not have to be immediately turned into physical action. In our clinical work we recognize how hard it is to work with patients who cannot hold their own intentionality in mind, but who need to evacuate it through some physical action. Our attempts to help them to contain and reflect on their desire can be seen as annihilating their very sense of self-agency because it is still so directly linked to action, a persistence of the teleological and earlier levels of self-agency.

Gallese and Umilta (2002) went on to discuss another key part of the construction of a sense of self, that of bodily perspective. They suggested that the self is a construct or model, experienced through key phenomena:

- Mineness: my body is my own.
- Selfhood: I am conscious of my own conscious thoughts and feelings.
- Perspectivalness: a sense of peripersonal space organized around a center.

They explored the last of these, perspectivalness, in some detail to show that each part of the body relies on different spatial frames of reference, supported by distinct neural circuits. In other words, our sense of peripersonal space (essentially, the space within reach of the part of the body in question) varies according to the part of the body we are currently using and the kind of action we are using it for. Peripersonal space will expand if we use a tool such as a rake, with the visual receptive field expanding to include the length of the rake and so to include formerly "far space as 'near' space." They concluded:

> Being a self depends on the acquired capacity to 1) recognize the existence of multiple frames of reference and 2) to put them in dynamic relation to each other by a continuous process of analogy and differentiation. . . . [T]he emergence of the self can be seen as the adaptive tool able to give coherence to these interacting levels of representation. (Gallese & Umilta, 2002, p. 37)

Gallese and Umilta argued that the research referred to above means that "space is represented according to the way we act in it" and therefore that agency is the glue that holds all the different embodied spatial frames of reference—reflecting the different intentional actions of different parts of our bodies—together. This view of agency, as the experience that unites all our differing bodily frames of reference together to give a coherent experience of self, has considerable implications when we link it with Gallese and Lakoff's hypothesis that abstract thought derives from the activity of secondary circuits linked to primary sensory-motor action chains, but which then become disconnected from those primary circuits—that thought and imagination are embodied metaphor rooted in, but decoupled from, motor action.

This view of agency, as the glue that holds our sense of self together at a physical spatial level, suggests that this could also be true at a meta-phorical level in relation to the emotional, representational, and inter-personal space in which we act. Our experience of relational space depends upon the way we act in it; for example, at the teleological level of self-agency, relational space can only be experienced through control and coercion. So the construct of a self must also be one that can inte-grate these metaphorical extensions of metaphorical personal space and in that context:

- recognize the existence of multiple frames of reference and
- put them in dynamic relation to each other by a continuous pro-cess of analogy and differentiation.

These multiple frames of reference for the emotional and representa-tional space within which we act and interact with others are the devel-opmental levels of self-agency identified above. A stable sense of self depends on the ability to integrate them and give coherence to these constantly interacting levels of self-agency, allowing us to go on know-ing who we are, to experience internal emotional and mental coherence as we move back and forth between physical, social, teleological, inten-tional, and representational levels of agency. In other words, self-agency becomes the generalized abstraction that gives meaning to all these spe-cific expressions of agency. Self-agency is the glue that holds different psychological experiences of self and emotional and psychological space together, just as Gallese and Umilta suggest it does in relation to physi-cal personal space.

In Chapter 3, I described the default network that a number of researchers consider to be central to the development of imagination (and so by implication to the capacity for all meaningful experience, as Johnson argued). Uddin et al. (2007) highlighted the fact that one of the most important aspects of imagination is that it allows us to disconnect our mental processes from actual physical events; imagi-nation allows us to mentally move events backward or forward in time and to invent or simulate any number of alternative outcomes to a given scenario. Imagination is a form of action and so of self-agency at the representational and autobiographical level. Imagining actions performed by oneself or by another activates shared mid-line and frontoparietal structures. So imagination seems to be the common representational domain between the cortical midline structures and mirror neuron system, allowing perspective taking at a representational level, and is also an important function of the default network.

Mentalization

One aspect of social relationships is the capacity to mentalize, to relate to the mental state of others. The capacity to mentalize is vital to the ability to experience self-agency at the representational level, because mentalizing requires a capacity to relate to one's own mind and emotions, as well as to those of others. Fonagy and Luyten have highlighted a distinction between explicit and implict mentalization:

> Explicit mentalization is typically interpreted, conscious, verbal, and reflective. It is a serial and slow process that requires attention, intention, awareness, and effort. By contrast, automatic or implicit mentalization is perceived, nonconscious, nonverbal, and unreflective. It is typified by mirroring. It presumes parallel and therefore much faster processing, is reflexive, and requires little effort, focused attention or intention. (2009, p. 1358)

They pointed out that nonverbally determined implicit mentalizing appears to be robust early in the second year or perhaps earlier, whereas verbal recognition of another's perspective is reliable only in the fourth. They also suggested that different brain areas may be recruited for automatic and controlled mentalizing. Automatic social cognition involves phylogenetically older brain circuits that rely heavily on sensory information. By contrast, controlled mentalization recruits phylogenetically newer brain circuits involved in processing of linguistic and symbolic material, including the medial prefrontal cortex (mPFC).

Their view accords with research showing that the midline structures that form part of the default network (especially the mPFC) are involved in representing the self and others in terms of mental states (Frith & Frith, 1999). So the move to psychological levels of self-agency, that link to mentalization and empathy, depends on the development of the mPFC and its connections to the rest of the default network.

Modinos et al. highlighted the fact that a number of regions that are known to be involved in self-awareness and social cognition strikingly overlap with the neural substrates of the default network:

> Recent functional neuroimaging studies have consistently shown brain activity within several cortical regions during self-referential tasks, particularly along the midline and including the prefrontal cortex (PFC), posterior cingulate cortex (PCC), and parietal regions. (2009, p. 1)

They summarized research that shows that these regions are involved in a number of self-related processes, namely self-reflection, encoding and retrieval of self-related information, self-related processing in sexual arousal, assessment of one's own personality and physical traits, self-referential decision making, and first-person perspective taking. They concluded:

> In this regard, the accumulating evidence for the existence of a default mode of brain function has derived from the observation of intrinsic activity in a neural architecture encompassing regions of the MPFC, PCC and medial precuneus, whose interaction would be intimately involved in self-awareness and conscious experience. (2009, p. 1)

Taken together, these studies suggest that the links between the insula (bilaterally activated by self-generated action) and the prefrontal cortex are crucial for the ability to evaluate events as relevant to one's goals or concerns and to mentalize. Without that ability to evaluate whether one's goals are being met, it is impossible to maintain a sense of representational agency, since there is no link between the outer event and the inner experience of intentionality, an essential aspect of the capacity to mentalize. Kampe, Frith, and Frith's study of mentalizing suggested that the right paracingulate gyrus also plays a crucial part in distinguishing the self's perspective from the other's perspective: "This suggests that it has a central role in the cortical circuits involved in attributing intentions to others or when these are highly relevant to the self's own action or reaction" (2003, p. 5262).

A study by Decety, Michalska, Akitsuki, and Lahey (2009) of adolescents with conduct disorder suggested that it is precisely this capacity to mentalize that is lacking. The neuroimaging studies suggest that they strongly empathize with someone in pain, in the sense that their own pain matrix is highly activated (the anterior cingulate cortex, insula, somatosensory cortex, supplementary motor area, and periaqueductal gray) and they also showed significantly greater amygdala, striatal, and temporal pole activation. But, compared with a control group who showed activation of the mPFC, lateral orbitofrontal cortex, and right temporoparietal junction (areas that regulate emotion), the conduct disorder group only exhibited activation in the insula and precentral gyrus. Furthermore, compared with the controls, their connections to the orbitofrontal cortex are lacking—they cannot downregulate their own distress, which becomes transformed into aggression toward the person in pain. They lack an ability to differentiate the other person's distress from their own, to maintain separate perspectives on self and other—in other words, to recognize each person's agency. In a sense, they experience the other person's distress as a coercive action, a reflection both of a failure to mentalize and also to disconnect mental experience from physical action, the two essential characteristics of self-agency at the representational level.

In Part II, I focus on some more detailed examples of the clinical problems that can be apparent in psychotherapy with adult patients whose development of self-agency has been inhibited or distorted, so that their sense of agency is still mainly expressed in physical action, or in more subtle forms of action, such as manipulation or emotional coercion.

PART II
Clinical Aspects of Self-Agency

5

When Words Do Not Mean What They Say: Self-Agency and the Coercive Use of Language

The speech we hear is an indication of that which we don't hear. It is a necessary avoidance, a violent, sly, anguished or mocking smoke screen which keeps the other in its place. . . . One way of looking at speech is to say it is a constant stratagem to cover nakedness.
(Pinter, 1999, p. 34)

HUMAN BEINGS PRIDE OURSELVES THAT WE ARE UNIQUE among animals in our ability to communicate with each other in a form of symbolic expression called language. We are reassured by the research that seems to demonstrate that however sophisticated the signal systems of other animals, they remain at the level of signs, not true symbols. Perhaps a slight glimmer of disquiet crosses our minds when we learn that a baby bonobo monkey called Kanzi, playing quietly in the background while researchers tried to teach his mother language, suddenly seemed to acquire the ability for symbolic expression and syntax, the essential features of language, while his mother never advanced beyond a simple signing system, a kind of reference list pointing to objects or actions (Savage-Rumbaugh & Lewin, 1994). But we can reassure ourselves that the language of animals such as Kanzi will never surpass that of a 3-year-old child, nor achieve the heights of expression, imagination, and rich symbolism in human literature and poetry.

That is, until Harold Pinter's plays hit the stage. In them we discovered that language can serve other purposes, often far less noble, purposes that are hidden in the prosody of the sentences, the rhythm and intonation, beneath their overt meaning. David Lodge has explored the masterly way Pinter uses language to convey the existential anxiety of the characters—the way they cling to a kind of meaningless conversation that must be kept going at all costs. Lodge highlighted the fact that this is an example of what Malinowski called "phatic communication," speech "whose primary function is not to communicate any information between the interlocutors, but to maintain the tenuous thread of human contact" (Lodge, 1997, p. 275).

In his excellent biography of Pinter, Michael Billington deconstructed the undercurrents of this kind of dialogue in the revue sketch "Last to Go," in which an all-night barman

> leaning on his counter, and an old newspaper seller, standing with his cup of coffee, engage in a desultory conversation that reveals a profound loneliness. . . . [W]hat you hear in the halting pause-ridden dialogue between the two men is fear: fear of being the last to go home, fear of being the one to break the slender conversational thread, fear of death. (2007, p. 108)

But Pinter then takes this form of dialogue a step further. In place of the anxiety expressed in mutual clinging, we find an increasing sense of menace and domination of one character by another, conveyed in the conversations between them. Billington highlighted the dynamics of power in Pinter's writing, the extent to which Pinter increasingly sees private life as a form of power politics full of invasion, retreats, subjugations, and deceptions. This is often conveyed in the rhythm of the characters' speech, a rhythm that subtly alters the meaning of the words themselves. On one now-famous occasion, Pinter said to the actor Michael Hordern, "Michael, I wrote dot, dot, dot and you're giving me dot, dot," by which he meant that the length of a pause is critical in conveying the degree of menace or tension behind the words (Billington, 2007, p. 141).

Until Pinter, theatrical dialogue largely conveyed the author's conscious message in a rather stylized way that does not reflect the way people actually talk to each other. We reply not so much to what the last person actually said but to what we can guess about that person's motive for saying it and the emotional signals we detect. Pinter deliberately leaves uncertainty about who the characters are, why they are there, and the meaning of what they say; this creates an atmosphere of anxiety and oppression that pervades the play and invades, confuses, and disturbs the audience. The uncertainty provides the context in which Pinter is able to highlight how humans use speech to coerce, manipulate, and control each other, through the messages that are hidden within, between, and beneath the actual words used, as an exchange in *The Caretaker* illustrates, where Aston asks the tramp, Davies, where he comes from and Davies evades even the simplest questions, even when Aston asks him directly where he was born:

> ASTON: Where were you born then?
> DAVIES: *(darkly)* What do you mean?
> ASTON: Where were you born?
> DAVIES: I was . . . uh . . . oh it's a bit hard, like to set your mind back
> . . . see what I mean . . . going back . . . a good way . . . lose a bit of
> track, like . . . you know . . . (Pinter, 1991 pp. 35–36)

Billington highlighted this exchange to illustrate that Davies "ducks and bobs and weaves under each enquiry as if no longer able to distinguish between prying officialdom and simple human curiosity" (2007, p. 125) and that:

> Pinter shows how language is a continuous battle-tactic; a potential weapon of domination, a defensive posture to secure one's position, a source of evasion to hide truth. . . . [W]hat Pinter sees is that the language we use is rarely innocent of hidden intention, that it is part of an endless negotiation for advantage or a source of emotional camouflage. (2007, p. 124)

Pinter is not alone in identifying the fact that language can become a vehicle for emotional and relational control over others. One particularly illuminating description comes from a literary theorist and critic, Roger Sell, who described the key characteristics of coercive communication:

> Where one communicant is thought of as sending a message to the other, who interprets it in the light of the context that is implied by the sender. So the sender is more active, the receiver more passive, the communication uni-directional and the context singular. (2007, p. 4)

Sell suggested that a great deal of communication that goes on in the world is of this type and we see it vividly enacted in Pinter's plays and in Orwell's chilling account of "Newspeak" in *1984*, which to my mind represents the ultimate form of this kind of coercion:

> The purpose of Newspeak was not only to provide a medium of expression for the world-view and mental habits proper to the devotees of Ingsoc, but to make all other modes of thought impossible. This was done . . . by eliminating undesirable words and by stripping such words as remained of unorthodox meanings, and so far as possible of all secondary meanings whatever. . . . Newspeak was designed not to extend but to diminish the range of thought and this purpose was indirectly assisted by cutting the choice of words down to a minimum. (Orwell, 1954, p. 241)

In Newspeak, a whole language was created that would itself coerce and control from inside the very mind of the person using it, by rendering any unorthodox thought impossible to express in words, because the thinker is simply a passive recipient of the thoughts of Ingsoc and has no other context or mind of his or her own.

Sell suggested that, in contrast, in noncoercive communication "the parties think of each other more or less as human equals, and are basically comparing notes about something as seen from their different points of view," and he went on to make the, to my mind, absolutely crucial point that:

> Non-coercive communication then, distributes agency more evenly, and is bi-directional and bi-contextual. Communicants each discuss whatever it is they are comparing notes about from within their life-world and the very difference between their life worlds is what makes the process interesting and valuable. (2007, p. 4)

These different kinds of communication derive from the fact that human language consists of signs, which may be related to the things they represent in a number of ways. Charles Peirce (1955), a philosopher, identified three kinds of signs in language: iconic, indexical, and symbolic. Iconic signs resemble the things they represent, like photographs. Indexical signs point to the thing they represent, like a signpost. Symbols bear no direct relationship to an object, other than that which has emerged by convention, such as a national flag. Thus, as Warren Colman wrote, symbolism is the "capacity to acknowledge the absence of what is imagined from the world of material actuality," so that a symbol "points to what it represents, without *being* what it represents" (2006b, pp. 21, 37).

Terrence Deacon (1997) has produced a very helpful diagram to demonstrate the distinction between indexical and symbolic communication. I reproduced that diagram in Chapter 4 (see Fig. 4.1). In symbolic communication, symbols acquire meaning through the multiple interconnections of meaning with other symbols (the top layer of the diagram). So far, only Kanzi seems to have been able to develop this capacity, and all other animal communication is at the indexical level, such as alarm calls pointing to a predator or an ant's pattern of movement, which indicates the location of food to other ants. The indexical pattern of relating clearly has survival value for infants. Their cries of alarm evoke a visceral response from the parent, who then rushes to protect the child. The indexical level of communication can be viewed as an embodied experience of self-agency in relationship that emerges in the first few days of the infant's life; the powerful, even coercive impact of infant's communication on the parent is essential for the survival of a helpless infant—it points the parent directly toward the infant's need for attention and care.

In contrast, a fully symbolic level of mental functioning is one of a rich network of thoughts, desires, beliefs, and fears that can be explored and related to for their own sakes, not primarily to evoke an action or emotional response in the other. It is a truly symbolic state of mind, in that eventually there is no coercion or manipulation of the other, who does not feel under emotional pressure to produce one specific response but feels free to reflect on the communication symbolically. There is no experience of "thought-action fusion" (Rachman & Shafran, 1999), which is the hallmark of the teleological level of self-agency.

So what do Pinter's plays and linguistic theory have to do with analytic practice? They both show us that human language can be used for indexical purposes as well as at the symbolic level. Deacon discussed the difference between symbolic and other kinds of communication, primarily in relation to language development (see Chapter 4), but he extended it to apply to emotional communication, which has some important implications for analytic theory and practice. Terrence Deacon's model offers a theoretical framework that helps us to understand how a person's communications can feel as though they coerce a particular emotional response from others. The crucial point Deacon highlighted is that in indexical communication, a communication is a sign that not only refers directly to a specific object but also successfully coerces a specific action from the other. It carries only one meaning for the recipient, in terms of the nature of a response.

Indexical communication is a pattern of relating in which any communication is coercive, in the way that an animal's alarm call ensures that all other animals flee the approaching predator; the signal does not just point to an object, but its function is also to evoke a specific behavioral or emotional response from the other person, without giving him any space to reflect on that response or choose an alternative. Deacon was clear that this coercion effect is not consciously intended, but the result of "a built in association between the production of these calls and a specific emotional state" (1997, p. 87). It is coercive because the response is automatic and involuntary.

The indexical level of communication can be viewed as an embodied experience of self-agency in relationship, which emerges in the first year of an infant's life. The powerful, even coercive impact the infant's communication has on the parent is essential not only for the survival of a helpless infant but also for his or her developing sense of self. This coercion is not, of course, consciously intended, but is an implicit relational interaction probably arising from the core-SELF emotional circuit that Panksepp described as the PANIC circuit, which is aroused by separation distress, which immediately causes the infant to make distress calls. Panksepp suggested that the "sounds of crying arouse distress circuits in parents that parallel the distress of the children" (1998, p. 267). The parent's response therefore probably also depends on the imitative function of mirror neuron systems, which are activated by the infant's visual and vocal distress signals. In humans it also depends on the capacity for imaginative empathy, which allows the parent to be aware of the respective agency of herself and her infant, which results from the activation of the right orbitofrontal cortex (Schore, 1994).

Indexical communication is an early stage in the development of the infant's expression of agency. To someone operating at the teleological level, mind and intention are unimportant in themselves; it is only the practical outcome that matters. In Bateman and Fonagy's words, "patients cannot accept anything other than a modification in the realm of the physical as a true index of the intentions of the other" (Bateman & Fonagy, 2004, p. 62). They suggested that this can create intense pressure on the analyst to abandon the analytic stance and provide concrete proof of his or her benign intent, in the form of physical contact and so forth, often leading to severe boundary violations. At the teleological level, one's own self-agency can also only be experienced by the practical emotional effect one creates in the other. An emotional response, even if only a facial expression, is in itself the visible goal that proves one's own agency. The other person's words would be irrelevant without the accompanying behavior.

To link this model to Deacon's terms, the teleological level of self-agency is put into action by the use of indexical communication, in which one person's signals guarantee a predictable emotional and behavioral response from the other. An infant feels that he creates the emotional response of his mother, not just her physical actions—indexical communication is about the need to control another sentient subjective being, not just a physical object. At this stage, as Winnicott (1975) pointed out, it would be catastrophic for the infant to be disillusioned about his role in creating the maternal response. In creating the mirroring response in the parent, the child discovers that he actually exists as a person with a mind and desires, through the direct impact he has on the other. This experience can be labeled as infantile omnipotence, but I think this pathologizes the infant's healthy discovery of self-agency, the absolute developmental necessity of this kind of emotional control of the other. It is as though the infant's experience is, "if I can't affect you, then I don't exist." The evidence that this is how the infant feels comes from the "still face" experiments that I described in Chapter 2 (Tronick, 2007). The mother's lack of emotional responsiveness, even for 3 minutes, creates a response of bewilderment, anxiety, shame, and depression in the infant, which has been shown to linger for several minutes afterward. Tronick also described the power of the infant's signals, how difficult it was for many mothers to maintain the still face experiment; their infants' attempts to elicit a response from them sometimes become irresistible and both mother and baby collapsed into laughter at the ludicrousness of the experiment, enjoying the child's success in forcing the mother to respond (Tronick, 2007, pp. 271–272).

When indexical communication persists into adult life, it reflects the fact that the patient's self-agency is stuck at the teleological level, in which he or she only feels real through having a direct behavioral or emotional impact on the analyst. When any developmental process is distorted or inhibited in childhood, it often emerges in adult life with greater intensity, and puts adult skills to use to meet infantile needs. So language becomes subverted from its symbolic function and is used in the service of indexical communication. Pinter understood this, that words become weapons rather than being messages for the other person to understand. Pinter's plays are indexical communication in action; the unconscious emotional signals each character uses, the body language, facial expression, and tone of voice, are a form of hidden coercion to another person to respond in one specific way, regardless of the conscious verbal message. In fact, the title of this chapter is misleading—instead of "When Words Do Not Mean What They Say," it could be "When Words Do Not Say What They Mean," because this conveys more clearly the fact that there are hidden additional and more powerful emotional resonances that override the overt syntax and meaning of the words themselves.

A powerful and chilling scene, "What's the most you ever lost on a coin toss?" from the Coen Brothers' film *No Country for Old Men*, vividly demonstrates coercive communication in action. The villain, Anton, stops to buy fuel and the storekeeper idly attempts to strike up a conversation about the weather. Anton either feels momentarily threatened that the storekeeper might identify him and so put him in danger, or decides to punish him for his presumption in treating him as a person who might be vulnerable to a friendly overture. He commands the storekeeper to call on a coin toss and calmly observes the terror of the storekeeper, who gradually realizes that his life depends on the toss of the coin. Anton remains impassive, his murderous intent obvious behind the blandness of his actual words.

In spite of the obvious unanalyzability of the psychopath in this terrifying dramatic example, these primitive stages of self-agency need to be recognized and worked through in analysis, just as much as early object relationships. Analysts believe that we do not condemn or pathologize the distorted or primitive transference projections our patients bring into the consulting room, but treat them as useful communications about the patient's unconscious object relationships. But I think analytic theories unduly objectify unconscious processes; they often imply that the patient has something bad inside, in the form of unconscious sadism associated with the death instinct, destructive internal objects, or negative archetypal imagery. If, as one colleague suggested, I seem to be unfairly implying that an object relations orientation carries a subtle moral disapproval toward the patient, I would point out that Ann Alvarez thought that some of her colleagues sometimes suggested "that people got the bad objects they deserved." She felt that in her clinical work with a psychotic boy, her interpretations of his increasing sadism "escalated this by seeming to accuse him of being totally responsible for this state of affairs" (Alvarez, 1997, p. 761). The more the analyst struggles to help the patient disidentify with these presumed negative internal structures, the more the patient experiences the analyst as negating his self-agency, which in its early developmental forms can often only be expressed destructively, as it is in a toddler's temper tantrum or in the sadism of Alvarez's patient; both need to discover that they can affect the parent but not destroy him or her. So I think we need to find new ways to relate analytically the patient's struggles to work through early developmental states of self-agency, especially when these are conveyed through coercive indexical communication, a sign that the teleological level of self-agency is still operating in the adult.

For our patients, a great deal therefore hangs on the analyst's theoretical framework for thinking about this kind of coercive communication and about the nature and purpose of projective identification. Patients who persistently rely on projective identification and emotional coercion are often identified as borderline; many analytic approaches attribute the patient's resistance to interpretation as a consequence of unconscious sadism and envy, based on an infantile longing for merger, which should be resisted. The patient's pressure to have an emotional impact on the analyst is seen as enactment, malignant regression, a failure of reflective function, or defenses of the self and so is pathologized, because the analyst's model defines the patient's need to evoke an emotional response in the analyst as a destructive denial of the necessary process of mourning and separation.

However, analytic theory is not always coherent or consistent in this respect. Both psychoanalysts and analytical psychologists have increasingly come to understand that in the process of analysis, both analyst and patient descend into mutual unconscious entanglements and projections, out of which individuation and understanding eventually emerge. In psychoanalysis, the work of Bion, Joseph, and Alvarez explored the role of projective identification as communication, the patient's need for the analyst to experience emotions "that the patient needs the analyst to have on his or her behalf" (Alvarez, 1997, p. 756). Their work is part of a paradigm shift in terms of the nature of psychoanalysis, with an increasing emphasis on facilitating and understanding unconscious relational processes and less on the accurate identification of specific mental content.

This is the point at which the apartheid between psychoanalysis and Jungian models of analysis is so clearly a lost opportunity. Jung's model of analysis explicitly stated that the analyst needs to be drawn in at a deep unconscious level and to use his or her emotional response as a countertransference guide (Jung, 1966c, para. 364–365). Michael Fordham extended Jung's research in this area, exploring countertransference as an expression of projective identification and as a useful source of information about the patient's state of mind. He went further to suggest that "an analyst might find himself behaving in ways that were out of line with what he knew of himself, but syntonic with what he knew of his patient" and concluded that "the whole analytic situation is a mass of illusions, delusions, displacements, projections and introjections" (Fordham, 1996b, pp. 165, 172).

Emerging research in attachment theory, neuroscience, and developmental psychology supports this view of analysis as a process in which the conscious and unconscious relationship with the analyst provides the essential foundation for individuation. The Boston Change Process Study group has offered a model that integrates these new disciplines with psychoanalytic practice (BCPSG, 2007), but this aspect has also long been a central feature of Jungian analysis. One Jungian analyst who has summarized this view is George Bright, who believes:

> The development of the capacity of the analyst to tolerate the experience of becoming muddled up or confused with his patient has been a significant clinical development. It implies a movement from ego-based work to an engagement whose basis is in unconscious processes. This approach is not, of course, without its considerable risks and dangers (2006, p. 2).

He went on to argue:

> Within analysis, place must be found to accommodate both a profound, sincere and possibly lengthy experience of psychotic fusion or at-oneness, characterized by refraining from

knowledge, and also an equally profound, sincere and essentially limitless process of misunderstanding, opposition and dialectic (2006, p. 6).

In spite of these developments in theory and practice, there has not yet, I think, been much recognition that a patient's compulsive need to "get inside" the analyst's mind might be more than symptomatic of infantile states of mind that need to be metabolized and outgrown, that it might actively serve healthy developmental needs that had previously been inhibited. This is not quite the same as the issue Warren Colman highlights, that the quality of compulsion characterizes the patient's omnipotent wish for an idealized object and that this must be distinguished from the genuine need for a good object (2006c).

The difference is that I am suggesting that the analyst's sense of being compelled is not necessarily a sign that a collusion is being demanded that should be resisted. The very experience of being compelled may indicate that there is a developmental need to relate, at least for a while, at the teleological level, through the use of indexical communication, in which the only thing that matters is the analyst's behavioral response. Frank Lachmann described such a situation with a suicidal patient who induced such intense anxiety in him that he decided to phone her 2 hours before each session to remind her of her appointment. He argued that his "enactment exactly matched the presymbolic quality" of her communications and it seems to have enabled her to begin to engage in the therapy in a way she had not done before (Beebe & Lachmann, 2002, p. 59). I think his description is of a patient functioning at the teleological level, at which the only evidence she felt she had of her own agency was his concrete behavioral response, which showed her that he held her in mind. This needed to be accepted and worked with before she could relinquish indexical communication and feel that her self-agency did not depend on coercive behavior but could be effective through words.

It is this intense involuntary pressure on the analyst to respond emotionally and behaviorally that makes analytic work so dangerous with teleological self-agency. It lies behind some of the severe boundary violations that authors such as Gabbard (2003) have so memorably described, with his account of his work with Dr N, an analyst who had allowed a desperate suicidal patient to stay overnight in his house and then, not surprisingly, ended up sleeping with her. But my argument is that an understanding of the developmental need for some form of enactment is precisely what enables the analyst to prevent this kind of extreme and severely damaging boundary violation. Dr N seems to have felt under intense emotional pressure to offer some kind of enactment but, perhaps because the only theories he could draw on were those that would pathologize that feeling as a countertransference collusion, he had no framework for finding a creative way for that need to be met. He could only resist, as he initially did, or capitulate disastrously to her unconscious belief that her agency would destroy her good object, as it indeed did when he slept with her.

One important consequence of the deficits in many analytic theories in relation to self-agency is that analysts who do not capitulate may instead resort to indexical communication themselves. Analysts do subtly coerce the patient to obey the analytic rules, mainly by insisting that the patient's attempts to force emotional responses from the analyst may undermine the analytic work unless they are recognized as regressed states of mind that must be analyzed and so eliminated. Even when enactments are accepted as an inevitable expression of the patient's regressed state, they are not seen as serving a necessary, even essential developmental purpose. Warren Colman has identified this as the functioning of the analytic superego, under whose influence

> the therapist fears being shown up and criticized for all the "enactments" he has missed and the transference dynamics s/he has failed to spot and/or interpret. Although it is recognized that "errors" will inevitably occur due to countertransference pressures, these are regarded as regrettable "failures" that the therapist should strive to avoid. (2006a, p. 106)

Even though Alvarez highlighted the dangers of unmasking defenses too early, she still suggests that the right words must be found, a "grammar of description" rather than a "grammar of explanation" (1997, p.755). The paradox inherent in all these injunctions is that the therapist's efforts to maintain the analytic boundaries through the exclusive use of interpretation may be experienced by the patient as indexical communications from the analyst—to prohibit the patient's use of indexical communication. I think that these analytic expectations come to be experienced as coercive by the patient who feels the analyst is demanding a level of self-agency and symbolic functioning that the patient unconsciously knows he or she is not yet able to achieve. If the analyst fails to understand this, an impasse can be reached, an unconscious battle between analyst and patient to control each other in which each feels they are fighting for survival, the analyst for survival of his or her analytic function and the patient for his or her very psychic existence.

The analyst often responds with ever more heroic attempts to break the impasse with increasingly radical interpretations. His or her supervisor may reinforce this approach by implying that any countertransference feeling of empathy in the analyst is a denial of the patient's sadism and a failure of the proper analytic stance. Some authors even suggest that it is better not to activate the attachment system when working with severe borderline personality disorder (Fonagy, 2007). In the worst case, the analyst's own frustration over professional impotence may lead to a decision to terminate the analysis. The analyst judges the patient to be unanalyzable since he or she does not seem to be able to conform to the analytic rules and regards this as a proper professional decision. It may indeed be so, if the analyst feels at the limit of his or her own capacity to tolerate and work through the impasse.

In this kind of impasse, with which I expect we are all familiar, both analyst and patient increasingly use words as controlling actions, not symbolic communications, and their relationship becomes increasingly mutually coercive, with each person attempting to force a specific kind of response from the other. The patient wants to force the analyst to be emotionally involved, and the analyst wants to force the patient to express his or her desire in words. Jessica Benjamin has discussed this kind of impasse as a complementary structure in which each person experiences the other as coercive: "indeed, coercive dependence that draws each into the orbit of the other's escalating reactivity is a salient characteristic of the impasse. . . . It is as if the essence of complementary relations—the relation of twoness—is that there appear to be only two choices: either submission or resistance to the other's demand" (2004, p. 9). Another way of putting this is that each is battling to assert their respective self-agency, to have a real impact on the other. Indeed, Benjamin recognized this crucial issue of agency, without using the specific word:

> In the doer/done-to mode, being the one who is actively hurtful feels involuntary, a position of helplessness. In any true sense of the word, our sense of self as subject is eviscerated when we are

with our "victim," who is also experienced as a victimizing object. (2004, p. 9)

I will give two brief clinical examples, one that illustrates the patient's indexical communication to the analyst and the second of which shows the patient's fear of the therapist's coercive intent. I am grateful to my colleague George Bright for his permission to quote the first vignette:

> The patient had, over a number of consecutive sessions, been complaining that she had no sense of my emotional presence for her, that I was distant and that my technique was inadequate, making me utterly useless to her. She persistently goaded me to tell her how I felt. This had the effect of making me even more tight-lipped and resistant to what I experienced as a ruthless whinging attack on me both as a person and as her analyst. Eventually, I could no longer hold my temper, and I told her exactly what I felt—how much I didn't look forward to her coming, how I hated her and her endless demands on me, and how deeply I cherished the thought of her ending her analysis. This was not beautiful, poetic or musical, but full of raw emotion. The patient burst into deep sobs for some minutes. When she recovered the power of speech she said "Thank God. You've come back from the dead." With hindsight I believe that, at a completely unconscious level, I had taken in and digested something of her of which both she and I were unconscious. What I gave her was digested in the sense that I had incorporated it into myself, and combined it with some aspect of me deeper than my consciousness, before giving it back to her. (Bright 2006, p.11)

To the patient, the analyst's words meant much more than they said, in telling her that she could get inside him and have a powerful emotional effect on him, that not only was he not dead, but also that she was not a dead object to him. The patient clearly felt that it was better to have even such a negative emotional impact than none at all. His violent response gave her back her self-agency. I doubt if in that case there would have been any response from the analyst that would have been so effective, because her self-agency was operating at the teleological level, so interpretations would probably only have made her feel utterly powerless to affect him. I think this illustrates the fact that a crucial part of our task as therapists is both to relate to and interpret the developmental trajectory of self-agency and that this can add a new and useful dimension to our understanding of this kind of experience of projective identification.

This may require a period of time in which the patient does relate mainly by control and coercion and the analyst accepts this without resistance. Alvarez suggested this may be the case with borderline patients, asking, "Are we in danger of producing premature integrations when we refuse to stay with their urgent imperative single-minded states?" (1997, p. 757). Beebe and Lachmann argued that "non-verbal interactions, like noninterpretative actions . . . provide a primary contribution to the patient's expectation of being understood" (2002, p. 47).

Jessica Benjamin agreed with their view that enactment interaction is sometimes the only route out of an impasse of mutual coercive communication, suggesting that the patient may need the analyst to assume the burden of badness and to be able to tolerate it. The analyst shoulders responsibility for hurting, even though her action represented an unavoidable piece of enactment. She continued:

> I also think of this as the moral third—reachable only through this experience of taking responsibility for bearing pain and shame. In taking such responsibility, the analyst is putting an end to the buck passing the patient has always experienced—that is, to the game of ping-pong wherein each member of the dyad tries to put the bad into the other. The analyst says, in effect, "I'll go first." In orienting to the moral third of responsibility, the analyst is also demonstrating the route out of helplessness. (Benjamin, 2004, p. 32)

She offered a way of thinking about the kind of enactment described by George Bright, but I would highlight the point implied by Benjamin, that an essential aspect of this exchange was that the analyst reclaimed his own self-agency and, in doing so, enabled the patient to reclaim her own. Indeed I would go further to argue that it is self-agency itself that is identified as the essence of badness by the patient and for a while Bright unconsciously colluded with that belief, until his violent explosion freed them both.

This second clinical example, which comes from a supervisee's account of a session, highlights the patient's assumption that the therapist's words are coercive communications. In this case the patient is projecting his experience of a fragile and fragmented mother who did not want him to become independent from her, but wanted to keep him as a castrated child who would always stay with her.

> The patient reminds the therapist of an interpretation she had made about his feeling emasculated and asks her if that is how she sees him. The therapist avoids the invitation to make a judgment, but says, "I sometimes think that's the way you feel." He responds with relief and tells her that her statement that he felt emasculated had made him angry. The therapist recognizes that he had not heard it as a neutral observation and asks, "Is it like having it done to you all over again, to hear me say something like that?" He replies that yes, it was a hurtful remark because his fear was that she wanted to castrate him, to make him one of the girls, because that is what women always want. He felt that she might be laughing at him and this made him feel furious, angry, and hopeless.

The patient did not hear her comment as an empathic observation about his state of mind, but as a controlling action, intended to make him feel castrated and belittled. In terms of self-agency, he assumed the therapist, like his mother, was operating at the teleological level, using words in the coercive way that Sell described, in which the sender is more active, the receiver more passive, the communication unidirectional, and the context singular. In this case the therapist rather neatly highlighted his feeling that in describing his humiliation, he felt that she was using indexical communication, making him feel castrated and so experience his loss of self-agency.

So it seems to me that one important reason why analysis breaks down is that the theoretical model the analyst relies on fails to address this particular range of developmental needs, the need to work through previously inhibited aspects of self-agency. Analytic approaches that focus purely on object relations leave this issue unanalyzed and leave the patient eventually feeling annihilated by the analyst's resistance to the patient's need to have a real emotional impact on the analyst. Jung spelled out the need for analysts to be changed as well as patients and the analysis of self-agency really does require analysts to be prepared to take something of the patient inside themselves and to be changed inside by it, in the way George Bright described. This is really the only way the patient can experience agency, through the same kind of unconscious communication that a baby experiences with his or her mother.

This has considerable implications for analytic theory and practice; the analyst needs to relate to, reflect on, and analyze the patient's unconscious sense of agency. Otherwise we risk seeing patients purely as the object of unconscious forces, which have them at their mercy until rescued by the analyst's interpretations. I think that when the analytic task centers on self-agency, it is vital for the analyst not to fall into the trap of trying to find the "correct" interpretation, which imposes the analyst's agency at the risk of denying that of the patient.

To give just one example, I will take Ron Britton's (1998b) excellent chapter "Subjectivity, Objectivity and Triangular Space" in *Belief and Imagination*. I entirely agree with his overall argument that the obliteration of the analyst's mind is felt to be a necessary defense against being seen as an object. However, he bases this on his argument that a failure of maternal containment renders the oedipal triangle persecutory, so that in infantile fantasy, the parental relationship creates a monstrous combined object. He suggests that this monstrous union is then experienced in fantasy as being consummated in the analyst's mind, so that, he wrote, "it was intolerable for such patients to feel that I was communing with myself about them. The mental communion I might have with ideas from other sources . . . would be for them a catastrophic union" (Britton, 1998b, p. 42).

This is a very powerful metaphor, one that intuitively fits the feel of this kind of experience. But Jessica Benjamin rejected Britton's model because it locates "the third as an oedipal construct, an observing function, conceiving the analyst's third as a relation to theory rather than a shared, co-created experience with the patient" (2004, p. 19). So when the central couple is located in the analyst's mind, the patient is excluded and Benjamin suggested that this view of the third, and the patient's awareness of being excluded, is itself the cause of the patient's attacks.

There an additional point I would add to Benjamin's critique, which is that Britton's model identifies the patient's struggles to engage the analyst at the teleological level of self-agency as not being about self-agency but about the operation of a malignant and alien object, the parental couple, embedded in the patient's psyche (which the patient then attributes to the analyst's mind). The wonderfully clear clinical description Britton gives of indexical communication, "where the need for agreement is absolute and paramount it can be achieved only by obedience or tyranny" (1998b, p. 57), attributes agency to the fantasied internal parental couple, thus denying the patient's own agency. Nor do I agree with his view that this comes from "a hypersensitivity to psychic difference, an allergy to the products of other minds" (p. 58), a view that once again denies the purposive nature of the patient's struggles to discover the nature of his or her impact on the analyst.

Regression in the Service of the Development of Self-Agency

So to bring this chapter to a conclusion, I want to highlight the role of regression in relation to the analysis of self-agency. One of the central tenets of many analytic models is that the patient needs to regress to access early and primitive object relationships in the transference and to gradually relinquish them. The fantasied omnipotent power they offer must be resisted by the analyst so that the patient can eventually relinquish them through the mourning process of analysis. In contrast, some post-Kleinian analysts, such as Donald Meltzer (1995, p. 127), regard regression as a dangerous process, a destructive re-creation of primitive undifferentiated, perverse sexual states of mind. But both of these approaches consider the patient's attempts to have an emotional impact on the analyst as the expression of primitive and pathological object relations, like an abscess, which in one model must be entered and cleaned for healing to take place, and in the Meltzer model must be carefully avoided to prevent the toxic contents from escaping. Those attachment-oriented psychoanalysts who have studied the teleological stance in relation to borderline personality seem to reach a rather similar conclusion to Meltzer, that regression is at odds with the predominant analytic task with such patients, namely the development of mentalization. The teleological enactments of the patient have to be tolerated but actively managed to reduce them to a minimum (Bateman & Fonagy, 2004).

But regression is also an analytic tool in the development of self-agency, and I think this may require a different response from the analyst to the patient's regressive attempts to influence him or her. I think this is where Jung's idea of *reculer pour mieux sauter* (regression in the service of development) is so useful and where the Jungian view of teleology as purposive and creative may merge with the narrower developmental definition of teleology as a particular level of self-agency. The analyst may need to accept that there may be a phase when the patient needs to create a real emotional reaction in the other in order to work through and move on from the teleological level of self-agency. This is not an invitation to violation of analytic boundaries. It requires the same kind of sensitive, intuitive response that a containing parent makes, for example, to the child's seductiveness in the oedipal stage, where the parent responds to and celebrates the child's physical beauty but does not violate it by abusive enactment.

But the absence of any emotional response at all is almost (not quite) as destructive as abusive violation, and I think the main practical implication of the issue of self-agency is that the analyst needs to accept that emotional reactions are enactments that may be as valuable as words, not just regrettable parameters. To give one brief example, an anonymous article by K described his wish to be, in his word, "welcomed . . . the kind of welcoming that has its roots in an utter, involuntary delight" (2008, p. 26). Note the word *involuntary* and his beautifully simple summary of all I have described here: " it is out of emotional engagement that mind comes" (K, 2008, p. 26). Lest this be taken as a naive plea for a corrective emotional experience, I would remind you that sometimes this emotional engagement takes the form of the angry outburst George Bright described, or the momentary disclosure of the analyst's anxiety that K recounted.

Welcoming does not imply collusive denial of hate and conflict. Grotstein wrote that "you first have to be bonded before you can be weaned" (1983, p. 496). Bonding and the sense of self-agency are interdependent—you can't have one without the other. So analysis of the transference implies understanding and working with self-agency. And at the teleological level of self-agency, actions do speak louder than words.

6

The Fear of Love: The Loss of Agency in Relationship

Tomas did not realize at the time that metaphors are dangerous. Metaphors are not to be trifled with. A single metaphor can give birth to love. (Kundera, 1984, p. 10)

THERE IS ONE PARTICULAR NARRATIVE that patients frequently bring to the psychotherapy consulting room and which helps the therapist to understand that an inhibited sense of self-agency is going to be a crucial aspect of the therapy with that patient. Sometimes the narrative is explicit, but more often it emerges between the lines, as it were, of the patient's description of the difficulties for which he or she is seeking help. It reveals the other pole of the relational dynamic I described in Chapter 5, in that the patient is mostly not coercive toward the analyst, but relates in a passive compliant way, apparently without any expression of self-agency, so that the therapist often ends up feeling, and sometimes becoming, coercive toward the patient—although, as Jessica Benjamin (2004) pointed out, in this "complementarity" the roles can suddenly reverse.

The essence of this narrative is the patient's childhood experience of parents who could not tolerate emotional separation and so attempted to retain perfect contingency with their infant, long after the infant needed to begin to separate and individuate. The child was a "self-object" for the parents, who needed others, including their own child, to constantly adapt to their emotional needs to sustain a sense of their own identity. This demand for "reverse parenting" often leads to a fear of any relationship, if the child finds that his or her love and attachment needs are manipulated by parents who prioritize their own emotional needs over those of the child. I explore the impact of this on the child's development of self-agency and I describe some clinical work with an adult patient whose history reflects this process.

In the Greek myth, Pandora's curiosity leads her to open the box the gods have given her and into which they have each put something harmful to humanity. As soon as she lifts the lid the evil contents escape, but she slams the lid down in time to keep Hope inside. We remember the myth mainly in terms of the enduring nature of hope, but its other message is that it is Pandora's sense of agency, her desire to find out for herself what the box contains rather than be obedient to the gods, that brings disaster.

The danger inherent in the wish to find and express our own agency, to explore and understand the world for ourselves rather than be subjugated to godlike parents whose every wish must be obeyed is a recurrent theme in religion and mythology. When Eve takes the apple from the Tree of Knowledge, the desire to know things for herself, to have a mind of her own, is an irredeemable sin for which humankind is banished forever from the garden of Eden—a story which conveys the terror a child feels that to assert her own agency will cause her expulsion from the paradise of parental love. Prometheus steals fire from the gods to give to the human race, and his temerity in attempting to give humans agency and control of their environment is brutally punished by a state of unending torture in which his insides are eaten away each day—a story that can imaginatively capture the child's experience of being the passive object of endless sadistic parental intrusions that eat away at his or her very self.

The message conveyed in these narratives is that the struggle to become an independent human, with one's own sense of self-agency, risks provoking catastrophic retaliation from parents who are unable to relate to their children as separate, independent beings. These are parents whose own failure to develop a secure sense of self-agency means that they depend on the responses of others, including their own child, to maintain a sense of their own identity (Fonagy, 1991). Kohut described this as relating to others as self-objects and suggested that this means that "the expected control over such (self-object) others is then closer to the concept of the control which a grown-up expects to have over his own body and mind than to the concept of control which he expects to have over others" (1971, p. 28); Kohut further described the effect this has on the person who is related to as a self-object: "the object of such narcissistic 'love' feels oppressed and enslaved by the subject's expectations and demands" (pp. 28, 32).

However, Kohut did not really develop this account of the effects of being on the receiving end of a self-object projection and the serious and damaging impact it can have on a child's psychic development. It leads to a relationship of reverse parenting, in which the child's unconscious belief is that his or her task is to contain the parents' anxieties and meet their needs. Such parents experience any difference or independence as rejection. The child learns that she must not have a mind of her own, that her own thoughts, needs, emotions, and desires are so dangerous for her parents that her own emerging independent sense of agency must be eliminated and she must always be exactly in tune with her parents' desires. It is the individuation process itself which such parents experience as threatening and which they seek to destroy.

This demand, either conscious or unconscious, for a child to remain totally attuned to the parent profoundly inhibits the development of the child's independence and sense of agency. Parents who fear their child's growing autonomy attack and undermine any independence of thought or action by which the child eventually develops into a mature adult with his or her own autonomy and agency. So, the child's curiosity, appetite, desire, love, or hate are all undermined, attacked, or invalidated, sometimes in quite subtle but devastating ways. The child ends up feeling that both to love and to be loved are equally dangerous. To be loved is to be a self-object for the parents and so to lose one's independent identity; to love seems to be too dangerous because it is a demand for an emotional response that is experienced as a threat by a parent whose own needs must always have priority.

I will focus on some of the more extreme manifestations of this relational dynamic, but it often appears in less dramatic forms in ordinary encounters. I can give one brief illustration from a chance observation of a father and child in a supermarket near my home. The child, a girl of about 8 or 9, was scanning in the purchases. The father, clearly impatient and irritable, could not allow her time to work out how to do it, but as she uncertainly picked out an item from the basket, said in an annoyed tone, "Pay attention—careful what you are doing," sighing loudly as she tried to scan the item and when the machine misread it, he immediately and triumphantly blamed the child, saying, "Now look what you've done," although it was clearly a machine error and not the child's fault. She picked up each further item with greater and greater hesitancy, her body language conveying her self-doubt, as she fumbled and glanced anxiously at her father each time; he responded with remarks such as, "Don't get it wrong again" and "This is rather a slow process—we haven't got all day," eventually taking over the job from her in exasperation. He certainly expected her to fail and my impression was that he needed to destroy her developing independent exploration of the world and perhaps even more important, her self-confidence and trust in her own judgment.

I would not suggest that occasional episodes of that kind of insensitivity offer proof of an unconscious envious attack on the child's self-agency, but would agree with a number of authors who have recognized that if such a pattern is repeated regularly it provides strong evidence of destructive intent (Khan, 1974; Miller, 1988). In this kind of experience, children come to believe that they are lovable only when they are exactly in tune with the parent—a masochistic sacrifice of self to protect the caregiver, whose needs are felt to be paramount. This places children in an impossible dilemma—to be loveable and loved, they must cease to exist in their own eyes and so must destroy all their own aliveness and agency. On the other hand, to experience oneself as a real person, with a sense of self and a capacity to make one's own choices brings the risk of violent retaliation, as Cordelia discovered when she did not say exactly what her father, King Lear, wanted to hear. It is an irresolvable impasse, which eventually leads the child to a state of despair. A total shutdown of the attachment system itself is felt to be the only means of survival, and no relationship ever feels safe because it risks activating loving feelings. This is the basis for the fear of love. To love means to exist and to want to have one's independent existence recognized and responded to by the loved other. But if those whom one loves fear and hate any psychic separateness that they cannot control, a terror of relationship and love seems to be the inevitable outcome, maintained by dissociative processes. All libido, all emotional intensity is avoided as a defense against relationship with a love object who is experienced as destructive of one's own sense of agency and identity.

This kind of experience does not particularly arise from acute trauma that overwhelms the processing capacities of the human mind but on much more everyday and less obvious painful experiences, whose harm lies in the message they convey to a child that his or her autonomy and self-agency are a threat to the parents. Parents who can only relate to others as self-objects cannot tolerate the child's need for recognition of his or her emotional needs, nor respond to their child's love in a way that fosters individuation and the development of self-agency.

Winnicott (1965a) described this kind of situation as a form of parental impingement that led the child to develop a "false self" to protect the "true self." But the use of the concept of self as a psychic structure is problematic; psychoanalytic writers, such as Kohut, Winnicott, Jung, and Fordham all defined *self* differently, so that integrating different models of the self is fraught with confusion. I have suggested elsewhere (Knox, 2007b) that some of these theoretical incompatibilities can be overcome if we reframe our models of the mind less in terms of psychic structures and more in terms of psychic and interpersonal processes. So, in attempting to understand the clinical material I shall shortly recount, I describe it in terms of an active and continuing process of self-agency and the ways in which this can become inhibited, rather than in terms of the self as a psychic structure.

Another difference from the false/true self formulation relates to the active internal attack on self-agency. It is not about a false self protecting a true self from impingement but about the child experiencing any self-agency as dangerous and destructive, as a direct consequence of identification with parental introjects. The badness is experienced as being inside and is identified with self-agency, rather than outside. Linked to this is the child's unconscious motivation for this identification, namely to protect the caregiver rather than his or her self. The caregiver's needs are prioritized over those of the child. Although Alice Miller (1988) highlighted the damaging effects of parental narcissistic demands, she described the resulting inhibition of the child's capacity to express hate, but only hinted at the child's experience that his or her love is a demand that parents cannot tolerate. It is the microanalytic studies of mother-infant interaction by Beebe, Tronick, and others, described in Chapter 2, that reveal the powerful inhibiting impact of this relational dynamic on the development of the child's self-agency. I remind the reader of Tronick's conclusion, quoted in Chapter 2, that "the infant develops a pattern of behavior that precludes human interchange, and in such withdrawal a denial of the child's self is produced" (2007, p. 261).

The damage caused to the infant's developing sense of self-agency when parents lack the capacity to mentalize, to relate to themselves and others as psychological and emotional beings, has also been highlighted by Fonagy and colleagues:

In general we might say that the self as agent arises out of the infant's perception of his presumed intentionality in the mind of the caregiver. Where parental caregiving is extremely insensitive and misattuned, we assume that a fault is created in the construction of the psychological self. We follow Winnicott's (1967) suggestion that the infant, failing to find himself in the mother's mind, finds the mother instead. But in such cases the internalized other remains alien and unconnected to the structures of the constitutional self. (2002, p. 11)

Fonagy et al. suggested that the "absence of a reflective object for the child's experience creates a vacuum within the self, where internal reality remains nameless, sometimes dreaded" (2002, p. 419). Internal reality includes infants' motivational world, their desire, curiosity, and expression of self-agency, which also therefore come to be experienced as alien and dangerous. So children cannot allow themselves to mentalize, to relate to their own mind and emotions, and so to experience or express self-agency in psychological or emotional terms. The unconscious purpose of this defensive system is to inhibit any expression of a child's self-agency because it is experienced as a threat by the child's key attachment figures. It is the clinical manifestation of the withdrawal from relationship described by Tronick and others, that I described in Chapter 2 and that Fairbairn also identified (see below). A number of authors have identified this core pattern of emotional and relational withdrawal and inhibition of self-agency in their description of the "as-if personality," and I think this is the concept that comes closest to the clinical picture I am describing here. Helene Deusch described the as-if person as one for whom "relationships are devoid of any trace of warmth, that all the expressions of emotion are formal, that all inner experience is completely excluded" (1942, p. 304) and went on to suggest that the person's apparently normal relationship to the world is based on mimicry. Hester Solomon expanded on this clinical picture:

> The "as if" personality concerns the action of defensive dissociation deriving from very early experiences of internalizing the presence of an absent object, creating the sense of an internal void at the core of the self. At the same time, the self is capable of acts of self creation through a succession of identifications and internalizations with other sources of environmental

> nourishment, which substitute for, and are constructed around, the original sense of internal emptiness. (2004, p. 635)

This unconscious dynamic underlies and contributes to a wide range of clinical phenomena, including eating disorders, self-harm, addictions, sexual perversions, and psychosomatic and borderline phenomena, sometimes contributing to a complete dissociation from any form of relationship or desire (Crowther, 2004; Seligman, 1982; Sidoli, 1993; Wilkinson, 2003). The states of mind associated with severe eating disorders seem to demonstrate very clearly the importance of the fear of love. Hilda Bruch viewed this dissociative state as fundamental in anorexia, quoting one of her anorexic patients: "I am completely isolated, I sit in a glass sphere. I see other people through a glass wall, their voices penetrate to me." (1973, p. 222). Ogden (1999, p. 183) suggested that the child's experience of the internal deadness in the mother or in the parental couple is internalized as an internal deadness in the child. Along similar lines, Andre Green (1986, p. 168) proposed that maternal depression is experienced by the infant as a mutual death.

What all these authors describe is a subjective experience of internal psychic deadness, but I do not think they adequately explain the unconscious logic that drives this state, the terror of domination by the internal other that sustains the malignant power of the denial of love and relationship. I think we can deepen our understanding of this clinical picture by identifying the underlying inhibited development of self-agency and the parent-infant relational patterns that contribute to this problem, for example, those demonstrated in the latest research by Beatrice Beebe et al. (2010). If parents themselves have no capacity to mentalize, no capacity to relate to their child's mind and emotions, their relationship with their child can only be based on a sense of having a direct behavioral or emotional impact on the child.

A mother whose self-agency is functioning at this teleological level (see Chapter 1), relies on indexical communication (the coercive form of communication described in Chapter 5) even when she is using words, which are, of course, symbols. The unconscious emotional signals the mother conveys, for example, in her body language, facial expression, and tone of voice, put pressure on the child to respond to her needs, as Beebe et al. have shown in the research studies I described in Chapter 2. The child feels coerced, manipulated, and constantly intruded upon.

The impact of this kind of parental intrusiveness can be to undermine and sometimes even annihilate the child's sense of self-agency and value as an independent person, as much as rejection or humiliation, contributing to the "the destruction of the personal spirit" so eloquently described by Don Kalsched (1996), but also by attachment theorists such as Hopper (1991).

Case Study

I want to explore in more depth the various forms this relational trauma may take and the nature of the defensive reactions they bring about, but first I describe some clinical illustrations of this kind of experience. I describe a former patient's dreams, before giving some of the background information that helps us to understand how he reached this position.

Dreams

1. The patient was in a boat with some colleagues from work. They were chugging along in a rather aimless way and he was not really involved with them—they seemed to be ignoring him. It was pleasant scenery but he was not really sure why he was there or where he was going.
2. He is in a large building full of Nazis. It feels frightening and dangerous. He has to go down an escalator but he does not want to because it leads down into black darkness, where he cannot see anything or find his way.
3. He is in a large English stately home, looking around. He comes to a narrow corridor that is partially obstructed by something. He is afraid he is too fat to get through but then finds he can. He meets the owner of the house (who looks like the head of a local education institute whom he recently saw playing in a pantomime). He tells the owner that it is difficult to find his way around and that it would be helpful to have signposts.

I think these three dreams illustrate clearly the patient's confusion about relationships, his fear of intimacy as persecutory, and his sense of being required to fit into a narrow set of expectations without anyone giving him any signposts about exactly what they expect of him. It is this Kafkaesque internal world that he brought into therapy, and his personal background will help us to understand how loving relationships have come to be so dangerous for him.

Personal History

This man, whom I call Alan, came to see me for help with his long-standing sadistic fantasies, which centered on the torture and sexual humiliation of women, involving biting their breasts and penetrating them with sharp objects. My patient felt ashamed of these fantasies and said with great emphasis during the first interview, "I am not a bad man," desperate to reassure me that he would never actually wish to enact the fantasies to harm or hurt anyone. The fantasies were only activated in the context of sexual arousal and masturbation.

His childhood was dominated by a mother who seemed to have become an internal Nazi. She was intensely anxious and intrusive, unable to allow Alan to be anything other than the person she needed him to be. During his analysis he remarked, "I simply did not want to be the kind of person I was supposed to be" and "My mother needed me there to fulfill her." She simply could not see another person's point of view and was puzzled and wounded by the slightest criticism. She alienated many people by her unconscious attitude of superiority to them and to any illness or failing. As an old lady she moved into a residential home and would introduce other people there to her son with phrases like, "This is Mrs Smith. She's got cancer." She seemed to reassure herself that she was stronger, less damaged than they were. She needed to believe that other people were impoverished compared with her. At the same time, she lived a life of dull, monotonous administrative work, which she hated, and she let her children know that she only did it to earn money for them because their father did not earn enough. Alan remembers feeling imprisoned on car journeys with her, feeling poisoned, literally, by her cigarette smoke or by her critical attacks on other family members.

Alan felt intensely involved with her as a child but he remembered finding her physically repellent from an early age—he felt that to be hugged by her was like being touched by a reptile. At other times, her presence felt like being cut by shards of broken glass. He could not look directly into her eyes because her face frightened him. He learned early in life that to disagree or challenge her was frightening and painful to her and that it made him feel he had been really bad. He said that she invaded his mind by controlling and planning his whole life. He learned to hide his feelings from her and ultimately from himself. He remembered waking up one night when he was about 6 or 7 and getting a glass of water and having the sudden impulse to wake her up by throwing it in her face while she slept, an impulse that he resisted. When he chose not to throw the glass of water at his mother, he was already learning to disconnect from loving relationship, deriving satisfaction from mastering his intense desire to have an impact on her. To have thrown it would have shown her how angry he was and by implication that she mattered to him. The other side of the picture is his fear of being abandoned—his earliest dream was of being left at the side of the road, with his parents driving away in a blue car.

His father was almost invisible as a person. He had no interests apart from his work. He ate whatever his wife gave him and seemed to have no preferences or opinions of his own at all and there were never any arguments between them. Alan said recently that his father had paid for the security he had in his marriage at the price of being castrated. Alan's father's own past was a mystery and he never spoke about his childhood or his family—he had broken off all contact with them. During the course of his analysis with me, Alan contacted a cousin whom he had not spoken to for decades and asked him about the paternal family history. He discovered that his father's father had been a sadistic tyrant and a cheat, bordering on criminality. Alan's father had left home at about 18 and, to Alan's knowledge, had only ever met him once since. Alan was married but only had a brief sexual relationship with his wife before the marriage. There had been no sex since and they adopted children.

The sadistic fantasies vividly conveyed his experience of intimacy as painful and sadistic, both to himself and others. He clearly identified with the tortured women and the fantasies reflected his fear of the persecutory mother, who needed to control him totally and who penetrated him with her anxiety and demands for total conformity to her views. The second dream, about the building full of Nazis, portrayed his persecutory inner object relationships and the death of his own sense of identity (going down the escalator into darkness) unconsciously demanded of him by his mother. The sadistic fantasies also represented his own sense that to be a separate person with needs and desires of his own would be acutely painful to his mother—it would be like torturing her and penetrating her with sharp objects. His unconscious fear was that his desire and sexuality would be painful and sadistically intrusive toward his wife, a view that she seemed to unconsciously share, in that the lack of sex had never been a real issue between them.

Alan's first analyst (whom he saw briefly in his 20s) made an interpretation that made a deep impact on him, when Alan asked him one day if he had any children. The analyst replied, "Do you mean, do I have any little slaves?," a comment that perfectly captured the quality of Alan's childhood experience that he existed to meet his mother's needs and expectations. The first analyst also conveyed that he felt Alan had experienced an oedipal triumph over his father—that he was his mother's intimate partner. The rage that accompanied this additional form of enslavement might well take the form of sadistic attacks on the women who aroused his sexual desire, which was unconsciously incestuous. It was small wonder that he was unable to have intercourse with his wife. Loving intimacy was impossible in the face of all that internalized anxiety and hate.

The Denial of Self in Relationships: Clinical and Developmental Aspects

Fairbairn recognized the despair that comes from feeling unlovable, worthless, or dangerous to those one most loves to be the fundamental anxiety behind schizoid withdrawal:

> It is the great tragedy of the schizoid individual that his love seems to destroy; and it is because his love seems so destructive that he experiences such difficulty in directing libido towards objects in outer reality. He becomes afraid to love; and therefore he erects barriers between his objects and himself. (1952b, p. 50)

In describing the erection of barriers between self and object, Fairbairn was describing a state of defensive dissociation. These barriers exist between the self and its internal, as well as external, objects. Mollon defined dissociation as a state that "requires a degree of detachment of part of the mind from what another part is experiencing" (1996, p. 4). I think the implications of this are wide-reaching, in that dissociative defenses therefore strip events and experience of meaning, since meaning depends on the integrative processes of the default network in the brain, which links new and old information together with self-experience and self-agency, a process that seems to have many similarities to Jung's

(1971) concept of the transcendent function and which I described in the discussion of the neurobiology of self-agency in Chapter 3. I have explored elsewhere and in Part I the way in which contemporary neuroscience and attachment theory help us to recognize these integrative processes as an essential part of the way the human mind evaluates information, analyzing similarity and difference and integrating the result into new forms of understanding (Knox, 2003). Appraisal is the name given by attachment theorists to this process, and research suggests that it is based on the integration of explicit and implicit knowledge (Fosshage, 2004; Siegel, 2003).

Dissociation strikes at the heart of this fundamental process by which new meaning and new symbolism develops, preventing the recognition of similarity and difference between a new event and past experience, between conscious, explicit and unconscious, implicit knowledge, between cognition and emotion, and, ultimately, between self and other. A rigid defensive system becomes elaborated that prevents any expression of agency. This denial of one's own or others' self-agency is a process that relies on a fundamental and wide-reaching assault on the meaning-making processes of the human mind, described by Bion (1965/1977, p. 54) as "linking" and by Jung (1970) as the transcendent function. Both the transcendent function and linking describe the mind's capacity to form connections between mental contents and it is this fundamental meaning-making process that is inhibited by dissociation.

I suggest that if a person's dominant and fundamental implicit relational experience is that he or she is not allowed to exist as an independent person in the eyes of the other, then the compensation provided by the unconscious in the form of dreams or other imagery is not in itself enough to overcome this dissociative denial of self-agency. Dreams, fantasies, or unconscious enactments are experienced as meaningful only when they are integrated with desire and excitement, the expression of self-agency in relation to other; otherwise the symbolic imagery of the unconscious begins to lose its life-giving qualities and is experienced as either dangerous or meaningless. The consequence is that the very creativity of the unconscious must be attacked and any experience of self-agency is repeatedly and triumphantly destroyed. I think this is the basis for the "addiction to near death" described by Betty Joseph (1982), although I offer a different etiological view, in suggesting that the destruction of the sense of one's own separate identity and one's own desire is a necessary sacrifice in order to be lovable to the other.

One of the most vivid literary accounts of this is given in a novel by Joanne Greenberg (1964), *I Never Promised You a Rose Garden*. It is a fictionalized account of her therapy with Freida Fromm-Reichmann that, while somewhat sentimental at times, powerfully conveys her terror of existing as a real person—someone with her own independent identity. The patient, Deborah (diagnosed then as schizophrenic, whereas she would be more likely now to be labeled as suffering from severe borderline personality disorder), has constructed a beautiful but terrifying imaginary world, Yr, peopled with gods, while the real world is one she can only see in flat monochrome and in which she does not exist as herself but simply as a robotic puppet. Any attempt to engage with the world, to love or enjoy anything or anyone in it, risks dire punishment from the gods and their agent, the Censor, because not only might the real world destroy her, she might destroy real people by any attempt at closeness or intimacy. She tells her analyst that she has destroyed her sister, then says, "I didn't mean to—she was exposed to my essence. It's called by an Yri name it's my selfness and it is poisonous. . . . [I]t's a quality of myself, a secretion, like sweat. It is the emanation of my Deborah-ness and it is poisonous." Deborah does not mean that she is selfish and so destructive, but rather, that she believes her very existence is poisonous to those she loves. Her sense of her self as destructive, which leads her to a denial of the reality of her own existence, leads to a splitting off of all her imagination and creativity into something separate from herself, a world that she experiences as separate and other, not as an imaginative construction of her own. To own it would be to acknowledge the unconscious symbolism and imagery as her own and her increasingly desperate attempts to deny these as expressions of her self lead the kingdom of Yr to become a steadily darker, more dangerous, and persecutory state in her mind.

This pattern of relating originates with the infant's experience of being on the receiving end of such coercive relating from his or her primary caregiver, but as the example of Deborah shows, it becomes internalized as a relational dynamic and as that infant grows, he or she may become equally coercive in subsequent relationships. As the example given by Alicia Lieberman (Chapter 2) shows, a mother whose self-agency functions at the teleological level, through action rather than reflection, does not provide an experience that allows her infant to progress beyond this coercive pattern of relationship.

I think this lies behind projective identification and the countertransference experience of being coerced or manipulated—it is an experience of the patient's sense of self-agency operating at the teleological (or in Deacon's terms, indexical) level. In this state of mind, thoughts and intentions are inseparable from the action they point to, or the emotional states they so powerfully elicit in the other person. Alan's mother's body language, tone of voice, and facial expression were all controlling signals to Alan conveying one message, that her survival depended on being constantly in a state of harmony and identity with him and so being validated by him in her role as his mother. Any criticism or rejection by him would destroy her.

In this context, Alan's fantasies convey his experience of relationships as persecutory and sadistic, as the second dream also shows. This arose from the intense intrusive anxiety of my patient's mother—a mother who related through fusion and was therefore totally unable to allow her husband or children to be separate people with minds and desires of their own. Such a mother is unable to mirror her baby's emotions, the importance of which Sue Gerhardt (2005) so vividly described in her book *Why Love Matters*. For someone whose unconscious fantasy or belief is that to be a self is a crime, making choices means having a mind of one's own, and this would invite punishment from the powerful other who can only relate to a self-object, by means of coercion or manipulation.

The first and third dreams convey Alan's bland withdrawal into non-relationship—where he is at sea, not knowing why he is there or what he is doing, probably based pretty much on his identification with his father's defensive mindlessness. The third dream is, I think, more to do with the analysis, his sense of having to fit into my expectations (the narrow corridor) and his anxious wish for me to give him a sense of direction, to tell him what I wanted him to do. It may also reflect his secret contempt for me, as someone taking part in an elaborate pantomime of relationship in which he wanted to play no part.

The developmental distortions that lie behind this defensive state of mindlessness arise from an inhibition of the transcendent function or, in attachment theory terms, appraisal, preventing the move from indexical to symbolic communication. Initially, the infant's developing sense of self, indeed his or her very survival, depends on being able to have a direct physical and behavioral impact on the caregiver, and so a perfectly contingent response in the first months of life is crucial; it allows the experience of the teleological sense of self to develop, through the infant's repeated experience of agency in creating the caregiver's predictable responses. In Deacon's terms, this relies on indexical communication, in which one person's signals guarantee a predictable response from the other. At this stage, as Winnicott (1975) pointed out, it would be catastrophic for the infant to be disillusioned about his or her role in creating the maternal response.

Increasing separation and individuation require an emotional response from the caregiver that is close to the infant's but not identical with it, thus allowing the infant to become aware that his or her desires have been communicated to another mind that has understood them, processed them, and responded in a way that reflects both the infant's and the caregiver's intentionality. A perfect attunement at this stage would fail to allow the sense of intentional and reflective self to develop because there would be no experience of dialogue with another, different mind, so vividly portrayed in the developmental research described in Chapter 2.

I think we can see that problems will arise at key points in the infant's development, if the mother lacks reflective function, basically the awareness of herself and her baby as separate mental and emotional beings. She can only relate at the teleological or indexical level, attempting to retain perfect contingency and total identity with the infant, long after the baby needs to start the process of separation and individuation. She feels she is only good and valuable if she is in total harmony with her baby and is using her baby as a substitute for her own absent internal reflective parent. Her communications to the infant remain at the indexical level, and so will be experienced by the infant as intrusive and coercive attempts to elicit specific emotional and behavioral responses that do not accord with his or her own state of mind. The alien sense of identity becomes installed in the child's psyche and is experienced as an alien self (Fonagy et al., 2002; Rotmann, 2002).

The child therefore experiences his mother as attacking any development if she rejects him when he begins to separate and so is no longer totally in tune with her. Separateness and indeed individuation itself come to be experienced as being bad, and this has a quality of absolute certainty. The child comes to believe that his or her task is to please the parent because there is only one mind—the parent's—whose needs and desires are always paramount. For Alan, the fear of loving and being loved originated in his experience that his mother expected him to be exactly in tune with her own desires. He could not have thoughts, desires, needs, emotions, or sexual identity of his own.

I suggest that it is the unconscious experience of self-as-object that determines and maintains this kind of state, as a defense against the unconscious belief that the parent's sense of self depends on the child's total compliance. But why would a child collude in the obliteration of self-agency? Perhaps to avoid becoming Prometheus, with parents parasitically devouring his aliveness to feed themselves. Parents who cannot find their own vitality in themselves appropriate all the child's vitality as their own; any sign of the child's own separate identity, whether in the form of emotional need or increasing autonomy, will be met with an envious attack of the kind I described happening in the supermarket.

The Analytic Task

The adult patient brings this childhood experience into the analytic process, which becomes subverted—it is no longer in the service of the patient gaining understanding but rather of being understood by the analyst and then of complying with that understanding. The analyst's communications are not experienced as being addressed to an independent mind that can use them for its own purposes but are experienced as instructions to the patient to comply with the therapist's needs. The patient believes that the analyst is functioning like the parent, through coercion or manipulation, operating at the indexical level. This leads to the kind of blandness I experienced with Alan—he simply did not allow himself to need anything from me, to make any demands on me. I frequently interpreted that for him to do so would be to risk putting himself in the power of a controlling mother again who needed to dominate him and who would humiliate him if he showed need, desire, or love.

In the analysis with me, he adopted a bland neutrality with emotional expression always subdued. There was no emotional intensity, except brief outbursts of narcissistic anger when he felt humiliated by others or by his own body's illnesses. At these times, he felt stirred up but also confused, as though his mind was in a fog, which I understood as a form of dissociation, a defensive avoidance of the emotional meaning of his experience. All his emotion remained secret, as it was from his mother. I think he secretly triumphed in the recognition that very little I said could penetrate his total emotional shutdown. He mostly successfully concealed both his love and his hate from me. I gradually came to realize that much of his emotional investment in the analysis went into trying to ensure, often successfully, that he had no emotional impact on me whatsoever. To arouse my interest in him would risk my becoming the controlling and intrusive mother endlessly picking at the inside of his mind, as the eagle did to Prometheus.

Alan had learned early in life to avoid giving his internal "Nazi" mother anything of himself for her to feed on and he re-created this in the analysis with me, which often made me feel at a loss about how to respond to him. I often seemed to have no thoughts or feelings of my own about him, as though I had become as bland and mindless as he was. As I became more aware of this, I began to point out the various ways in which I felt that he diverted my attention away from his internal world, such as the frequent occasions when he would seem to invite me to join him in critical comments about other people, a pattern that replicated his collusion with his mother's criticism of other people in order to divert her negativity away from himself. As a result, he began to acknowledge his terror of being vulnerable; for example, he almost always arrived about 10 minutes before the session and would sit in his car in the drive thinking about what he would talk about. I said that he seemed to need to bring me only material that he had prepared in advance and so could present to me in a way that kept it under his control. When he brought dreams to his sessions, he would describe the dream and then immediately offer his own interpretation of it, preempting any interpretation I might wish to offer, as though afraid that I would become a penetrating intrusive Nazi-mother, taking over and controlling his symbolic products. No symbolic process could therefore be allowed to come alive in the room between us—there could be no intercourse and so no living experience created between us.

His fear was that any spontaneous emotion or thought would place him at the mercy of the meaning that I would make of it. For a person whose unconscious belief is that the analyst or parent cannot tolerate any evidence of the patient's independent psychic existence, there is a very real danger that the analyst's interpretations will be experienced as coercive or manipulative. The harder the analyst tries to offer them as factual objective observations, the more the patient feels annihilated by the perceived demand to become the object the analyst seems to be describing, rather than the subject he or she so desperately needs to allow to exist.

In Jungian theory, the route out of this deadness is through the activation of the shadow, the aspects of our identity that we find unacceptable and so relegate to the unconscious. However, Alan had learned from an early age to suppress any expression of his shadow; resisting the impulse to throw the glass of water at his mother was an early example. In the analysis, he was adept at avoiding any conflict with me, by negating my interpretations with a variety of responses, such as bewilderment, incomprehension, or a kind of amused tolerance at the strange things that analysts sometimes say. Initially, his avoidance of separateness was successful in reducing me to a position of masochistic analytic silence, in that I could not find a way to speak about the deadness in the analytic relationship. Attempts to offer interpretations that might penetrate his blandness felt coercive, as though I was forcing him to respond and be changed by them. It seemed impossible to establish a dialogue in which the patient and analyst are separate, each with minds of their own, and in which words are open communications, which the analyst offers for the patient's own mind to use as he wishes. We remained stuck in an indexical level of relationship, in which Alan's communications, as well as mine, were controlling and manipulative actions.

What I needed to do to change this situation was to become more aware of the extent to which I had identified with the projection of the Nazi mother and so that any attempt to penetrate his defensive system was actually a sadistic assault, which would expose his weakness and humiliate him, just as his mother did with her remarks such as, "This is Mrs. Smith. She's got cancer." As I became more aware of the real power this projection had held and the degree to which I had sometimes felt contemptuous or patronising toward him, it became possible to speak about his experience of humiliation without enacting the sadism.

It was the repeated experience of the symbolic, rather than the indexical, level of communication that needed to be allowed to develop in the analysis. The first place this work needed to be done was in my own countertransference, on my unconscious identification with the coercive indexical communications of his mother. I needed to become free to speak from my own self, without feeling that I was torturing and penetrating him with my words. Only then could we begin to engage with his fear that I would parasitically feed off his aliveness, devouring him for my own purposes and destroying him in the process.

I have explored the consequences when the development of a fully mature and reflective sense of self-agency is inhibited and how this gives rise to a fear of love and relationship. I have suggested that these linked problems emerge when parents are fearful of their infant's separation-individuation process and need the infant to remain as a psychic mirror for themselves. As infants grow, they then fear all subsequent relationships as potentially destructive of their subjectivity and also fear that their own self-agency will threaten their key attachment figures.

The underlying fear of allowing oneself to exist as a subject rather than as an object can contribute to any of the patterns of insecure attachment—avoidance, ambivalence, or disorganization—and to a whole range of clinical problems. Impenetrable defenses of the self can be expressed in bland nonrelationship or in cycles of intense attempts at merger and fusion with the analyst, followed by violent attempts at separation, often fueled by self-harm in the form of alcohol or drug abuse or self-injury. What I have attempted to show with this particular clinical example is the developmental inhibition of self-agency, which underpins the fear of love. It is rooted in the person's experience that relationship is always coercive, that one person is directly controlling and dominating another. This experience is maintained by the predominance of an indexical form of communication, in which words are controlling actions, not truly symbolic communications.

In analytic work, it is therefore vital for the analyst to be demonstrably open to the possibility of alternative meanings in any exchange between analyst and patient, rather than trying to impose a particular view of the patient's unconscious intentions on him. Otherwise an analytic impasse is inevitable, in which analytic work deteriorates into a battle in which both analyst and patient are fighting for survival, the analyst for survival of the analytic function and the patient for his or her very psychic existence. Indeed, the analyst's countertransference feeling that his own survival as an analyst is at stake can alert him to the fact that, for the patient, the analyst is another parental figure who requires total subjugation to his needs and the annihilation of the patient's own self-agency.

In spite of the fact that some degree of enactment of this impasse may be inevitable, an analyst who is open to exploring multiple symbolic meanings and to understanding the material from the patient's perspective, rather than imposing his own, offers a new experience within which the patient can gradually relinquish her defensive mindlessness. The projection of the controlling, devouring parent can gradually be withdrawn as the analyst demonstrates again and again his own reflective function, the awareness of the patient as a separate psychological and emotional being. This experience is gradually internalized, activating the compare-and-contrast integrative processes, allowing the patient to begin to relate to her own mind as a separate and symbolic psychic space that can integrate conscious experience, unconscious symbolism, and the sense of self-agency.

7

The Abuse of an Object and Relating Through Incorporation

The pain of living and the drug of dreams. (Eliot, 1936)

IN THIS CHAPTER, I EXAMINE how an inhibited development of self-agency can contribute to many forms of addiction. In his powerfully evocative poem "Animula," T. S. Eliot (1936) drew a mournful picture of human development and of the slow destruction of hope, pleasure, and playfulness as the small child learns the harsh realities of life. The poem describes the infant's initial delight in discovering a magical world—the brilliance of a Christmas tree, the wind, the sunlight, and the sea. But gradually a warped and damaged child emerges, who can take no pleasure in life or relationships, who retreats from the world of new and exciting sensations, denying his own desires and need for relationships, becoming selfish and emotionally stunted, and taking refuge from the pain of living in "the drug of dreams."

I think this poem speaks directly to the avoidance of separation-individuation and the inability to experience real relationship that lie behind the fear of love that I described in Chapter 6. But it also contributes to much addictive behavior. In an article about the unconscious processes that contribute to alcoholism (Knox, 1995), I suggested that people who have become afraid of the pain of relationships with other people in the real world retreat into a fantasy of fusion with their objects "to sustain a delusional fantasy of fusion between self and object as a defence against separateness." I drew on the work of Fordham, Gordon, Balint, and Rosenfeld to suggest that "fusionary wishes are a reflection of intense separation anxiety with accompanying fears within the patient of annihilation" (1995, p. 167). I suggested that alcohol seems to provide a direct and almost magical route to regressive fantasies of fusion and of omnipotent control of objects—these are the dreams that act like an addictive drug, as Eliot so well understood, and the actual substance used to achieve this state of mind is not in itself the goal, but merely the vehicle to bring it about. I explored the implications this had for analytic work, particularly with patients who misuse alcohol:

> Thus the analyst cannot be allowed to be separate and to make interpretations which can penetrate the patient and in doing so confirm that the analyst is indeed a separate and independently functioning person. If the analyst is recognized as separate then the analyst's interpretations are new experiences and the patient may be affected and changed by them; in regressive states of fantasied fusion, all change is dangerous because it involves loss and activates depressive anxiety. (Knox, 1995, p. 167)

In this state of mind, separateness and loss are experienced as catastrophic threats, mobilizing the most extreme forms of defense, which Fordham (1985) described as "defences of the self," the kind of defenses that prevent any new experience from being taken in, because all new events threaten the fantasy of total merger with, and control of, one's love objects. In that article I was focusing specifically on the addiction to alcohol, but the same pattern can easily be identified in relation to a whole range of other addictive substances and patterns of behavior, such as pornography, gambling, shoplifting, or even the apparently more ordinary risk taking in extreme sports.

These addictive substances and activities can always be used as a total defense against the painfulness of everyday reality, in which we have to experience separation, loss, and ultimately our own helplessness to prevent old age, illness, and, ultimately, death. Addictions offer an illusion of omnipotence through the artificial feelings of well-being, ranging from calm content to manic excitement that can be summoned each time the addiction is indulged, depending on the effect of the drug or activity. Under the influence of any mind-altering substance, the delusion of fusion never has to be confronted, nor the pain and anxiety involved in experiencing separation, loss, vulnerability, or helplessness. Whenever stress or anxiety threatens, the addiction can be used as an escape route from reality.

Addiction and Self-Agency

I would like to extend this view of addiction as a defense against experiencing the pain, terrors, and disappointments of real life by linking it with the development of self-agency and with Winnicott's ideas about a person's capacity to function as an integrated whole—to achieve "unit status" (1965b, p. 44). What Winnicott meant by the idea of unit status is the stage reached when the child can say, "Here I am. What is inside me is me and what is outside me is not me" (1971a, p. 130). Winnicott then links this with:

1. The capacity to be alone
2. A new capacity for object relating, one based on an interchange between external reality and psychic reality
3. The child's use of symbols and a capacity for creative play

Winnicott showed extraordinary understanding in his account of the kind of parenting required to enable the development of unit status. Attachment research has explored the same territory in more scientific terms, accumulating a wealth of evidence to suggest the three crucial areas of psychic development that lead to unit status are affect regulation, the development of the capacity for mentalization (the basis for reflective function), and the emergence of a truly psychic sense of self-agency. I discuss these in more detail in Chapter 8.

But the developmental and neurobiological studies I described in Part I lend support to the argument that self-agency is the most fundamental of these three developmental processes. The extent to which the development of self-agency underpins both the capacity for mentalization and affect regulation is the focus for some current key developmental research, particularly the studies by Beatrice Beebe and colleagues that I referred to in Chapter 2. Their work suggests that the development of self-agency is a fundamental organizing force in psychic development, demonstrating that infants discover their sense of agency through the emotional and behavioral impact they have on their primary caregiver. The complex turn-taking behavior between infant and caregiver, in which the infant can repair disruptions, is the foundation of the sense of self-agency. In a healthy relationship, the caregiver responds positively to, encourages, and enjoys the infant's capacity to communicate needs and emotions. So the infant's emotions form an integral part of the expression of agency and sense of self.

Initially the infant needs a mother who can provide a quality of attunement in which her responses almost perfectly mirror the infant's needs. In Winnicott's words, the infant is not forced to ask whether the breast was given or whether he created it. The infant's sense of self-agency depends on being able to have a direct physical and behavioral impact on the caregiver; it allows the experience of self-agency at a physical level (e.g., milk being produced as the infant sucks). At the social level of self-agency, the infant begins to recognize his actions having an effect in a different, less direct way, namely, creating behavioral responses in others, for example, his mother smiling and talking in a turn-taking way. The complex nature of these interactions, the rhythms of disruption and repair, are essential to healthy communication. At the teleological sense of self, one person feels that she directly creates and controls a predictable response from the other. In infancy, this is the stage of narcissistic grandiosity, the sense of omnipotent and magical control over the object world, and this is essential as a form of psychic protection against the terrifying awareness of one's helplessness. However, in order to move from the teleological level, its gradual erosion is also essential, even though the painfulness of the accompanying disillusionment contributes to the tantrums and rage of toddlerhood.

At the intentional level, forbidden desires or wishes may feel dangerously powerful, able to create wishes and desires in the other. The difference from the teleological level is that it is not behavior but intention that controls the other—so desire in one person's mind brings about not only action by the other person but desire in the other person's mind. For example, the toddler's unconscious incestuous wishes will feel dangerous because desire itself is seen to cause desire in the other, and so the child's oedipal desires are experienced by him or her, in fantasy, as seducing the parent who will then enact them.

At the most mature level of self-agency, the representational level, agency can be expressed and communicated in language, without the coercion or magical omnipotence of the more primitive, action-based levels. These different developmental stages of self-agency play a central role in determining the nature and function of both conscious and unconscious fantasy. This has considerable implications for our understanding of the kind of borderline experiences and primitive defenses that underpin substance abuse. The central theme in this chapter is that the kind of regressive fusion fantasies that seem to predominate with substance abuse are expressions of the person's self-agency at the teleological and intentional level, at which there is not yet a fully developed sense of one's own separate identity.

These are people who have not experienced relationships with a caregiver whose responses adapted to the different stages of their developing self-agency. For example, a mother whose self-agency is functioning at the teleological level can only relate to her child as a self-object, who is not recognized as having a mind of his or her own. The mother's relationships are based on a primitive level of self-agency in which she only feels real when she is having a direct behavioral or emotional impact on her infant. She can only relate by attempting to retain perfect and total identity with her infant, long after the baby needs to start the process of separation and individuation. She feels she is only good and valuable if she is in total harmony with her baby and is probably using the baby as a substitute for her own absent internal reflective parent. Her communications to the infant are intrusive, coercive, or manipulative, and so will be experienced as attempts to elicit specific emotional and behavioral responses that do not accord with his own state of mind. As I described in the previous chapter, she experiences a fantasized state of fusion with her baby, one in which there is no difference between them, no separateness.

If brought up by this kind of mother who lacks reflective function and is unable to relate to her baby as a separate mental and emotional being, the child experiences his mother as attacking any development if she rejects him when he begins to separate and so is no longer totally in tune with her. Separateness and indeed individuation itself comes to be experienced as being bad. The child feels coerced, manipulated, and constantly intruded upon by a mother who relates through fusion and is therefore totally unable to allow her children to be separate people with minds and desires of their own. Such a mother is unable to mirror her baby's emotions, the importance of which has been so clearly demonstrated by Allan Schore (1994, 2001). The child comes to feel that having a mind of one's own is in itself bad. An essential component of this experience of badness seems to be the experience that any emotion that is not exactly in tune with the caregiver's emotional state is dangerous and destructive to the caregiver. For example, Beatrice Beebe has shown that mothers of future disorganized infants cannot mirror their infant's distress, as I described in Chapter 2. They create a false cheerfulness and a refusal to recognize negative emotions in the child, because it activates their own distress. They convey this to their baby by subtle nonverbal signals, which can be seen when videotapes of mother-infant interactions are run in slow motion.

If parents only feel real when they are controlling the actions or feelings of another person, then it becomes much harder for the child to separate and to develop a separate identity. The child internalizes this kind of relationship and also remains stuck at the teleological level of self-agency. For a child who has had this kind of parent, it is impossible to say, "Here I am. What is inside me is me and what is outside me is not me." There is an absence of the capacity to be alone, an inability to genuinely relate to others and a lack of the capacity for creative play (Winnicott, 1971a, p. 131).

So how does the infant achieve unit status, the move from levels of self-agency that depend on the manipulation or coercion of the other to a true sense of the autobiographical self and the accompanying capacity to relate to others as separate people with their own minds and emotions? Increasing separation and individuation requires an emotional response from the caregiver that is close to the infant's but not identical with it, thus allowing the infant to become aware that his or her desires have been communicated to another mind that has understood them, processed them, and responded in a way that reflects both the infant's and the caregiver's intentionality. One way the primary caregiver achieves this is by marking, a term used to describe a mother's exaggeration of her response to her baby. It has been suggested that this allows the baby to recognize her reaction as a response to him (Gergely & Watson, 1996). But this is also a way in which the caregiver highlights the turn-taking exchanges between them, in which the turns convey the mother's state of mind as well as that of the infant. It is an experience of dialogue with another, different mind, in which both can express emotion and respond to the emotion of the other.

However, this in itself may not be enough. It was Winnicott who recognized the crucial role of destructiveness in the "subject's placing of the object outside the area of the subject's omnipotent control" (1971b, p. 89). Winnicott argued that the object's repeated survival of destruction enables the subject to recognize the object as an independent entity in its own right. Winnicott suggested that for many patients the main analytic task is to help the patient to acquire the capacity to use the analyst:

> The analyst, the analytic technique, and the analytic setting all come in as surviving or not surviving the patient's destructive attacks. This destructive activity is the patient's attempt to place

the analyst outside the area of omnipotent control, that is, out in
the world. (1971b, p. 91)

Viewed from the perspective of self-development, the repeated destruction, in fantasy, of the object and the gradual recognition that the object
survives such attacks and goes on being is not only the basis for the
sense of object constancy, it is also the means by which infants become
increasingly secure in the knowledge that they also exist separately and
independently of their effect on the object. If the object survives the
attack, the subject can discover that being is separate from doing, and
existence is independent of one's physical actions. A child goes on existing and knowing he exists even when having to recognize the continuing and independent physical and psychic survival of the other person,
whom he has just tried to destroy.

The object's survival of destructive attacks drives the move from the
teleological and intentional level of self-agency, in which one knows
one exists only through the physical or emotional impact one has on
the other, to the true psychic autonomy of the representational level, at
which mind can reflect on its own processes rather than automatically
convert them into physical or emotional action. In this sense, true psychic separateness and autonomy directly depend on the recognition of
one's powerlessness to control or coerce others.

This is precisely the experience that is most feared by someone who
cannot bear to give up the fantasy of fusion, to relate to others as separate and independent people. Many patients with problems of addiction
cling desperately to relationships based on fusion, and so to their addictions, because they have not had the experience of the object surviving
their destructive attacks. For them, their attempts at separation have
succeeded in destroying the object, for the reasons I have suggested in
Chapter 6—their experience of a parent whose sense of self depends on
the capacity to coerce or manipulate the baby and so who does really feel
destroyed by the separation-individuation process in the child.

Addictions as Symptoms of the Inhibited
Development of Self-Agency

In Chapter 5, I described a patient who had withdrawn from relationships almost entirely—he related to the objects in his internal world
through sadistic fantasies. He succeeded in insulating himself almost

completely from real relationship while maintaining a fantasy of fusion in his sadistic fantasies. But for others there needs to be a more concrete enactment of addiction, in the form of relating through incorporation, which leads to a range of addictive behavior. Since both of these patterns are defenses against expected intrusiveness in relationships, it may never be possible to identify why one person adopts a pattern of relationship of schizoid withdrawal and another person becomes drawn to addiction. Indeed, the two often go together, in the sense that real relationships are avoided while the intense longing for fusion and merger are met through the addictive behavior.

So the fear of real relationship plays a major part in a range of clinical phenomena, such as eating disorders, self-harm, and addictions, sometimes contributing to a complete dissociation from any form of relationship or desire and sometimes to a devouring desire to be merged and fused with the desired other, to swallow the loved object or be swallowed by it. This is frequently the case with people who use addiction as a defense to maintain fantasies of fusion, to defend against the experience of psychic separateness, and who relate to others by means of coercion and manipulation. This is relating through incorporation, the obliteration of the sense of the subjectivity of the other, the denial of their independent identity. Addicts of any kind do not just abuse a substance—alcohol, drugs, food, money—they often also abuse other people, treating them as mindless self-objects to be controlled, coerced, and manipulated at will. It demonstrates self-agency at the teleological level, when people only feel they exist when they are directly controlling another. The darkest aspect of this level of self-agency may be the capacity to torture another person—an addictive behavior in itself, in which the torturer needs an escalating degree of sadism to experience a sense of self-agency.

For an addict, it is a massive task to move on from this fantasy of fusion in relationships. Any relationship with another person threatens the denial of otherness, because it would require recognition of the other person as someone with needs and desires of her own. To recognize this can so easily lead to the projection of the addict's own unsatisfied need into the other, who then becomes the devouring carrier of the addict's own limitless greed, or alternatively to a devouring desire to be merged and fused with the desired other, to swallow the loved object or be swallowed by it.

For example, Catherine Crowther explored anorexia as one

manifestation of addictive states of mind, in which there is an overwhelming longing for love and relationship that must be displaced and
managed in relation to food:

> The anorexic person, feeling neediness as an unbearable ten-
> sion, unable to disentangle emotional hunger from bodily greed,
> deflects her dangerous desires away from her human object
> (almost invariably her mother) and projects her greed into the
> food. She has the delusion that her actual self is being gobbled
> up and swallowed down by the food if it is allowed inside her
> body. What comes through in the transference is that any need
> of another person is felt as a loss of self-control and as complete
> capitulation to the person who could fulfill that need, who threat-
> ens almost to devour her. In other words it is a terror of normal
> dependence. (2004)

Crowther viewed schizoid withdrawal as a form of catastrophic defense
in response to this terror:

> This claustrophobia prompts her to withdraw emotionally from
> the relationship, to a safe distance, professing self-sufficiency—
> i.e. a narcissistic flight. This in turn becomes a place of aban-
> doned isolation and terrifying separateness, with extremely
> painful affects, leading full circle back to the longings for the safe
> blissful union with another. (2004)

So these people do really feel that their attempts to separate, partly
through destructive attacks, succeed in destroying the object. They
remain stuck at the teleological level of self-agency in which they experience either their own omnipotent power to destroy a loved other by any
attempt to separate, or the reverse—the other's power to destroy their
independent identity. This coercive pattern of relating is brought into
the analytic process, which becomes subverted; the patient who relates
at the teleological level has the unconscious assumption that the analytic task is not that the patient gains understanding but rather that only
one person can have a mind and the other has to comply. The analyst's
interpretations are not experienced as being addressed to an independent mind that can use them for its own purposes but are experienced
as instructions to the patient to comply with the therapist's needs. The

patient believes that the analyst is functioning like the parent, through coercion or manipulation, operating at the teleological level. Initially the patient hopes that being understood by the analyst and then complying with that understanding will bring about a magical cure. However, this fairly quickly activates the opposite fear, that to be merged with the analyst in this way is a form of annihilation and all the analyst's attempts to communicate are seen as coercive or manipulative and so are destroyed. So an analytic impasse is very quickly reached in which the analyst's words do not mean what they say, but what the patient fears they mean.

In my view, these are the kind of patients for whom interpretation is not enough—indeed, a classical interpretive stance is doomed to failure because it demands a level of self-agency in the patient that the patient has not yet achieved. Increasingly frantic attempts at interpretation will only make things worse. They convey the message that the patient ought to be able to relate to and take in the interpretations—but the patient does not hear them as reflections. For a person whose unconscious belief is that the analyst or parent cannot tolerate any evidence of the patient's independent psychic existence, there is a very real danger that the analyst's interpretations will be experienced as a demand for the patient to see things in exactly the same way as the analyst. They are experienced as coercive or manipulative and the harder the analyst tries to offer them as factual objective observations, the more the patient feels annihilated by the perceived demand to become the object the analyst seems to be describing, rather than the subject he or she so desperately needs to allow to exist (Alvarez, 1997; Benjamin, 2009).

Clinical Illustration

I would like to look at the implications of an approach centered on self-agency for clinical work, especially with those addicted to alcohol or other substances, drawing on my work with a patient, Josephine, a single woman in her 30s, a middle child of a large family. She was often aware of feelings of insatiable need, so that when she started to drink, she would want more and more. She had had the same feeling in the past about smoking, eating, and sex, so that each would become compulsive but still unsatisfying activities for her at times. She would drink herself into unconsciousness, or chain smoke, unable to stop, or binge on food, all compulsive activities but that still left her feeling that she was insatiable and could never be satisfied.

These expressions of her unconscious regressive longing for fusion started in childhood. She remembered occasions when she was a child, about 5 years old, in church with her family on a Sunday. She would develop an intense thirst; she knew that it was not water that she wanted, and she had an ill-defined sense that it was a need that could never be met, and that it had something to do with the need for love. She thought that it might be a religious experience and accepted my interpretation that it seemed as though she wanted to find the blissful closeness of a baby feeding at the breast.

It did seem that the birth of her sister at around this time, when Josephine was 5 years old, had caused her intense feelings of jealousy, deprivation, and abandonment, feelings that made her long to be the baby getting the satisfying food and love from her mother, not her new baby sister. Watching her sister being breast-fed and being special to her mother in the way she longed to be, and once was, seems to have been unbearable for her. She had once been the adored baby, but her position was usurped, and it does seem as though her mother loved babies but could not relate so easily to her children as they grew older.

She often complained that her intensity seemed too much for everyone and drove them away; although I did interpret this in transference terms, as her experience of me as the mother who could not cope with her, this seemed to get nowhere and simply irritated her because it seemed so formulaic, which indeed I think it was. I think I would focus much more now on her unconscious fear of self-agency, her fantasy that to have any emotional effect on anyone, including me, was to either destroy or be destroyed by them. This was apparent in one of her dreams:

> She was in a classroom with a teacher who was writing incomprehensible questions on a blackboard for an exam; everyone else was writing down answers but Josephine stood up and challenged the teacher, telling her the questions were nonsense. The teacher collapsed in tears, admitting that she was no good and indicating that she would immediately resign.

I think this dream reflected her fear that I really would collapse if she challenged anything I said, however incomprehensible it seemed. I would probably now say something not just about her need to make me feel how useless I was as an analyst, but about her dilemma that she needed to get through to me in order to know that she could have an impact and so was real, but also about her fear that if she did she would destroy me. She simply did not feel safe enough to attack me in order to find out that I could survive, so she could not discover that she was not able to control and coerce me, that her self-agency was not as powerful and dangerous to her objects as her dream suggests. My interpretations about her wish to make me feel ineffectual simply reinforced her fear that I would find that unbearable and as though I was telling her that any attack on me would be intolerable for me.

She told me two dreams which I think illustrate rather well the origins of her fear of her own self-agency and the extent to which the development of a fully mature reflective level of self-agency had been inhibited by her parents' inability to allow her to develop her own identity, to have a mind of her own:

> In this dream, her parents were cycling along on a tandem, carrying a doll which they had bought to put outside their house as a decoration. On the way they met an autistic child, who was unable to speak or communicate her feelings to them in any way.

Josephine could see that she was both the compliant doll and the autistic child, whose real feelings were locked inside. Another dream showed how entrenched her passivity had become and how out of touch she was with an active sense of self:

> She was walking along a road, carrying a heavy baby. The baby became too heavy, partly because it was so floppy—its head was lolling down almost to the pavement. Josephine felt she could not manage it and had to sit down, but then got up again because she knew she had to get home, but the baby was so heavy she was afraid she would drop it.

Not surprisingly, these patterns emerged in the relationship between us as the analysis progressed. Although she acquiesced to my interpretations, it was clear that they also did not satisfy her and she complained more and more, but in a rather passive way, about her feeling that the analysis was not helping her and making me feel increasingly useless and guilty for being so ineffectual. She became increasingly frustrated with my interpretations of her dreams and other material in terms of infant needs. She experienced these comments as manipulative, as my attempts, like her mother's, to keep her in a dependent state, like a doll, that I did not want her to grow up and become independent of me, or to have a mind of her own. She quoted a newspaper article she had read about a patient who had been in analysis for 9 years and said that she thought that the analyst had kept the patient in a dependent state, just like his mother, who had wrapped him too tightly in blankets as a baby, so that he developed a lifelong sensitivity to being physically constricted. The more I interpreted this as resistance to and fear of regression, the more she heard it as a demand from me for her to remain in that state. However, my theoretical stance at that time was that all this protest was resistance and I should simply continue my line of interpretation. I think that for a while we reached the kind of impasse I described earlier in this chapter.

Paradoxically, she also felt that she wanted me to know her mind as if from the inside, to understand her experience completely without her having to use words to describe it. She was not able to experience her agency at the representational level, in that she had no conviction that her verbal account of her experience would have any effect on me. It was as though the only way I could understand any particular experience she described would be for me to be there and see it for myself—then I would know the truth of it. She felt that her perceptions and feelings were irrelevant. This was an expression of her fear of her own psychological agency, of allowing herself to form her own judgment and opinions. It was as though the only judgment that mattered was mine and all she could do was comply with the views that I offered her.

This was a toxic combination of my belief that interpretation would bring about change and her belief that she just needed to wait for me to reveal truths to her that she would then accept. I did not take sufficient notice of my guilt and feelings of inadequacy as countertransference clues to her need to have an impact on me, to experience herself as an agent, through her emotional effect on me. This did happen on occasion, but on those days, each time it did, I felt that I had broken an analytic rule. For example, she once said that she was always repeating herself—I must get so bored. In fact this comment seemed to interrupt a rather important story she was telling and I said, rather irritably, that she was not repeating herself. She seemed relieved to have evoked a real spontaneous reaction from me for once, just as the patient did in the more explosive example I gave in Chapter 5. However, such spontaneous responses on my part were rare and I think she gave me many clues in her material that I was failing her and that she was becoming more and more angry with me, but also afraid of her own anger and how destructive it might be. She needed to find that she could attack me and that I would survive—that she could have an impact on me but not totally control me nor destroy me, as Winnicott suggested.

However, she was terrified that her dream might become reality, that her thoughts would automatically become actions and that she really might destroy me—she thought on a couple of occasions that she saw tears in my eyes at the end of a session and she described her horror at the thought that she might have hurt or upset me. She might even have to end the analysis if she felt she could harm me in that way, as though I was a fragile mother who must be protected at all costs. I now feel that I should have said quite openly that she was right, that I did sometimes have tears in my eyes and felt strong emotions about some of the things she told me. I think that it would have enabled her to feel that she could affect me without destroying me and my attempts to maintain an analytic neutrality and not reveal my emotional reactions simply reinforced her feelings of shame and guilt about affecting me in that way. It does seem as though her mother was too fragile to withstand any confrontation or to cope with any emotional demand. Another dream seemed, once again, to illustrate her fear of having any real emotional impact on her mother:

> She was walking with her mother who suddenly turned round and spat out at her the words, "Don't you dare give me anything," in a venomous tone and then lashed out at her with long catlike claws.

This dream conveyed her sense that her mother wanted her to be a "cloned self" (Wilkinson, 2003), not to be a separate person who could give her anything that she did not have or know already. So her solution was to retreat into a state of passive and mindless confusion, endlessly needy and endlessly unsatisfied, with food or drink or sex providing the action-based experience of agency at the teleological level. Once again, a dream illustrates the issues:

> She was walking along with a male friend (who, in reality, wanted a sexual relationship with her, a desire she did not reciprocate).

There was a fog ahead of them and suddenly a group of galloping horses emerged from the fog toward them. She was frightened of being knocked down and had to jump out of the way. Then she and C went into the fog and when she came out the other side, C had gone. She was quite relieved and felt she had lost him deliberately.

This dream seems to illustrate very well her fear of her own desire and power and the way in which she avoided her own agency by being in a mental and emotional fog, not knowing what she wanted or felt. It felt like a relief to get rid of any relationship that might force her to know her own mind and her own desire.

What Josephine needed to discover in her relationship with me was that she could be her own self with me and not just a stuffed doll or an autistic child. For this to happen, she needed me to be emotionally responsive, without turning that responsiveness into manipulative actions. It is only through this experience of me as a person with real emotional responses that she could discover that she could become increasingly confident that her self-agency could affect me but not destroy me. She needed to discover over and over again that there were two minds at work, that she and I were separate, each with minds of our own, and that words are open communications, which I offered for her to use as she wished, not coercive actions to which she was forced to respond and be changed by.

About 15 years after the end of the analysis, I had a conversation with Josephine about her experience of our work together. She said that it had been enormously important to have someone who would listen to her in a way her mother had never done and that that experience had been very helpful. But she said that she felt some disappointment that she had not really developed the capacity to take initiative, to have a sense of power and direction in her life and to know her own mind. She often felt that she was not really sure what her opinions were. She remembered how vivid her dreams had been during the analysis and said that she had not really dreamed since. She reminded me of a dream she remembered having during the analysis, of a powerful tiger leaping up from the ground onto a high wall. She would have loved to have that kind of power and sense of agency in herself.

My discussion with my former patient confirmed my feeling that an important area of work, that of self-agency, had not really been as fully explored as either of us might have wished. I do not think that I then understood the importance of the role of analysis in facilitating the development of the patient's self-agency, to enable her to find expression of her agency in the relationship with me. My focus at that time on interpretation as the main tool for change made me less open to the possibility of alternative ways of responding to her, which would have perhaps given more scope for her to repair the disruptions between us and so experience more of a sense of agency. My interpretations seemed to impose one particular view of the patient's unconscious intentions on her, which led her often to experience me as another parental figure who required total subjugation to my view.

In contrast, I would now focus on creating the conditions that allow the patient's own sense of agency to be mobilized, initially through the implicit relational exchanges between us, the "moments of meeting" described by the Boston Change Process Study Group (BCPSG, 2007). The pattern of ongoing regulation, disruption, and repair and heightened affective moments are coconstructed through repeated turn-taking exchanges in therapy, just as they are in infancy. So the experience of agency in therapy is also the foundation for the capacity to experience strong emotion without fearing it as destructive—in other words, the capacity for affect regulation. Self-agency is also the capacity for self-reflection and awareness of the mental and emotional separateness of self and other. It is the repeated experience of the truly symbolic, rather than the teleological level of communication that needs to be allowed to develop in analysis.

Otherwise an analytic impasse is inevitable, in which analytic work deteriorates into a battle in which both analyst and patient are fighting for survival, the analyst for survival of his analytic function and the patient for her very psychic existence. In contrast, an analyst who is emotionally involved but does not feel threatened by the patient's need to assert agency offers a new experience within which the patient can gradually relinquish her desperate attempts to avoid separation and individuation. The projection of the controlling, devouring parent can gradually be withdrawn as the analyst demonstrates again and again his own reflective function, the awareness of the patient as a separate psychological and emotional being.

8

The Analytic Relationship: Integrating Psychodynamic, Attachment Theory, and Developmental Perspectives

Experience is never limited, and it is never complete; it is an immense sensibility, a kind of huge spider-web of the finest silken threads suspended in the chamber of consciousness, and catching every air-borne particle in its tissue. It is the very atmosphere of the mind; and when the mind is imaginative, it takes to itself the faintest hints of life. (James, 1951, p. 31)

Analytic Theories and Clinical Practice

In a number of publications I have argued that Jung's view that the relationship between analyst and patient lies at the heart of psychotherapy anticipated the emphasis on the implicit unconscious relationship between therapist and patient in contemporary relational and attachment theory (Knox, 2003, 2007b). His view was that in any effective therapy, both analyst and patient descend into mutual unconscious entanglements and projections, out of which individuation and understanding will eventually emerge. It requires the analyst to be drawn in at a deep unconscious level and to use his or her emotional responses as a countertransference guide to define the analytic task (Jung, 1966c, p. 176). Jung was clear that analysis required the whole person of the analyst, who had therefore to guard against "the danger of succumbing to the infection of the patient's condition" (p. 176).

In contrast, the early psychoanalytic model of analysis was one in which a thoroughly analyzed analyst would cure the patient by carefully timed and accurate interpretations of unconscious drives, fantasies, and defenses. Countertransference phenomena were seen by early psychoanalysts (with notable exceptions such as Ferenczi) as unanalyzed aspects of the analyst in question, and it was not until the work of Betty Joseph and Paula Heimann that they began to be more widely understood as containing important communicative potential for the analysis (Heimann, 1973, p. 122).

Psychoanalysis has of course, subsequently developed this approach as a central aspect of object relations theory; the work of Bion, Heimann, Joseph, Alvarez, and others explores the role of projective identification as communication, the patient's need for the analyst to experience emotions "that the patient needs the analyst to have on his or her behalf" (Alvarez, 1997, p. 754). Their work is part of a paradigm shift in the approach of many psychoanalysts, who place an increasing emphasis on facilitating and understanding unconscious relational processes and less on the accurate identification of specific mental content.

Nevertheless, there remain sharp divisions between different groups in the more traditional branches of psychoanalysis and analytical psychology about the relative importance of the relational and interpretative aspects of analytic work. These divisions partly reflect the differing perceptions of the nature of the unconscious. Analysts who consider unconscious content to be significantly influenced by objective processes such as instinctual drives or archetypes tend toward a more interpretative stance, whereas those who view early relationships and subjective personal experience as the main contributor to the formation of unconscious content tend toward a more relational interpersonal approach (Eagle & Wakefield, 2004). The latter view is, of course, central to attachment-based and relational schools of psychoanalytic psychotherapy (Beebe & Lachmann, 2002; Benjamin, 2004; Reis, 2005; Schore, 2003b).

A Historical Contribution to a Relational Model: Jung's Study of Alchemy

Jung's detailed study of alchemy, which he used to explore the conscious and unconscious processes at work between analyst and patient, is a powerful metaphor for a relational approach to psychotherapy. This work will be largely unfamiliar to non-Jungian readers of this book and it can be adequately understood only by reading Jung's own extensive discussion (Jung 1966a, 1968).

Jung argued that the alchemists knew that they were not practicing ordinary chemistry, but that, while exploring the nature of matter though his experiments, the alchemist "had certain psychic experiences which appeared to him as the particular behaviour of the chemical process" (1968, p. 244). Jung suggested that these experiences were projections, that the alchemist "experienced his projection as a property of matter; but what he was in reality experiencing was his own unconscious" (p. 244). Jung concluded that "alchemy had a double face: on the one hand, the practical chemical work in the laboratory, on the other a psychological process, in part consciously psychic, in part unconsciously projected and seen in the various transformations of matter" (p. 270). An essential condition of alchemical work was that the mind of the alchemist must be in harmony with the work and that he "must keep the eyes of the mind and soul well open" (p. 270).

It was this emphasis on the psychic condition and mental attitude of the alchemist that led Jung to draw on alchemy as a historical and philosophical framework for understanding the changing stages in the analytic process and in the relationship between analyst and patient at each stage. Jung thought that the 16th series of alchemical pictures, the *Rosarium philosophorum*, demonstrated the stages of the analytic relationship and that "everything the doctor experiences when analysing the unconscious of his patient coincides in the most remarkable way with the content of these pictures" (1966a, p. 200). For example, he wrote:

> The alchemical image of the conunctio . . . is equally valuable from the psychological point of view; that is to say, it plays the same role in the exploration of the darkness of the psyche as it played in the investigation of the riddle of matter. (Jung, 1966a, p. 169)

The main point I want to highlight about Jung's exploration of alchemy is his use of it as a metaphor, to emphasize the "mutual unconsciousness" that develops in the analytic relationship:

> The patient, by bringing an activated unconscious content to bear upon the doctor, constellates the corresponding unconscious material in him, owing to the inductive effect which always emanates from projections to greater or lesser degree. Doctor and

patient thus find themselves in a relationship founded on mutual unconsciousness. (Jung, 1966a, p. 176)

The Relational Aspects of Analysis

A number of analytical psychologists, especially Michael Fordham, continued Jung's focus on the unconscious relationship between therapist and patient, the transference and countertransference, by linking Jung's ideas to the work of Klein, Bion, and others on projective identification. Fordham finally came to consider countertransference as an expression of projective identification and as a useful source of information about the patient's state of mind, if the analyst accepts that "an analyst might find himself behaving in ways that were out of line with what he knew of himself, but syntonic with what he knew of his patient" (1996b, p. 165). He suggested that "something of the same nature might be contained in countertransference illusions" and concluded that "the whole analytic situation is a mass of illusions, delusions, displacements, projections and introjections" (1996b, p. 172). What Fordham was outlining here was that an essentially relational process is the necessary basis for understanding and interpretation, a view very much in keeping with contemporary relational and attachment models for the process of change in psychotherapy (described in previous chapters).

Recent research in attachment theory, neuroscience, and developmental psychology supports Jung's view of analysis as a process in which the conscious and unconscious relationship with the analyst provides the essential foundation for individuation, the process of development of each person's individual unique identity (Jung, 1971, p. 448). Jung's understanding of the analytic relationship, which anticipated many of these insights in contemporary attachment-based psychoanalysis, offers a helpful historical context to these more recent developments (Knox, 2007b).

The empirical research and theoretical developments within these new disciplines are also accelerating the shift in psychoanalytic theory toward facilitating and understanding unconscious relational processes (BCPSG, 2007). It may be argued that many of these developments in psychoanalysis emerged quite separately from and do not depend on the research in the newer and more empirically based disciplines. Bion, Klein, Meltzer, Joseph, Winnicott, Fairbairn, Balint, and Guntrip are some of the key figures who developed the object relations model of psychoanalysis. But of these, only Fairbairn, Balint, and Guntrip clearly rejected the theory that instinctual drive is the major determinant of the internal object world, and instead placed object seeking as the infant's primary motivation. And even Fairbairn (1952a, p. 74) conceived of analysis as a struggle to overcome the patient's attachment to his internal bad objects through interpretation. The idea that the unconscious and the self contribute actively to psychic recovery originates with Jung, who argued that "the collaboration of the unconscious is intelligent and purposive, and even when it acts in opposition to consciousness its expression is still compensatory in an intelligent way, as if it were trying to restore a lost balance" (1969, p. 282).

This view of the unconscious has reemerged more recently in the relational, attachment theory, and developmental schools, which highlight, for example, the importance of the infant and the adult patient's unconscious but active contribution to the interactive dynamic process of disruption and repair in relationships (Beebe & Lachmann, 2002). This increasing body of research helps us to take a truly developmental approach to the analytic process itself and to define more clearly the different ways in which the analytic relationship can be used in the service of individuation. Attachment theory research gives new depth and precision to Jung's concept of individuation, clarifying the self-organizing nature of the psyche and the developmental processes that contribute to psychological and emotional maturity. It supports the view that the analytic relationship needs to be more flexible than either the classical psychoanalytic interpretative or the classical Jungian archetypal models would allow; in place of the uncovering of specific mental content (e.g., repressed oedipal material or archetypes), an attachment-oriented analyst accompanies the patient on a developmental journey, one that will sometimes require interpretation of such material but will also allow for new experiences to emerge in the analytic relationship.

This developmental approach therefore demands that the analyst's use of technique needs to be attuned to the analysand's current unconscious developmental tasks. Joseph Sandler (1976, p. 44) coined the phrase "role responsiveness" to describe the way in which an analyst allows the patient to project a particular role onto him or her, a view that resonates with Fordham's view, outlined above, that projective identification is not a force to be resisted by the analyst, but one that provides a useful source of information via the analyst's countertransference reactions. I would extend this idea by suggesting that "developmental attunement" requires the analyst to use his or her countertransference reactions to identify the particular nature of developmental inhibition that the patient brings to the analysis and to use the appropriate analytic techniques in response. This does not mean a total identification with a particular projective identification. It sometimes requires an attuned affective response or a countertransference feeling from which an interpretation will be made.

So what does attachment-based research tell us about the processes that contribute to individuation, which includes both the capacity to function as an independent differentiated individual and also to relate to the collective aspects of our humanity and of the particular society we live in? As I have indicated in Part I, there is an extensive literature, with authors focusing variously on different aspects of neurophysiology, interpersonal relationship, and self-development. But there seem to me to be three fundamental developmental tasks described in this range of research, which I suggest are the elements that together lead to what Winnicott (1965b, p. 44) identified as unit status. These are the development of affect regulation, the capacity for mentalization, and a secure sense of self. But it seems to me that the last of these is rather a less precise concept than the other two and it is the development of self-agency that more accurately describes this particular developmental task. I suggest, therefore, that the therapeutic relationship can provide the context for the development of:

- Affect regulation
- The capacity for mentalization (the basis for reflective function)
- A sense of self-agency

In practice, these developmental tasks are mutually interdependent in their trajectories, so that progress in one area depends critically on progress in the other two. It is also the case that therapeutic work in each of these three areas will make different demands on the analytic relationship at different stages of the analysis, sometimes requiring a state of unconscious entanglement between analyst and analysand and sometimes a process of increasing separation and differentiation.

Affect Regulation

One of the functions of any therapy is to help the patient develop the capacity for affect regulation in the context of an intense relationship.

Allan Schore has summarized much interdisciplinary research evidence, which indicates that therapist-patient transference-countertransference communications, occurring at levels beneath awareness, represent rapid right-hemisphere-to-right-hemisphere nonverbal affective transactions and that the therapist's facial expression, spontaneous gestures, and emotional tone of voice play a key part in that unconscious emotional interaction. These "dyadic affective transactions within the working alliance co-create an intersubjective context that allows for the structural expansion of the patient's orbito-frontal system and its cortical and subcortical connections" (Schore, 2003b, p. 264).

In other words, change in therapy crucially depends on the affect regulation that gradually develops from relational interaction; the emotional regulation offered by the relationship creates the conditions necessary for the neural development in the orbitofrontal cortex and other areas, on which affect regulation depends. From a different theoretical perspective, Ferrari and Lombardi suggest that this is not a transference issue as such, but one that involves the infant's or individual's relation with himself rather than the other, with the other playing a facilitating role (Lombardi, 2002, pp. 363–381). This view has some similarities with that of attachment theorists who suggest that the infant does not internalize an object; rather, what is internalized is the particular repeated relational dynamic between self and other (Beebe & Lachmann, 2002).

In practice, a great many aspects of the analytic relationship can therefore help to promote the process of affect regulation. When the patient's emotions are out of control, consciousness becomes flooded with inchoate emotions and bodily experiences, and at that moment the analyst's attempts to create a process of self-reflection through interpretation, including interpretation of the transference, will be unlikely to succeed. Interpretation depends upon words which, by the very fact that we need to use them, convey the separateness of one mind from another and so may be unbearable to someone who cannot yet be sure that he or she can be allowed to have a much more direct emotional impact on the analyst. The patient needs to discover that the therapist is not afraid of the patient's need for emotional closeness, and that this need will not destroy the therapist and his or her therapeutic function.

In these situations, the analyst's tone of voice, body language, and facial expression play a crucial part in affect regulation. Sometimes an attuned response, a Kohutian mirroring, may create a new experience of object relationship and offer containment through the therapist's instinctive downward modulation of affect. This would be largely an intuitive and unconscious response by the therapist, the equivalent in psychotherapy of the parent's attuned response to a baby's cues (Beebe & Lachmann, 2002). Attachment theory and neuroscience lend strong support to the argument that this attuned, empathic attitude from the therapist is a necessary precondition for the mourning process, which is an integral part of analytic understanding (Schore, 2003b, pp. 52–57). Separation and loss must occur at the pace the infant or adult patient can manage. If they are forced or imposed too early, they lead not to cycles of deintegration and reintegration but to disintegration, dissociation, and encapsulated autistic states of mind, which become more and more impenetrable (Fordham, 1996a).

But affect regulation also develops out of containment created in other ways in the analytic relationship. This includes the clear structure and boundaries of the therapeutic setting, the therapist's consistency and reliability, and his or her focus on symbolic meaning rather than concrete enactment. When the patient's capacity for affect regulation is highly unstable, the simple act of naming emotions, identifying the cues that trigger them, and helping the patient to anticipate their impact on the self and on others all contribute to the capacity for affect regula- tion. The ability to self-regulate in psychotherapy is inextricably bound up with the interactive regulation offered by a consistent, empathic, but also boundaried and reflective therapist. When affect regulation is already more firmly established, the task of understanding and inter- preting the patient's unconscious internal world contributes to the development of reflective function and so to further affect regulation. The direct interpretation of transference then becomes the main focus for this work.

Clinical Illustration

A female patient arrived for a session slightly late and in a flus- tered state. She exhaled deeply and launched into a rapid descrip- tion of how pressured she felt and how much was going on in her life. Her husband had bought her a new phone but she could not make it work and thought she broke it, as well as wasting precious time trying to get it to work. At this point I made an interpretation that my offering her new ways to communicate in the therapy were not working for her and made her more anxious because she did not feel she knew how to use them. I wondered if people who try to help seem to her to make things worse, not better.

She scarcely heard me but went straight on to say that she feared she gave off so much anxiety that it might actually affect a machine, such as a phone, and make it break down. She went into a long account of all the things she had to do and how she almost dreaded going on holiday because she would have nothing to do except read and think and she was not sure how she would cope with that. I responded by saying, "You are afraid of what will happen if you have time to stop and think here," attempting to shift from her focus on the concrete external reality of her holiday to the current, more symbolic fear of her own internal processes.

She reacted by talking about fragile parents, hers and her husband's, who needed to be looked after. She constantly worried that one of them would collapse, especially when she tried to contact them and did not immediately get a reply. Once again, I interpreted her immediate fear in the room, saying, "You are afraid that you might put too much pressure on me and make me break down, and it makes you especially anxious if I do not respond immediately." At this point she became calmer and more reflective and acknowledged both her anxiety that she might overwhelm me and her sense that she needed to protect me from the pressure she might put me under.

The therapist must, of course, have developed the capacity to self-regulate, to manage his or her own affective responses to the patient. This includes paying careful attention to countertransference reactions, since attunement also involves the countertransference experience from which interpretation is drawn. Jung's own example of his dream about a female patient in a tower on a high hill, whom he had come to find rather irritating and boring, revealed to him the unconscious contempt he had felt for her, and he recognized the compensatory function of the dream, that he should "look up" to her more. This demonstrated his capacity to reflect on and to use his own emotional reactions to understand the unconscious aspects of the analytic relationship (Jung, 1966a, p. 332). His exploration of alchemy was the earliest detailed research into transference-countertransference dynamics and the way these aspects of the analytic relationship contribute to the analytic task of individuation (Jung, 1966c).

Mentalization and Reflective Function

One of the main tools for developing affect regulation is the therapist's use of reflective function, by which he or she makes sense of the patient's conscious and unconscious experience through interpretation. The simple act of identifying and naming feelings is containing in itself, just as is a parent's naming of the infant's sensations. Psychotherapy provides a framework for the development of the capacity for mentalization and reflective function, the ability to relate to and make sense of ourselves and each other in mental and emotional, not just behavioral, terms (Fonagy, 1991; Bateman & Fonagy, 2004). This depends both on transference experience and also on the detailed exploration of personal history and the gradual construction of coherent autobiographical narratives, which depend on an understanding of one's own and other people's desires, needs, and beliefs.

The capacity to link experiences in a meaningful way is a crucial part of human psychological development and is intuitively nurtured by parents in the early development of their children. Stories are crucial vehicles for the development of mentalization. One of the defining features of any bedtime story is that it links events in a meaningful way through the desires and intentions of the people who play the various roles in the story, whether fictional or not. In any narrative, it is minds that are the agents of change, giving rise to decisions, choices, and actions that produce effects and link events into a coherent structure. Without mental agency, there would be no story, no meaningful thread tying events together, and those events would appear random and meaningless.

Holmes coined the term "narrative competence" to describe this ability to make sense of experiences and linked deficits in the development of narrative capacity to differing patterns of insecure attachment. Holmes also highlighted the fact that narrative is a dialogue: "There is always another to whom the Self is telling his or her story, even if in adults this takes the form of an internal dialogue" (2001, p. 85). This dialogue is also itself a constructive process of increasing complexity in which a story is created first by one person and then taken over and retold on a new level by the other. It is a direct expression of the collaborative turn-taking and repair of ruptures and misunderstandings that are fundamental to all human interaction, whether verbal or nonverbal, as Enfield and Levinson (2006) described. They pointed out that

turn-taking and repair of ruptures are the major guarantors of intersubjectivity, of shared understandings:

> When what I say reveals a misunderstanding of what you said,
> you get an immediate opportunity to correct it. . . .such a system
> has emergent properties, shifting the burden of explanation away
> from properties of the individual to the shared activity. We can
> "read" other minds in part because human interaction is orga-
> nized so as to engender intersubjective understanding. (2006, pp.
> 9–10)

The essential distinction between this kind of human intersubjective
interaction and that of animals is its basis in Gricean communication:
Person A's behavior conveys a certain intent to person B because person
A wants to convey to person B that that is what A intends it to mean. In
contrast to indexical communication, there is no predetermined or fixed
meaning to the behavior; the meaning is reached by consensus between
A and B, that A intends it that way and B accepts that intention.

This process, whereby the narrative initially belonging to the parent
is then taken over by the child, is also mirrored in the therapeutic dialogue. Psychotherapy theories are themselves narratives of a sort, which
we construct so that we can find meaning in our patients' verbal and
nonverbal communications, often when patients themselves cannot yet
do so. A successful therapeutic narrative is one that can become meaningful to patients so that they can take it over, use it for themselves,
and adapt it to establish their own sense of psychic causality, the links
between intrapsychic experiences and the external world.

Clinical Illustration

A supervisee had been seeing a female patient who presented with
a psychotic belief that she had a devil or demon inside her, who
controlled her like a puppet, and that this demon was so powerful
and dangerous that it could destroy anyone who tried to rescue
her, including her therapist.

The patient was contemptuous of any of her friends, family,
or doctors who did not believe in the reality of the demon. She
could not think about the demon in psychological terms, as a
symbolic expression of some aspect of her mental state, her belief
that her thoughts were evil and destructive, but was convinced

that the demon really existed. She believed that she could therefore never have children herself, that the demon inside her meant
that she would not even be able to give birth to a healthy child or
to be a good enough mother if she did. At one point she then told
her therapist that her mother had had several abortions before
she herself was born, and the patient felt that her mother had
always been strongly ambivalent toward her and might not even
have wanted her to be born.

My supervisee was then able to make a link between the
patient's experience of her mother's murderousness and to suggest that this had been internalized by the patient and was experienced as a murderous demon. In this way, he was able to create a
narrative that accepted the reality of the demon as an internalization of a real murderous parent. The patient could make sense of
her experience of a demon inside her by seeing it as an image of
her mother's unconscious hostility toward her and her implicit
awareness of that hostility.

Following these sessions, the patient tried to talk to her
mother about her past. Her mother avoided any discussion of
the abortions, but did describe her own mother's indifference
toward her, including one occasion when she was sent to school
while suffering from acute appendicitis, which resulted in a rup-
tured appendix and emergency surgery. The patient could see
that her mother had also been the object of murderousness from
the patient's grandmother, and this again helped to lessen her
delusional beliefs by recognizing them as a reflection of parental
anxiety, abuse, and neglect handed on from one generation to
another.

Holmes described the psychotherapist's role in this respect as that of an
"assistant autobiographer," whose role is to find stories that correspond
to experience. This role starts in the assessment interview, where the
therapist will "use her narrative competence to help the patient shape
the story into a more coherent pattern" (Holmes, 2001, p. 86). Holmes
suggested that the patient then gradually "learns to build up a 'story-
telling function,' which takes experience from 'below' and, in the light of
overall meanings 'from above' (which can be seen as themselves stored
or condensed stories) supplied by the therapist, fashions a new narrative
about her self and her world" (2001, p. 85).

This aspect of the analytic relationship is very familiar to Jungians across the spectrum of our theoretical orientations. The active and creative role of the unconscious, shown through dreams, fantasies, paintings, sand play, and other forms of symbolic expression, has regularly been given careful attention in Jungian clinical practice. A developmental Jungian analysis may result in analyst and patient coconstructing a different kind of narrative from that which emerges in a more classical Jungian analysis, but in both approaches the patient's unconscious is seen as playing an active and creative role in the emergence of a meaningful analytic story, as the "demon" did in the clinical example above.

The crucial aspect of this process is the coconstruction of shared meanings between therapist and patient. If the therapist's theory and practice are not collaborative, they will not serve the purpose of conveying that the therapist's intention is to empathize with the patient's subjective experience and facilitate the development of self-agency. Instead it will convey that the therapist wishes to impose on the patient a particular view of his or her unconscious, which the patient is required to accept. If the patient does not, it is simply treated as resistance. A clinical example of such an exchange is given in the Postscript.

A Sense of Self-Agency

Psychotherapy is also a context in which the inhibited development of self-agency can be overcome. An increasingly complex and psychic self-agency can emerge, in which the sense of self does not depend on the direct physical or emotional impact one has on another person but on the capacity for self-reflection and awareness of the mental and emotional separateness of self and other.

A sense of self-agency develops in a series of stages, summarized by Fonagy and colleagues, described in Chapter 1. These stages of self-agency are levels of psychic organization, nonconscious implicit internal working models that structure experience, while themselves remaining outside awareness. The earlier stages in the development of self-agency are not fully replaced or erased by later developmental stages but remain hidden behind them until some psychic breakdown allows them to predominate again if later stages of self-agency—the stages of reflective and autobiographical self—are insecurely established or fail to develop. Jung (1966a, p. 15) recognized the importance of this process of *reculer pour mieux sauter*, which he defined as a purposive backward movement of libido in order to access and activate unconscious contents and processes that are essential to the process of individuation.

I suggest that the patient's level of self-agency will profoundly influence the effectiveness of the therapist's approach, requiring the developmental attunement I referred to earlier in this chapter. The analyst needs to focus intuitively on the therapeutic technique that is most appropriate to the level of self-agency that unconsciously predominates, and this is a complex and constantly shifting skill developed during many years of clinical practice. If a person's sense of self-agency is functioning at a level at which only actions matter or make a difference, then interpretations that rely on that person's reflective function will be doomed to failure. A clinical example from a colleague's practice powerfully illustrates this. Warren Colman explored with great sensitivity the need for the therapist to enter into a symbolic enactment, which, he argued, "when consciously undertaken albeit not consciously understood, can have inestimable value for the analytic process, opening up possibilities that may be stifled by a more strict adherence to analytic abstinence" (2010, p. 276).

Clinical Illustration

Anna arrived at the session with an ugli fruit, which she wanted to give me. She had no idea why she had brought it and did not want to think about it. I commented that it might be an image of herself, which she accepted, saying that she'd always liked ugli fruits, though they're not very popular. They're ugly on the outside but juicy and exotic to eat.

For a while there was a complete absence of feeling in the session, even when she referred to someone who was dying of cancer in the Far East, alone and apparently unmourned by his family. Eventually, we returned to the ugli fruit and she said she was afraid I wouldn't accept it. Uncertain of its meaning, particularly the potentially seductive implications of being offered her juicy exotic fruit, I hesitated about whether I should keep it. However, the quality of unspeakable distress that followed made it clear that oedipal sexuality was not the issue here and that the fruit represented something far more fundamental about "the self," which made it absolutely vital that I accept her gift. She was overwhelmed with a dreadful feeling that she shouldn't have brought it and had an image of herself as a little ugli fruit on legs running out of the door. Eventually she was able to say that if she took it away with her, she would throw it in the bin (cf. bulimia) but if I kept it, she would be involving me and this was unendurable. This spoke directly to the feeling I had had in the initial consultation that she wanted to do the analysis herself without involving me, as a way of avoiding all the unbearable risks of rejection, betrayal, and abandonment. And yet I knew that it was only through an intense mutual emotional engagement between us that the area in herself that was as yet unknown and unthinkable could come into being through being emotionally contained and digested within my mind. In one sense, bringing an actual piece of food for me to eat was a very concrete representation of this process; yet insofar as the ugli fruit was an embodiment of a dream image that represented her self, it was at the same time symbolic, in just the way that the Mass is symbolic even if it is asserted that the bread and wine are the body and blood of Jesus, since what is symbolic is the transformation that takes place in the recipient through ingestion.

I knew too what I must do with Anna's gift, though I could not say how I knew. I took it home and ate it, making a point of sharing it with my family in a way that felt to me like a ritual celebration (even though it was an ordinary enough event for them). It was something precious and sharing it seemed to me an acknowledgment of the nourishment and enjoyment that Anna could bring, implicitly transforming her sense of herself as hateful and unwanted. A few months later, Anna mentioned that she had given ugli fruits to her own children when they were young, which made further sense of the need I felt to share it with mine.

Although the ugli fruit was spoken about between us from time to time, it belonged to the area in Anna that was not yet known or understood. Its potency as a symbol was apparent and was felt by both of us, but its meaning remained unknown. Yet I also knew that there was something sacrosanct about the ugli fruit and that I must not speak of it to anyone—and have not done so until now, despite having a particular interest in symbolic objects brought to analysis.

Of course, I did not tell Anna what I had done and for a long time she continued to worry about whether I might have thrown it in the bin. After all, it was not like other gifts of wood and stone, for example, that I might keep in a drawer or on my desk. It had either to be eaten or, like a human body, it would rot. So perhaps eating it might also have meant something akin to a burial ceremony in which the body is ingested by Mother Earth (Gordon, 1978, p. 82). Her worry also reflected her belief that she was rubbish, linked to her own disgust at her fat body. This aspect of the transference was the very thing that needed to be digested and perhaps detoxified though internal contact with my sense of the preciousness of her ugli fruit self. (Colman, 2010, pp. 281–283)

Jung spelt out the need for an alchemical process to take place in analysis, in which the analyst is changed as well as the patient and Colman's example demonstrates that the analysis of self-agency really does require the analyst to be prepared to take something of the patient inside himself and to be changed inside by it. This is really the only way the patient can experience agency, through the same kind of unconscious communication that a baby experiences with his or her mother. The actual eating of the ugli fruit was exactly the symbolic enactment that Colman described. The implicit relational need was for the analyst to enjoy the inside of the fruit, not collude with the patient's identification with the "ugli" exterior. This enactment on her part could also be seen as a form of teleological self-agency, her need to make an emotional impact on the analyst, so that he would not just hold her in mind, but really enjoy her. Her catastrophic response to the hint that the analyst might not accept the fruit seems to support this—she was afraid that to have an impact on the analyst would make him hate Anna and her "ugli" gift. At that stage of agency she could only know the impact she had through an action, both hers and the analyst's, and her core assumption was that any expression of her self-agency would make the analyst reject her.

This has considerable implications for analytic theory and practice; the analyst needs to tune in to, reflect on, and analyze the patient's unconscious sense of agency. Otherwise we risk seeing the patient purely as the object of unconscious forces, which have the patient at their mercy until rescued by the analyst's interpretations. I think that when the analytic task centers on self-agency, it is vital for the analyst not to fall into the trap of trying to find the "correct" interpretation, which imposes the analyst's agency at the risk of denying the patient's.

I have explored elsewhere (Knox, 2005, 2007a) some of the lifelong consequences when the development of self-agency has been impaired in infancy. There I suggested that the most serious problems arise when a child grows up with the fear that to have any emotional impact on another person is bad and destructive. This is based on the experience of parents who could not bear any awareness of the child's own emotional needs and hence could not relate to him or her as someone with a separate identity. The child comes to fear that to love is to drive the other person away.

It seems that this might be exactly the situation in which the analytic relationship needs to recreate the highly attuned, near-perfectly contingent mirroring that was lacking in that person's infancy. This is not a simplistic tactic to provide a corrective emotional experience. It is a form of analytic containment necessary to allow regression to a developmental stage that provides the secure sense of self-agency that is the essential foundation for separation and the individuation process. Neuroscience and attachment theory tell us that the sense of self is fundamentally relational, requiring an internalization of the mirroring other for a secure sense of self and self-agency to develop, and that this is based on right-brain-to-right-brain communication from the earliest moments of infancy. This lends support to the view that a confirming relationship must be the basis for any analytic work with an analysand whose early experiences have not provided the foundation for a secure sense of self.

Later stages of self-agency require a different approach, in which the emphasis is on separation rather than close attunement. It was Winnicott who recognized the crucial role of destructiveness in the "subject's placing of the object outside the area of the subject's omnipotent control" (1971b, p. 89). Winnicott argued that the object's repeated survival of destruction enables the subject to recognize the object as an independent entity in its own right.

In infancy, narcissistic grandiosity—the sense of omnipotent and magical control over the object world—is essential as a form of psychic protection against the terrifying awareness of helplessness. However, to move from the teleological level, its gradual erosion is also essential, even though the painfulness of the accompanying disillusionment contributes to the tantrums and rage of toddlerhood. For many people who come to analysis, it is also necessary to go through a similar experience of rage in adult life, as analysts know especially from work with patients with a history of severe trauma. The analytic relationship needs to be one that allows for the patient's repeated destructive attacks on the analyst, which both analyst and patient can survive. This intensive work with negative transference enables the patient gradually to relinquish the coercive control of the analyst, which accompanies the teleological and intentional levels, and to allow the experience of separation and difference, which reflect truly psychological and symbolic self-agency. I would remind the reader of the point I made in the previous chapter that if the other person survives the attack, the child discovers that being is separate from doing, and one's sense of self can be independent of one's physical actions. Children go on existing and knowing they exist even when having to recognize the continuing and independent physical and psychic survival of the other person, whom they have just tried to destroy. The recognition of one's powerlessness to control or coerce others is the means by which a person gradually achieves true psychic separateness and autonomy.

But this kind of working through of a person's previously inhibited self-agency can only take place on the foundations of the kind of developmental attunement and symbolic enactment that Warren Colman described and that is also powerfully evident in the case illustration by Frieda Fordham (Chapter 9).

The Analytic Relationship and the Process of Individuation

At the heart of all these aspects of analysis is the relational dynamic that Jung called the transcendent function. Jung's view was that in symbols "the union of conscious and unconscious is consummated" (1969, p. 289). In attachment theory terms, the transcendent function can be understood as a constant dynamic process of comparison and integration of explicit conscious information and memories with the more generalized knowledge that we accumulate unconsciously in the internal working models of implicit memory, a key part of which constitutes the sense of self. This process of comparing and contrasting—in attachment theory called appraisal—is an unconscious process by which experiences are constantly screened and evaluated to determine their meaning and significance.

> Sensory inflow goes through many stages of selection, interpretation and appraisal before it can have any influence on behavior, either immediately or later. This processing occurs in a succession of stages, all but the preliminary of which require that the

> inflow be related to matching information already stored in long-term memory. (Bowlby, 1980, p. 45)

New experience is therefore constantly being organized by unconscious internal working models, and unconscious implicit patterns are constantly being identified in conscious language. Jung's theories about self-regulation and compensation thus anticipated the contemporary concept of appraisal, in that he considered self-regulation to be a process in which unconscious compensation is a balancing or supplementing of the conscious orientation. From a relational perspective, James Fosshage (2004) has described psychoanalytic therapy as an "implicit-explicit dance," in which there is a constant two-way flow of information between explicit and implicit memory systems. Siegel offers neuroscientific support for the central role of emotion in this process, suggesting that "such an *integrative process* may be at the core of what emotion *does* and indeed what emotion *is*" (1998, p. 7).

Meaningful experience, therefore, depends on the transcendent function, a process that compares and integrates the following:

- Internal objects (the internalized other) and the self
- A new event and past experience
- Explicit and implicit knowledge
- Cognition and emotion
- Left brain and right brain
- Orbitofrontal cortex and subcortical networks

Consciousness or unconsciousness are not fixed attributes of either pole of these dyads but are distributed in varying degrees between the two poles, reflecting the variety of ways in which mental content may be processed and stored.

The essence of the mechanism underlying self-organization, from an attachment perspective, is one of comparing and contrasting, the constant evaluation of similarity and difference between new information and existing knowledge. The alchemical metaphor highlights the fact that some patients need to regress to a state of merger, a mutual descent into unconsciousness. This analytic experience is focused on regression to infantile experiences of perfect contingency (Gergely & Watson, 1996), when similarities rather than differences are discovered and explored, and when the illusion of fusion is not challenged but allowed to run its course. Marcus West (2007) has drawn on Matte Blanco's model to suggest that an affective appraisal mechanism is predominantly an unconscious preference for sameness, so that too much difference is at first ignored (giving the impression of primary narcissism) but then gradually sought or allowed.

Gergely and Watson suggested that this stage is followed by increasing separation, as infants begin to be more interested in "imperfect contingency," which means that their interest shifts from similarity to difference. Others, such as Tronick and Beebe, differ somewhat from Gergely and Watson in suggesting that disruption and repair are as essential to the unconscious attachment dynamics of mother and infant as regularity and predictability, even in the earliest weeks of infancy, as part of the process of unconscious categorization that is fundamental to the development of meaning.

In both models, however, these developmental processes eventually lead to the achievement of unit status, the recognition of the complex and ever-shifting similarity and difference between self and other, which forms the basis for the capacity to have deep emotional relationships without fearing a catastrophic loss of self. Similarly, in adult analysis the unconscious exploration of similarity and difference are inseparable from each other and also from affect regulation. For example, emotional stress seems to lead to a position of preferring sameness and resisting change. Exploration, the curiosity about difference, gives way to the retreat to a secure base—that which is safe and familiar—because stress indicates danger.

An Integrated View of the Tasks of the Analytic Relationship

I suggest that the wealth of information from other disciplines does, for the first time, put us in the position where we can attune the analytic process and the analytic relationship to the developmental task a patient is struggling with at any point in the process. We can construct a table including the three main analytic goals I described at the start of this chapter (Table 8.1):

- Activating the attachment system to facilitate the development of secure attachment
- Developing the capacity for mentalization and reflective function
- Facilitating the development of self-agency

These goals can be correlated with three main therapeutic approaches:

- Interpretation, allowing conscious awareness of repressed or dissociated mental contents
- New relational experiences, in which the analyst is a new object for the patient
- Facilitating regression (*reculer pour mieux sauter*)

Table 8.1 then allows us to place a variety of specific analytic techniques in the context of the particular task and the particular broad analytic approach that the analyst feels most closely corresponds to the task.

TABLE 8.1. ANALYTIC GOALS AND TECHNIQUES

	INTERPRETATION (narrative linking)	**NEW EXPERIENCE** (analyst as new object)	**FACILITATING REGRESSION**
Developing secure attachment	Transference interpretation in the here and now	Empathic mirroring Attunement Containment	Enabling projection: experiencing the past in the present
Developing reflective function	Transference interation linking past and present	Analyst's focus on symbolic rather than concrete	Recalling and working through painful past experiencet
Development self-agency	Interpretation of dreams, fantasies, symptoms as intentional/creative	Analyst's survival of destructive attacks	Active imagination Art, sand play

With this kind of multivectored model, different analytic theories can be seen to reflect differing emphases among analytic groups on their own particular view of the analytic relationship. But these tasks and techniques are not mutually exclusive, so that in any psychotherapy process, all of these tasks and techniques may be in action simultaneously. This is why a developmental, process-based model becomes essential to improve our understanding of the analytic relationship, because it can encompass a range of analytic approaches. It also places a responsibility on the analyst to give up the secure base, the safe territory of familiar analytic models, and to explore difference and the ideas generated by other analytic approaches and other disciplines, including neuroscience and attachment theory. We need to be able to adapt our analytic approach to each patient and not to impose a one size fits all model of the analytic relationship in our clinical practices. Just as infants guide their parents' responses to attune to their developmental needs, so our analytic patients can guide us in the analytic relationship.

9

The Effect of the Therapist's Clinical Approach on the Patient's Sense of Self-Agency

WHEN RESEARCHERS STUDY THE EFFECTIVENESS of psychotherapy in general or compare one kind of therapy with another, a consistent finding is that psychological interventions of all kinds are better than no treatment at all—"the average treated person is better off than 80% of people who have not been treated" (Lepper & Riding, 2006, p. 9). A number of meta-analyses have come to similar conclusions (Lipsey & Wilson, 1993; Shapiro, Barkham, Hardy, & Morrison, 1990; Smith & Glass, 1977). The use of randomized controlled trials in an attempt to discover whether one type of psychotherapy can be shown to be better than another has so far failed to demonstrate any clear advantage of any one particular approach, a finding known as the Dodo effect: "Everybody has won and all must have prizes" (Lepper & Riding, 2006, p. 10; Luborsky, Singer, & Luborsky, 1975; Shedler, 2010, p. 104).

Luborsky et al. (1999) have shown that, even when a particular study does seem to demonstrate that one treatment appears to be more effective, the therapeutic allegiance of the researchers creates a systematic bias in favor of their preferred treatment modality, thus calling into question the validity of the research findings. This kind of "investigator allegiance" effect means that some outcome research studies do not provide any more reliable information about therapeutic effectiveness than therapists' intuition that a patient's progress in therapy results from the particular theory and clinical approach they adhere to, the "enumerative inductivism" described by Fonagy and Tallindini-Shallice (1993).

In addition, the actual clinical practice of psychotherapists and analysts is not necessarily in accord with their own theories. One research study (Vaughan, Spitzer, Davies, & Roose, 1997) found that a group of senior analysts could not even agree on the criteria by which to define whether an analytic process was taking place in a session; so the very concepts that are considered fundamental to the process and effectiveness of psychoanalysis elude consensus within the profession. Lambert, Garfield, and Bergin (2003) have shown that observing actual clinical practice across modalities reveals that "regardless of the type of therapy, it will include cognitive, emotional, behavior and relationships elements" (Lepper & Riding, 2006, p. 15). Jonathan Shedler has reviewed the empirical evidence that clearly demonstrates:

> There are also profound differences in the way therapists practice, even therapists ostensibly providing the same treatment. What takes place in the clinical consulting room reflects the qualities and style of the individual therapist, the individual patient, and the unique patterns of interaction that develop between them. Even in controlled studies designed to compare manualized treatments, therapists interact with patients in different ways, implement interventions differently, and introduce processes not specified by the treatment manuals (Elkin et al., 1989). In some cases, investigators have had difficulty determining from verbatim session transcripts which manualized treatment was being provided (Shedler, 2010, p. 103)

Shedler (2010) suggested that this means that randomized controlled trials that evaluate a therapy as a "package" do not necessarily provide support for its theoretical premises or the specific interventions that derive from them. For these reasons, studies of therapy "brand names" can be highly misleading.

In the light of this kind of evidence, David Tuckett asks the inevitable question—whether the absence of any clear evidence that any one particular practice of psychotherapy is demonstrably better than another means that anything goes:

> If we are to have disciplined pluralism in psychoanalysis, the question is whether we can find "good enough" ways to know when psychoanalytic practice is more or less competent. Or are judgements of excellence and competence in the case of

psychoanalytic practice inextricably tied to conflicting conceptions of the psychoanalytic enterprise? Are psychoanalytic stan-
dards just political? Does anything go? (2005, p. 32)

The answers relevant to this question are slowly emerging from research
studies that explore what actually happens between patient and therapist, often based on session videotapes or transcripts. Research of this
kind is increasingly demonstrating that a number of factors determine
the outcome of psychotherapy, but these are independent of any particular analytic theory; the active ingredients of therapy are not necessarily
those presumed by the theory or treatment model (Shedler, 2010).

The first study of the effectiveness of psychotherapy, the Menninger
Foundation Psychotherapy Research Project (Wallerstein, 1989)
tracked two cohorts of patients over 30 years and showed substantial
improvements for patients both in psychoanalysis and in psychodynamic psychotherapy; the major curative factor identified was "therapist
support." A positive dependent transference, corrective emotional experiences, assistance with reality testing, and other supportive measures
correlated with a good outcome, but interpretation by the therapist or
insight on the patient's part (the essential trademarks of psychoanalytic
theory) showed no such correlation with outcome. Elliot et al. (1994)
undertook a further study of the part that insight might play in relation
to improvement in psychotherapy. They found that a common factor
in all the "insight events" they identified in session transcripts was the
creation of a "meaning bridge," "the forging of links between a reaction
and its context, enabled by an intervention by the therapist" (Lepper,
2009b, p. 354).

One study is particularly illuminating because it shows that it is relational factors that determine successful therapy outcome for depression,
even when that therapy is not psychodynamic but cognitive therapy:

> (a) working alliance predicted patient improvement on all out-
> come measures; (b) psychodynamic process ("experiencing")
> predicted patient improvement on all outcome measures; and (c)
> therapist adherence to the cognitive treatment model (i.e., focus-
> ing on distorted cognitions) predicted poorer outcome. A subse-
> quent study using different methodology replicated the finding
> that interventions aimed at cognitive change predicted poorer
> outcome (Hayes, Castonguay, & Goldfried, 1996). However,

> discussion of interpersonal relations and exploration of past expe-
> riences with early caregivers—both core features of psychody-
> namic technique—predicted successful outcome. (Shedler, 2010,
> p. 104)

Shedler was careful to point out that these findings should not be interpreted as indicating that cognitive techniques are harmful, and that
other studies have reported positive relations between cognitive-behavioral therapy technique and outcome. But qualitative analysis of the ver-
batim session transcripts suggested that the poorer outcomes associated
with cognitive interventions were due to implementation of the cognitive treatment model in dogmatic, rigidly insensitive ways by certain
therapists (Castonguay et al., 1996). So these findings indicate that the
more effective therapists facilitated relational processes such as a positive
working alliance, enabled the patient to "experience" (focus on emotions and thoughts about self), discussed interpersonal relationships, and
explored relationships with early caregivers. All these are aspects of a
relational approach that also facilitates the patient's own sense of self-
agency both in relationship with the therapist and in terms of making
sense of (creating a meaning bridge) in relation to his or her own emotions and past relational experience.

Shedler pointed out that the danger of applying a therapeutic model
too rigidly applies to psychodynamic therapy as much as to cognitive
therapy. The equivalent in psychoanalytic therapy of "too rigid adherence to the cognitions" (that predicts poor outcome in cognitive therapy) is the overreliance on interpretations, and Wallerstein (1989) has
shown that interpretation shows no correlation with good outcome. It
is the relational factors described above that make a difference, not the
analyst's interpretation. The danger of too great a reliance on authori-
tative interpretation by the therapist is that the patient's own struggle
to coconstruct, with the therapist, a meaningful narrative of his past
and present experience is sidelined or discounted and so his sense of
self-agency is gradually undermined, especially if those interpretations
are based on psychoanalytic theories that assume that the therapist has
privileged knowledge of the contents of the patient's unconscious, for
example, in terms of the content of unconscious fantasy or archetypal
imagery.

It could be argued that so long as a therapist works clinically in a
relational way, analytic theory could be seen merely as a useful metaphor

for the therapist to draw on in her own mind. But the research evidence which demonstrates that too great a reliance on interpretation is either ineffective or, if applied too rigidly, unhelpful, means that the theory of mental content the therapist uses does matter (even if it is not the theory itself that underpins change in therapy), because in most psychodynamic theories, the model of the mind is closely coupled to and prescriptive of specific clinical techniques. The key issue is whether the theory and accompanying technique are compatible with the research evidence that I have referred to above, in relation to the clinical factors that correlate with good outcome. For example, Klein's view of the nature of unconscious content is not just a theoretical model of the mind but also a prescription for a particular clinical technique, centered on deep and early interpretation, specifically in relation to negative transference as, ultimately, an expression of the death instinct, as Hinshelwood spelled out. He specified this tight link in a Kleinian approach between the theory and clinical practice:

> The negative transference is also important on theoretical grounds. Since derivatives of the death instinct are the problem, aggression and destructiveness need to be brought into the transference for investigation and interpretation. (Hinshelwood, 1989 p. 16)

In Chapter 1, I pointed out that the belief that the main analytic task is to make conscious, modify, and integrate innate unconscious contents is not unique to Kleinian theory. A significant proportion of Freudian and Jungian therapists also hold to the view that consistent interpretation of innate infantile fantasies is transformative, rather than the relational interactions that research has actually shown to be the effective factors in psychotherapy. There are a number of potential dangers in these assumptions, dangers that depend on the way the analyst applies these theories about innate unconscious content:

1. The therapist may be seen as having privileged knowledge of the patient's unconscious, so that the patient's conscious subjective experience and attempts to create his or her own meaning bridge may be treated as irrelevant or, worse, as resistance, because the therapist understands the patient's unconscious better than the patient does.

2. If the underlying theory assumes and focuses on negative unconscious intentionality, such as the death instinct, as Hinshelwood suggested, this kind of negative view of the patient's unconscious may have damaging effects on the patient's sense of self and of self-agency, as I discuss in more detail below.
3. The therapist's belief that transference interpretation is the vehicle for bringing about change means that positive relational experiences, which research has shown to be so important for the patient's improvement, are also treated as irrelevant or as resistance. The therapy is inevitably handicapped if it is deprived of the clinical tools that research shows are actually most effective.
4. Therapists can end up struggling with a constant tension between working in the way prescribed by some theories and their intuitive sense of what is actually effective with each patient—as Warren Colman has described and as Frieda Fordham put it in the case discussion given below, "It was rather alarming to have departed so far from what at that time I took to be the right kind of thing to say in an analysis."

A clinical example illustrates the damage that can be done if a therapist does not engage in any kind of coconstructive relational process with the patient. It was given to me by a colleague, recounting her own experience of meeting a new therapist for the first time.

Clinical Illustration

One evening I went along to an unfamiliar part of London, to meet my new therapist. She answered the door but beyond establishing my name, said nothing and ushered me into a large room, lit by a harsh central ceiling light. The room was shabby and depressing. She indicated the chair I should take, which was a hard low wooden chair with a padded seat. She herself sat some distance away. Her face was expressionless. Silence descended.

I felt more and more uncomfortable, feeling vulnerable and small. Eventually I realized that she expected me to talk, so I began to fill what felt like the vast chasm between us. But I soon began to feel that I was babbling. I wasn't getting any feedback. I was disoriented.

I suppose that eventually she must have made some response but I can't remember it. I remember longing to get away from her. When the session ended, I felt bad. I thought I must be a very inadequate sort of analysand. I had not done it well. There was something wrong with me. I was pathetic and stupid. Then I began to feel angry; actually she had not been kind, not understanding. I realized there was no way on earth I would ever go back to that bleak room again.

This kind of experience is not uncommon and could simply be seen as an expression of transference. But even if my colleague's perception of the therapist and the room was distorted by her own projections, the way the therapist conducted herself amplified any such projections to such an extent that it became impossible for the patient to tolerate the experience. The therapist was so unresponsive that my colleague felt she was not getting through to her at all, and this lack of a sense of agency in relation to the therapist was a profoundly undermining experience, which was fatal to the establishment of any therapeutic alliance, making it impossible for my colleague to feel she would be listened to or understood. Many of my colleagues have seen patients who describe their distress at this kind of encounter with a previous therapist who works in this way. It is based on a view that the therapist's role is to be a neutral and objective interpreter of the patient's unconscious (particularly its negative aspects) as it apparently manifests in the transference, as Hinshelwood's discussion of Kleinian theory, described above, spells out. But this is based on theories about the human mind that are inaccurate and outdated, as the research described in Part I shows, and it fails to draw on the relational factors that are actually the key to successful therapy.

So if the theory the therapist uses is not the mutative factor in therapy, the reader might wonder why I draw on a theory of self-agency in this book to support my argument for a particular relational approach in therapy. But the theory of self-agency is a theory about certain kinds of relational experience, not a theory about specific unconscious mental content. It is also rooted in a wealth of observational studies, such as those of Beebe, Schore, Tronick, and Fonagy, about the nature of healthy and unhealthy relational interactions in parent-infant dyads and the long-term consequences of adverse relational experience in early life, of the kind that I described in detail in Part I. The focus on self-agency is an attempt to explain how these relational factors in psychotherapy might bring about psychic change in the patient, just as those infant research studies show how central the experience of agency is for the infant's healthy psychological and emotional development.

To illustrate the direct relevance of some of these issues for clinical practice in more detail, I give the account of Frieda Fordham, a Jungian analyst, of her work with one of her patients, described in an unpublished paper given over 50 years ago at a scientific meeting. Fordham did recognize that preconceived theories hold dangers for the way the therapist functions, and her paper was given to explore the unfamiliar ways in which archetypes might manifest themselves in a patient's material:

> One tends to have preconceived ideas of how archetypes manifest themselves, to welcome them if they appear in a familiar form, and even to try to impose such a form by subtle suggestion or enthusiasm about certain kinds of material. (1958)

Fordham went on to explore these ideas in relation to the psychoanalytic theory of a patient's "ruthless greed," drawing on the work of Melanie Klein:

> Mrs. Klein's early book, The Psychoanalysis of Children (Envy and Gratitude was not published then), contributed something to the understanding of my patients, for the feeling and fantasies they had were comparable to the infantile fantasies she describes, especially the aggressive and destructive ones such as biting, scooping out and destroying the breast, tearing the mother's body, soiling it with excrement, and poisoning and destroying her babies. (Fordham, 1958)

Fordham therefore used the material to argue that infantile aspects of archetypal imagery show remarkable similarity to Kleinian fantasy. She illustrated this point by linking Melanie Klein's ideas to a Finnish folktale, "Killervo," which she felt expressed the primitive savagery and ruthlessness of the child's unconscious and which she saw emerging repeatedly in her patient's fantasies. She very specifically linked archetypes to Klein's concept of innate unconscious fantasy, writing: "One can see in the Killervo story similarities to the infantile fantasies described by Mrs. Klein and would therefore be justified in assuming that she was describing an archetype, as also were my patients" (1958). In other words, she used the material, at least in part, to support a

Jungian-Kleinian hybrid model of innate forces at work in the human psyche. For example, she stated, "We do think that the archetypes do the work and that our job is to help create the conditions where they can manifest themselves, as well as making the patient aware, i.e. conscious, of them so far as it possible, and develop an attitude towards them," and stated later that for a successful analysis, the patient "had to experience the instinctual pole of the archetype."

Clinical Case Description by Frieda Fordham

This case was presented at a scientific meeting of the Society of Analytical Psychology, Feburary 1958. A shorter version was published in *Harvest 9*, 1963, with the title "Myth, Archetypes and Pattern of Childhood.".

> My first patient came with quite a clear conception of what a Jungian analysis should be, as she had read books about it. To her great distress, however, she found herself unable to stick to any of the imagined rules. There was a crisis in her life at this time, one of those insoluble problems which people often bring to analysis, and she talked a lot about it. Eventually all that could be said about was said, there was nothing left but a terrible dilemma, for she could neither bear herself or myself to be silent. When I tried to find what lay behind this she became quite frantic, shouted at me and finally burst into tears. This happened more than once.
>
> She found it impossible to sit still for long, and would walk about the room, often hugging the cushion from the back of the chair. When she did sit down she either tore something to pieces or else flung herself about in the chair and told me she felt like smashing something. She could not stand any interpretations, feeling them to be brutal or sadistic attacks on my part, or if I occasionally seemed to be understanding she would accept it for a moment and then turn on me with jeering remarks, such as "You think you're very clever don't you?" or "Think you've scored a bull's eye, but you haven't." She obviously felt from this that I was penetrating her in a dangerous way. She complained bitterly of her tenseness, of her lack of any kind of feeling, of her family, her situation, and about not having any archetypal dreams, till at last I asked her what she meant by an archetypal dream? She was

vague about this so I said, "Well, supposing you could choose what do you think it would be?" After a moment's thought she answered, "Well, about Romulus and Remus."

She had no association to this except a rather vague idea that they were twins suckled by a wolf, but almost immediately she remarked there was a baby crying in the house, didn't I hear it? She was quite anxious because I didn't seem to. However, I remembered her saying something of the kind before: there was a baby crying somewhere, where was it? in the house? outside? it sounded awful and someone should do something about it. Whilst I was remembering this and wondering how it fitted in she was going on talking, and I was half listening, not hearing the words properly but noticing the tone of her voice. Suddenly it flashed across me how like the sound of a whimpering baby it was and I felt myself just like a mother trying to get a recalcitrant child to feed, I did not realise myself to be the wolf-mother, but my response to a cry of need conveyed by the tones of a voice.

She had told me of her bad relationship with her mother, and in fact one of her comments had been, "My mother had to die so that I could live." As a baby, she said, her mother had got to hate the sight, or perhaps the sound, of her. There had been feeding difficulties though she didn't know anything about them only that she had cried perpetually, and this crying was often referred to later in her childhood. Also later on in her life she had half starved herself over a long period, going down to child's weight and becoming really ill in the end, I expect this knowledge conditioned my response, but what I said came involuntarily. It was, "I have lots of good milk to give, why can't you take it?"

It was rather alarming to have departed so far from what at that time I took to be the right kind of thing to say in an analysis, but the remark immediately evoked a response from my patient, and though she could not answer my question there was give and take between us for the rest of the hour, which seemed in retrospect not unlike a satisfactory feed.

Looking back it seems that this was the session when the self was first constellated, and this is why it became so meaningful and set the stage for the future work. With the fantasy of Romulus and Remus the Divine Child had appeared on the scene, but it could not be treated as an abstraction, rather the drama had to be lived as if it were a real child or flesh and blood, and as if it were the patient's own lost childhood, as indeed it may well have been.

Up to this point an ordinary technique had been used in as much as I had remained passive and interpreted the material when I could, but now I found that for a long time I had to adapt myself to my patient as though she were in fact a hungry wailing baby, and I had to evolve a method of dealing with it. Her needs became absolute and I had to adapt myself to them.

She herself refers to this period as her hungry, devouring, dependant stage. Though she consciously tried to be otherwise, she was in fact quite ruthless in her demands on my time. The session had to be at a certain hour, which could not be changed. I did not accept this at first but found the distress caused by a change and the hindrance to analytic work so great as not to be worthwhile. Nor could she be kept waiting without sinking into despair and feeling utterly rejected. Any change in the room caused agitation, as did real or fancied changes in my appearance. There was nearly always a threat as to whether she would leave or not at the end of the hour, and though this was never actually carried into effect on some occasions it was a near thing. Holidays were a source of distress to her. My first one was almost a disaster; after that, when I had realised more clearly what the situation was I treated it just as if I were leaving a very young child and sent daily postcards.

Eventually we settled down to a routine of regular hours, broken by weekends which she could just tolerate by freezing the situation and carrying on as if half alive. She herself named the session "the morning feed" or "the fill up," which just enabled her to carry through the rest of the day.

It was not, however, an easy feed. For a long time she felt persecuted by me and quite unable to be convinced of any good will. These feelings mostly centred round what she called "my technique." This meant that I was manipulating her according to a formula and did not really care about her at all. I sometimes wondered if my patient's babyhood had been like this, I certainly had good grounds from her history in assuming that her mother was likely too rigid and un-spontaneous in relation to her children's needs.

The greedy nature of her feelings, i.e. the patient, slowly

became apparent; as well as demanding my time and my active interest, she devoured me with her eyes, or by asking innumerable questions. Other patients were intolerable—she wanted me for herself alone, there were to be no rivals, but so insecure was she in her possession of me that even a noise outside was a threat to it. The chair cushion became hers and had to be kept for her alone. She mostly buried her face in it, but also pummelled and beat it, getting very angry on one occasion when it smelt as if someone else had used it. She used this cushion first as substitute for my breast and later as what Winnicott calls a transitional object, i.e. an object which is both more and less than a substitute for the breast. It is less because unlike a bottle it does not provide food, and it is more because it carries the libido previously invested entirely in the breast over into other objects. Most mothers are familiar with this stage of development, when the baby has a special toy or bit of blanket or its thumb which it sucks for comfort and as a defence against anxiety.

After a time her hungry feelings were sufficiently conscious to be expressed in words. She complained of aching with emptiness, of her sides sticking together because she was so empty, and also of strange feelings in her mouth and tongue, and of being "all mouth." She said she was desperately hungry and I *must* get her a drink though complaining of hunger, and also that she eventually confessed to getting quite excited by the number of bottles of milk on the door step when she arrived. The demand that I should get a drink for her continued for a very long time in spite of my attempts to analyse it, and many fantasies about my breasts occurred; they were sucked, the nipples were bitten and chewed, and the breast themselves savaged, that is to say cannibalistically attacked.

She always took her shoes off at the beginning of the session, and very often she wrapped herself in my rug. This was ostensibly to keep warm, and it represented my loving arms, but later it became clear a safeguard against the attack she both feared and wanted to make on me. This attack was also projected on to the things in my room which she would like to smash. At one time she kept thinking I was going to have a baby and this aroused murderous feelings of the kind described by Mrs. Klein. There were also anal and urethral fantasies. These were mostly about soiling and damaging my room, but were also directed against my body and its fantasised contents.

Lastly there were fantasies of my having a penis, and sometimes herself having a penis. I am calling these fantasies, but at the moment of experiencing them conviction would be a truer word. Almost all her fantasies were of this nature, and were experienced in the session as realities. This was often so painful to her that she tried in all sorts of ways to circumvent the experience. For instance to avoid her ravenous hunger she would have a large meal before coming, but this dodge rarely worked.

Along with destructive and aggressive feelings, concern for me began to develop, at first in a rather fantastic form and eventually as a recognition that I had needs as well as herself. At first I was thought to look pale or ill, or exhausted, even when my actual appearance flatly contradicted this. When I became ill nothing would convince my patient that she was not the direct cause (a point worth noticing here is the omnipotent attitude so expressed) and she suffered terrible remorse. She then began to offer to do things for me, mostly things that would have been impossible, like the small girl offering to do things for mother well beyond her capacity, but sometimes more real. She also gave presents to me, for instance she produced a sweet out of her pocket, which I accepted because I thought it was connected with her need to make up to me for her greediness and the harm she feared it had done me, and this, when analysed later turned out to be the case.

Eventually she began to discover how much love as well as aggression there was in her biting feelings, and in her urge to attack me. I have not said much about myself as the terrible mother, but you will realise that I often appeared in this guise, I was thought to be cold, angry, demanding, expecting too much of her, and more fantastically I had knives in my stomach going round like a mincing machine which would mince anyone up, and also I was beating her unmercifully and jeering at her too. I appeared in pictures she painted as the wolf mother—not however the friendly one who suckled the children, but a much more sinister figure of the Red Riding Hood story type; there were also pictures of me as a devilish looking coloured woman, and a black one which was called "The Shit Queen." In the early days of analysis she also painted many pictures of anonymous naked women with a kind of phallic breast, upturned and very sharply pointed at the nipple, breasts which were more likely to impale a child than to feed it. Later the pictures turned to full round breasts with babies feeding contentedly, and she modelled a beautiful mother and child in clay.

Discussion: A Relational Perspective on the Case Study

Frieda Fordham's case example clearly illustrates her intuitive understanding of the dilemma highlighted by Shedler, that the active ingredients of therapy are not necessarily those presumed by the treatment model. Frieda Fordham was not a Kleinian, but was drawing on Kleinian theory to support her view that the patient's material demonstrated a link between archetypes and infantile unconscious fantasies of ruthless greed. And, as I have already indicated, Klein's view of the nature of unconscious content is not just a theoretical model of the mind, but also a prescription for a particular clinical technique, centered on deep and early interpretation, specifically in relation to negative transference as, ultimately, an expression of the death instinct.

So Frieda Fordham was drawing on Kleinian theory but found that the clinical approach that the theory prescribes was not proving helpful. Her own reactions to the patient became essentially relational rather than purely interpretative, showing her willingness to adapt to the patient's need to feel that she could have a real emotional impact on her therapist, as I described in Chapter 5. If she believed that the patient's material reflected instinctual unconscious fantasies of ruthless greed, as Klein proposed, then that theoretical model would prescribe a purely interpretative approach, and Fordham makes clear her unease about diverging from this approach.

But it seems clear from Fordham's own account that it was the points at which she responded in an intuitive and relational way that enabled her patient to experience and express her own self-agency in the therapy. Just as Warren Colman described (in the example in Chapter 8), Fordham recognized that her patient needed her "symbolic enactments," by which I suggest that the analyst allows the patient to express self-agency at the teleological level. She needed to discover that the analyst understood and accepted her need for omnipotent control, that her need to have such a powerful effect on the analyst did not drive her away, the effect it seems to have had on her mother.

This patient clearly suffered from an extremely traumatizing childhood. She felt that "her mother had got to hate the sight or perhaps the sound of her," a clear experience of hostile caregiving, an extreme example of the kind that Broussard and Cassidy (2010) have shown causes lifelong difficulties (the research described in Chapter 4). This early relational trauma, the experience of being profoundly rejected and, at times, even hated by her mother, would in itself be sufficient to create feeding difficulties in infancy and then severe anorexia in later life. The myth of Romulus and Remus she referred to is the story of two abandoned children, rescued by a wolf-mother, and the real abandonment she must have suffered at the hands of a mother who could not attune to her, nor meet her most basic needs for survival, erupted in a hallucination of a baby crying, which could well be a dissociative experience of the terrified neglected crying child part of herself, a kind of dissociative flashback to her own infant experience. The fantasies are expressed in this form, the hallucination of a baby crying, because the very early infantile trauma remains split off and unintegrated, so can only be experienced in sensory form (Brewin, Dalgleish, & Joseph, 1996). The focus on feeding in the patient's fantasies probably reflects the real deprivation she suffered while struggling to feed in childhood.

This awareness of her mother's hostile caregiving would also lead to the patient's terror of taking in anything from her or later from any maternal figure, including the therapist. She seems to have experienced exactly the kind of failure of specific aspects of empathy that Beebe et al. (2010) have so clearly shown to be predictive of disorganized attachment. Beebe et al. showed that these mothers closed up their faces, smiled fixedly, or turned away when their infants were distressed, and Fordham's patient seems to have experienced exactly this kind of withdrawal and hostility to her distress from her mother. The patient demonstrated some of the classic aspects of borderline personality disorder, the result of this early infantile trauma, that lead to a combination of a desperate clinging alternating with violent hostility and rejection, which Fordham so evocatively described. The patient was initially terrified to internalize anything Fordham said, seeing her interpretations as sadistic, brutal, and dangerous. She really does seem to have believed that Fordham was dangerous, ruthlessly manipulative, cold angry, and demanding and wanted to beat her up or cut her into pieces, so vividly conveyed in her fantasy that Fordham had knives in her stomach that would make mincemeat of her.

To interpret such terrifying images as the product of innate processes, such as instinctual drive or the collective unconscious, does not do justice to the reality of the relational trauma created by the patient's mother's real hostility to her. The patient's devouring attention to Fordham can be seen, not just as greed, but as the hypervigilance shown by so many people who have been on the receiving end of hostile caregiving in childhood, a constant state of alertness to expected rejection or hostility by the caregiver, in the hope that anticipating it may enable the child to mitigate it.

Not only was the patient terrified that her therapist wanted to destroy her, she was also terrified that she was damaging to her therapist. She was afraid that her overwhelming need would actually make her therapist ill—that to have any effect on her, to allow herself any expression of agency would be intolerable to Fordham and would harm her as she seemed to have felt that it harmed her mother. She was convinced that she would make Fordham ill or indeed was the cause of any illness Fordham did, in reality, experience. Her mother's hostility and rejection of the patient as a baby were almost certainly the consequence of the mother's own significant psychological disturbance. Mothers of disorganized infants are women who suffer from unresolved loss, abuse, or trauma themselves are and preoccupied with their own emotional distress (Lyons-Ruth, 1999). Beebe et al. described the psychological fragility of mothers of infants who develop disorganized attachment (future D infants):

> Out of her own unresolved fears about intimate relating, and her fears of being re-traumatized by the infant's distress, at specific moments the mother of the future D infant mobilizes complex contradictory behavioural tendencies, that derail the infant. (2010, p. 93)

One of the main reactions these mothers have to their infant's distress is to withdraw, with a "closed" face, or a fixed cheerful expression, or by looking away (Beebe et al., 2010). The infant is left in his own distress uncontained and with the implicit knowledge that he has directly caused the mother's distress. No wonder the patient was convinced that any expression of distress would make Fordham ill. Wrapping herself in the rug was not only holding herself together in an attempt to manage her own distress, but was also a way of protecting Fordham from any effect she might have on her. It seems as though the patient could not tell the difference between expressing her self-agency in a relationship, thus having an effect on another person, and doing that person harm. It was probably the case that there was no real difference between having an emotional effect on her mother and causing her real distress—as Beebe et al. stated about mothers whose infants develop disorganized attachment: "The infant's distress may be so over-arousing and terrifying to the future D mother that she repeats aspects of her own childhood feelings . . . or defends herself against re-experiencing them" (2010, p. 93).

It is exactly a person's history as an infant, of this kind of maternal withdrawal and distress, that makes a relational approach in psychotherapy essential, so that such a patient can gradually express self-agency and realize that it does not damage the therapist or the relationship between them. Fordham intuitively knew that she had to be willing to adapt to her patient's need to control her and her reassurance that the patient would not drain or destroy her by her need for such exact attunement seems to have eventually enabled the patient to regress and to work through the teleological level of self-agency. Her need to control her therapist's behavior was something that Fordham accepted, recognizing the need to adapt herself to her patient as though she were in fact a hungry wailing baby, whose needs were for absolute attunement. The teleological level of agency can only be experienced through action and behavior, and Fordham showed her enormous skill as a therapist in recognizing this and adapting her approach accordingly to attune to the patient's developmental need, rather than sticking rigidly to theory. She recognized that the patient found any experience of separation deeply threatening—as though to recognize that Frieda Fordham had a life of her own was unbearable. In essence, there was a period of time in which the patient could only relate through absolute fusion and total control, as though to allow Fordham any self-agency of her own would mean that the patient would be abandoned. So the session had to be at a certain hour, which could not be changed because of the intolerable distress this caused. To be kept waiting, or to find any changes in the room or in her therapist, were experienced by the patient as rejection and abandonment.

There seems to have been a moment of meeting, of the kind described by the BCPSG (discussed in Chapter 2), one based on an implicit relational knowing, when Frieda Fordham suddenly found herself differentiating herself from the depressed, hostile, neglectful mother when she made her involuntary remark, "I have lots of good milk to give, why can't you take it?" This remark would have conveyed a number of implicit messages to the patient, that Fordham was not a depressed, exhausted, depleted mother who would feel drained by her baby's needs. It must have been an enormous relief to the patient to be told that Fordham felt that she had plenty to give her, in contrast to her experience of her mother, from whom she could not feed. Fordham also intuitively recognized the essential role of turn-taking in therapy, saying that following her remark an experience of "give and take was established between us, which in retrospect was not unlike a satisfactory feed." It was, of course, exactly like a satisfactory feed, in replicating the turn-taking that is first expressed in the burst-pause-burst pattern of feeding that Hendriks-Jansen described and that I referred to in Part I.

Postscript: Negative Attribution in Infancy and in Psychotherapy

THE RANGE OF RESEARCH that I described in Part I, drawn from a range of different disciplines, demonstrates how vulnerable children are to the impact of their parents' perception of them and how dangerous and damaging it is for an infant's developing sense of self when parents fail to engage in the communicative turn-taking that forms the foundation of healthy human psychological and emotional development. One form this failure takes is that the parent misreads the child's communications and attributes intentions to the infant that he or she is not yet developmentally capable of. The parent assumes that the infant has conscious plans and intentions as adults do, and does not understand that the ability to relate to the parent as a separate individual with his or her own emotions and needs only begins to develop at around 3 years of age. Alicia Lieberman has described the toxic effect of negative maternal attribution on a toddler's sense of self, and I shall quote again the striking example she gave of this kind of parental misattribution:

> One mother, for example, perceived her 3-month-old baby daughter as so "cunning" that, according to the mother, the baby jumped from her crib to the adjacent parental bed to sneak a feeding at the breast while the mother was asleep and then jumped back to her crib. This was the only explanation the mother could find for her breasts feeling rather empty of milk when she woke up in the morning. (1999, p. 739)

Lieberman revealed that the mother was unable to relate to her own inner feelings of emptiness, rooted in her own childhood deprivation and to her fear of not having enough to give her daughter. Instead, she experienced her emotional emptiness in a concrete and behavioral way, as breasts empty of milk, and decided that the baby's actions must be the cause, even though such behavior would clearly be impossible for a 3-month-old baby.

Although this mother's attribution of negative intentionality to her infant has a psychotic quality, parent-infant psychotherapists do often see mothers who regularly attribute negative meaning to their infants' attempts to communicate. This kind of parental misattribution is evident in the research by Beatrice Beebe et al. (2010, p. 100), where there are examples of mothers, whose babies were later identified as disorganized, who would misread their infants' distress signals as "fussing," as deliberate attempts to control the mother's mood, or as accusations that she is a bad mother. One example given me by a colleague was that of a mother who said her 7-week-old son "keeps all his screaming for me and his smiles for other people." Sue Gerhardt (2010, pp. 90–91) described a mother who complained that her toddler stuck to her like glue and said that she couldn't wait to get rid of her at day care.

This kind of misunderstanding of infants' developmental need to experience agency in relation to their caregivers can lead to the terrible damage done by inappropriate advice to parents, such as the notorious Truby King method, where parents were given strict injunctions by so-called experts to adhere to a strict 4-hour feeding routine and to ignore their babies' desperate cries at all other times. This kind of advice is so out of keeping with the research evidence of the huge value of a parent's sensitive responsiveness to her baby that it should have been consigned to the dustbin forever. However, it has regrettably recently seen a renaissance in the approach advocated by Gina Ford (2001), who advocates a similar rigid imposition of routines on the baby, regardless of his or her expressed emotional needs. Sadly, psychotherapists often see patients who have been damaged by this kind of rule-driven parenting, which rides roughshod over the turn-taking exchanges that Tronick, Beebe, Schore, Stern, and others have shown to be so central to the psychological and emotional development of the human infant.

Hostile Caregiving in Psychotherapy: Negative Therapeutic Attribution and the Effect on the Patient's Sense of Self

Psychotherapy patients often arrive in the consulting room with distorted views of their own motivation, for example, seeing themselves as greedy, lazy, or envious or just bad. Sometimes this is the consequence of overt negative parental attributions, as Lieberman (1999) and Broussard and Cassidy (2010) described, which the child internalizes and comes to feel are true reflections of his or her personality. In other cases, it may be the result of specific, detailed, and fine-tuned relational interactions in early infancy, for example, when the mother cannot bear to relate to her infant's distress because it causes her too much distress, as Beebe et al. (2010) described. The infant may grow up feeling guilty and a bad person for causing such maternal distress. The clinical experience of many therapists who work with patients who show disorganized attachment and borderline personality is that such patients have a deep sense of themselves as bad. So there is a very real danger for such a person who comes into therapy and finds that the therapist also works from a theoretical position of negative attribution, in relation to the patient's intentionality and agency.

But tragically this kind of negative attribution, in relation to the patient's need to experience agency in the therapeutic relationship, is also apparent in psychotherapy theories and practice that focus on negative unconscious fantasy as an expression of the death instinct, rather than on constructive relational interactions between therapist and patient. Just as a parent's misunderstanding of her infant's intentions can profoundly damage the child's developing sense of self-agency, the same can also be true in a psychotherapy relationship. If a therapist's clinical approach is based on theories that focus on unconscious "destructiveness," that therapist's constant negative attribution of intentionality is experienced by the patient as a denial or pathologizing of the patient's relational needs. For example, one therapist told a story about a patient who one day brought her a present of a loaf of bread the patient had made. The therapist did not take the bread but simply let it drop on the floor between them, treating the gift as a manipulative seduction. There is a real danger that the patient will experience this as the same kind of hostile caregiving that Frieda Fordham's patient experienced from her mother, or the baby in Alicia Lieberman's example.

Such a therapist focuses on interpreting the negative transference and sees no need to coconstruct a dialogue and a relationship with the patient that will create a safe framework within which painful material can be explored. It is a toxic combination of a failure of turn-taking with a negative perception of the person's intentionality.

The therapist's failure to recognize the importance of the patient's need to express self-agency, combined with the negative perception of the patient's intentionality inherent in the concept of innate destructive fantasy, is experienced by many patients as deeply alienating, especially those who have suffered from early relational trauma and negative parental attribution in childhood, of the kind that has already made them feel like bad people.

It so often leads to the kind of therapeutic impasse described in previous chapters, which turns into a battle between a therapist determined to stick to his or her interpretations of a patient's unconscious envy or sadism and a patient struggling to experience a sense of agency in relation to the therapist—to feel that the need for relationship is not bad, but is accepted as real and healthy by the therapist. This theoretical approach also neglects most of the criteria for effective therapy described by Shedler (2010). It takes no account of the need for the therapist to facilitate a process of disruption and repair (Beebe & Lachmann, 2002), in which the patient has an opportunity to correct the therapist's misattunements (Benjamin, 2009).

But even if the therapist does not always focus on negative interpretation, the emphasis on unconscious fantasy itself, the idea that patients do not know their own mind and that the analyst is in a better position to deduce what is occurring unconsciously, undermines patients' sense of self and self-agency. Even worse is when analysts confuse their interpretations with factual knowledge and do not distinguish what the patient says from what the analyst thinks. It is the idea that the therapist's own attribution is privileged knowledge that undermines self-agency. An analyst who regards interpretation as the only effective analytic tool is in danger of adding to the patient's relational trauma and of preventing an experience of agency in the therapeutic relationship.

Extracts from a transcript of an analytic session demonstrate the destructiveness of this kind of impasse. In this example, the patient is objecting to the fact that everything he says is interpreted as an expression of his unconscious feeling towards the analyst. While this may be seen as an extreme example, this session takes place shortly before the final breakdown of the therapy and so the exchanges have a particular intensity and powerfully illustrate the patient's frustration with the analyst and the painfulness of his feeling that there was no room for him to assert self-agency in the relationship. I have the patient's permission to use the transcript.

Clinical Illustration

The patient starts the session by objecting that the therapist does not seem interested in his account of his experiences with other people outside the consulting room. The therapist responds:

> ANALYST: I'm trying to stress to you that what I am helping you to do is to be aware of the truth of what you think and feel at the deepest levels of your mind, unconsciously, at any one moment, which is here in this moment.

The analyst then makes the point a few sentences later that when the patient talks about something outside the room, that he is actually communicating something else entirely:

> ANALYST: You say you are talking about work. I want to talk about what you said means, according to me, about how you feel here and now. . . . Because I'm saying to you, look, if you think you are talking about work. . . . If I make an interpretation about something different it is because I think that *is* the meaning, the pressing meaning of the communication here and now.
> PATIENT: But my problem is that almost without exception . . . , when I tell you something about work you invariably find a meaning for it here.

Over a series of increasingly heated exchanges the patient continues:

> PATIENT: What I am saying is that someone who always comes up with the same answer [speaking over the analyst's voice], whatever the question, seems to me that they've got a theory which is impenetrable, unfalsifiable and not to be trusted.

The analyst responds a couple of exchanges later by reiterating the point that he is interpreting the patient's unconscious in the here and now:

> ANALYST: I am pointing out to you that whatever interpretation I make to you, and I could make one now, is based on what I think you are doing unconsciously.

Shortly after, the patient makes a further attempt to get the analyst to see his point of view and to enter into a dialogue with him that could help to begin to build a meaning-bridge between past and present:

> PATIENT: Now what I would like to make clear, to make the point again which you ignored and always ignored throughout the many times that I've raised it, is that you have only one interpretation, one sort of interpretation of my unconscious. . . . You've never given me an interpretation, what I would call a proper transference interpretation . . . where you've actually said, "At this moment you are feeling I'm a father who will not tell you what to do, which is why you're thrashing around trying to find an identity." Your interpretations are solely and exclusively reductions of everything to a hypothetical intense unconscious relationship that I have with you and that is the sole focus of your interpretations. . . . "

But the analyst rejects the patient's invitation to find meaning in their exchanges in terms of the influence of past relationships on the present and so to repair the profound misunderstanding between them. Their battle continues, going around the same circles, with the patient trying to assert self-agency and to get the analyst to listen to his subjective experience, while the analyst is only interested in interpreting the patient's supposed immediate unconscious feeling toward him:

> ANALYST: I wish to interpret not how you think you are or claim that you are, but how you actually are behaving, by the way that you're communicating to me.
>
> PATIENT: You can talk about how I actually am behaving and communicating to you today but I would like you to answer the question. How can we be remotely confident that tells us anything very much about how I was 5 hours ago or how I've been in the last 24 hours since I last saw you?
>
> ANALYST: That's not a question that interests me.
>
> PATIENT: But it is the question I'm addressing.

The patient goes on to question the analyst's certainty that he is the authority on the true nature of the patient's unconscious, making the point that the analyst's own conscious and unconscious may affect his perceptions:

PATIENT: There is always a countertransference and there is always the reality of two personalities involved and two intellects involved. I mean I can't go on submitting myself to your preoccupations in this way. I have to feel that there is some connection between my experience outside of here and what goes on in here and I don't feel at all happy that there is, so much is going by the board.

After continuing in this vein for the rest of the session, toward the end the patient challenges the analyst:

PATIENT: Your basic premise is that I'm here to help you find out what's in my unconscious.
ANALYST: Yes.
PATIENT: And I say that is not how I perceive your role and I do not want to employ a psychoanalyst to do that. I want to employ a psychoanalyst to help *me* to find out what is in *my* unconscious.

The analyst's refusal to consider that the patient's conscious perception of himself has any relevance for the analytic work is experienced by the patient as so destructive of his subjectivity and agency that the work quickly reaches a stalemate. The patient had an enduring belief that he was, in essence, a bad person, an experience that a subsequent analysis revealed to be partly rooted in his early childhood experience of a depressed disorganized mother who could scarcely hold herself together at times, retreating to bed, where she would curl up in a fetal position with one arm under the pillow and the other over her head, as though she was afraid of being hit. At such times the patient was told, "Mummy must not be disturbed," and he somehow knew that she was feeling suicidal. He came to feel that any emotional demand was too much for her and caused her distress and that he was a bad person for wanting his emotional needs to be met. This belief, that any expression of his self-agency in terms of a need for emotional engagement and relationship was bad, meant that the analytic experience described above was simply disastrous for him, reinforcing his belief that his need for relationship and dialogue produced catastrophic defensiveness and withdrawal from his analyst. If the analyst had helped him to make a meaning-bridge (Eliott et al., 1994) of this kind between past childhood experience and the analytic relationship, it might have been possible for the work to proceed. But the absence of such contextualization, or of any coconstruction of shared understanding, fatally undermined any potential therapeutic alliance.

Conclusion

The research studies I described in the first half of this book show that the idea that the human mind has innate mental contents or structures, patterns of unconscious imagery and thought (or fantasy) that are largely autonomous of personal experience, becomes increasingly untenable as we discover the relational and developmental, emergent nature of the human unconscious. I have highlighted some of the key research in developmental psychology and neuroscience that convincingly demonstrates that the human infant is not born with predetermined unconscious fantasies or structures, but that relational experiences are internalized and organized into unconscious schemas of self in relationship. The child's development of self-agency is inextricably rooted in intersubjectivity.

The case studies I have described in this chapter demonstrate how essential it is for the therapist to facilitate the patient's development of self-agency in the therapeutic dialogue and how catastrophic it can be for many patients if this is not permitted by the therapist. But this does often place therapists in an uneasy position, that Fordham, Colman, and I myself describe, in which we somehow felt that we were not really observing the rules of proper analytic practice. So we urgently need the research evidence that is rapidly accumulating to provide the theoretical foundations for effective clinical practice. One relevant study is that of Shedler, who pinpointed the key factors in a therapeutic process that correlate with a good outcome. This research adds another fundamental challenge to some of the theoretical assumptions used to justify the clinical approach demonstrated in the transcript above. Shedler suggested that the factors that are present in effective psychotherapy involve the patient's active role in gaining understanding about:

> How the person views self and others, interprets and makes sense of experience, avoids aspects of experience, or interferes with a potential capacity to find greater enjoyment and meaning in life. (2010, p. 100)

This is a cooperative meaning-making effort on the part of therapist and patient that is far removed from the patient as a passive recipient of the analyst's interpretation of unconscious fantasies, a model in which the patient's own views are seen as irrelevant. Relationship is also at the heart of the conversational model of psychotherapy developed by Hobson (1985) and Meares (2004). This is an intersubjective approach, whose central aim is to foster a form of relatedness called "aloneness-togertheness." For Meares, this aim went beyond that of correcting habitual and distorted maladaptive forms of relatedness and his view was that " therapeutic interventions directed at "insight" and the "unconscious" risk invalidation and the creation of dependence" (Meares 2004, p. 52). Instead the aim of the conversational method is for patient and therapist to build a jointly created imaginative narrative, arising out of play-like, non-linear mental activity: "its purpose was the generation of self, which was understood as a dynamism, a process, arising in conversation as a third thing, between people" (Meares 2004, p. 52). In this kind of relational approach, the patient's experience of self-agency plays a vital role, in keeping with Shedler's view:

> The goals of psychodynamic therapy include, but extend beyond, symptom remission. Successful treatment should not only relieve symptoms (i.e., get rid of something) but also foster the positive presence of psychological capacities and resources. Depending on the person and the circumstances, these might include the capacity to have more fulfilling relationships, make more effective use of one's talents and abilities, maintain a realistically based sense of self-esteem, tolerate a wider range of affect, have more satisfying sexual experiences, understand self and others in more nuanced and sophisticated ways, and face life's challenges with greater freedom and flexibility. Such ends are pursued through a process of self-reflection, self-exploration, and self-discovery that takes place in the context of a safe and deeply authentic relationship between therapist and patient. (2010, p. 100)

This is an eloquent description of the three main therapeutic outcomes I described in Chapter 9, the development of affect regulation, mentalization, and mature self-agency—and also of the processes of interpretation, new relational experience, and the experience of regression that together contribute to effective psychotherapy.

I hope that in this book, I have convinced the reader that infant developmental research and psychotherapy process and outcome studies demonstrate the central role of self-agency in the relational processes that contribute to healthy psychological and emotional development in childhood development and in also in psychotherapy.

References

Ablon, J. S., & Jones, E. E. (2002). Validity of controlled clinical trials of psychotherapy: Findings from the NIMH Treatment of Depression Collaborative Research Program. *American Journal of Psychiatry, 159,* 775–783.

Alvarez, A. (1971). *The savage god: A study of suicide.* London: Weidenfeld & Nicolson.

Alvarez, A. (1997). Projective identification as a communication: Its grammar in borderline psychotic children. *Psychoanalytic Dialogues, 7,* 753–768.

Astington, J. W. (2002). The developmental interdependence of theory of mind and language. In N. J. Enfield & S. C. Levinson (Eds.), *Roots of human sociality: Culture, cognition and interaction* (Chapter 6). Oxford: Berg.

Atwood, G., & Stolorow, R. (1984). *Structures of subjectivity: Explorations in psychoanalytic phenomenology.* Hillsdale, NJ: Analytic Press.

Bahrick, L. R., & Watson, J. S. (1985). Detection of intermodal proprioceptive-visual contingency as a potential basis of self-perception in infancy. *Developmental Psychology, 21,* 963–973.

Bakhtin, M. M. (1973). *Problems of Dostoevsky's poetics* (R. W. Rostel, Trans.). Ann Arbor, MI: Ardis.

Balint, M. (1968). *The basic fault: Therapeutic aspects of regression.* London: Tavistock.

Bandura, A. (2001). Social cognitive theory: An agentic perspective. *Annual Revue of Psychology, 52,* 1–26.

Baressi, J. (2002). From "The thought is the thinker" to "the voice is the speaker." *Theory and Psychology, 12*(2), 237–250.

Barkow, J. H., Cosmides, J., & Tooby, L. (1992). *The adapted mind:*

Evolutionary psychology and the generation of culture. New York: Oxford University Press.

Bateman, A., & Fonagy, P. (2004). *Psychotherapy for borderline personality disorder: Mentalization-based treatment.* New York: Oxford University Press.

BCPSG. (2007). The foundational level of psychodynamic meaning: Implicit process in relation to conflict, defence and the dynamic unconscious. *International Journal of Psychoanalysis, 88,* 843–860.

Beebe, B., Jaffe, J., Buck, K., Chen, H., Cohen, P., Blatt, S., et al. (2007). Six-week postpartum maternal self-criticism and dependency and 4-month mother-infant self- and interactive contingency. *Infant Mental Health Journal, 29,* 442–471.

Beebe, B., Jaffe, J., Markese, S., Buck, K., Chen, H., Cohen, P., et al. (2010). The origins of 12-month attachment: A microanalysis of 4-month mother-infant interaction. *Attachment and Human Development, 12,* 1–135.

Beebe, B., & Lachmann, F. (1994). Representation and internalization in infancy: Three principles of salience. *Psychoanalytic Psychology, 11,* 127–165.

Beebe, B., & Lachmann, F. (2002). *Infant research and adult treatment: Co-constructing interactions.* Hillsdale, NJ: Analytic Press.

Benjamin, J. (1995). *Like subjects, love objects: Essays on recognition and sexual difference.* New Haven, CT: Yale University Press.

Benjamin, J. (2004). Beyond doer and done to: An intersubjective view of thirdness. *Psychoanalytic Quarterly, 73,* 5–46.

Benjamin, J. (2009). A relational psychoanalysis perspective on the necessity of acknowledging failure in order to restore the facilitating and containing features of the intersubjective relationship (the shared third). *International Journal of Psychoanalysis, 90*(3), 441–450.

Billington, M. (2007). *Harold Pinter.* London: Faber & Faber.

Bion, W. (1977). Transformations. In *Seven servants.* New York: Jason Aronson. (Original work published 1965)

Biven, L., Panksepp, J. (2007). Commentary on "Toward a neuroscience of empathy: Integrating affective and cognitive perspectives." *Neuropsychoanalysis, 9,* 141–146.

Blum, H. (1980). The borderline childhood of the Wolf Man. In M. Kanzer & J. Glenn (Eds.), *Freud and his patients.* New York: Jason Aronson.

Bollas, C. (1987). *The shadow of the object: Psychoanalysis of the unthought known.* London: Free Association.

Borg, E. (2007). If mirror neurons are the answer, what was the question? *Journal of Consciousness Studies, 14*(8), 5–19.

Bourne, V. J., & Todd, B. K. (2004). When left means right: An explanation of the left cradling bias in terms of right hemisphere specializations. *Developmental Science, 7*, 19–24.

Bowlby, J. (1980). *Attachment and loss, 3. Loss: Sadness and depression.* London: Hogarth Press.

Bowlby, J. (1988). *A secure base: Clinical applications of attachment theory.* London: Routledge.

Bradshaw, G. A., & Schore, A. N. (2007). How elephants are opening doors: Developmental neuroethology, attachment and social context. *Ethology, 113*, 426–436.

Bretherton, I. (1995). The origins of attachment theory. In *Attachment theory: Social developmental and clinical perspectives.* Hillsdale, NJ: Analytic Press.

Brewin, C., Dalgleish, T., & Joseph, S. (1996). A dual representation theory of post-traumatic stress disorder. *Psychological Review, 103*, 4, 670–676.

Bright, G. (2006) Unpublished manuscript.

Britton, R. (1998a). The suspension of belief and the "as-if" syndrome. In *Belief and imagination: Explorations in psychoanalysis.* London: Routledge.

Britton, R. (1998b). Subjectivity, objectivity and triangular space. In *Belief and imagination: Explorations in psychoanalysis.* London: Routledge.

Broucek, F. (1979). Efficacy in infancy: A review of some experimental studies and their possible implications for clinical theory. *International Journal of Psychoanalysis, 60*, 311–316.

Broussard, E.R. (1976) Neonatal prediction and outcome at 10/11 years. *Child Psychiatry and Human Development, 7*, 8593.

Broussard, E, Cassidy, J. (2010). Maternal perception of newborns predicts attachment organization in middle adulthood. *Attachment and Human Development, 12*, 1–2, pp.159–173.

Bruch, H. (1973). *Eating disorders.* New York: Basic Books.

Bruschweiler-Stern, N., Harrison, A. M., Lyons-Ruth, K., Morgan, A. C., Nahum, J. P., Sander, L. W., et al. (2002). Explicating the implicit: The local level and the microprocess of change in the analytic situation. *International Journal of Psychoanalysis, 83*, 1051–1062.

Buccino, G., Riggio, L., Melli, G., Binkofski, F., Gallese, V., & Rizzolatti, G. (2005). Listening to action-related sentences modulates the activity of the motor system: A combined TMS and behavioural study. *Cognitive Brain Research, 24,* 355–363.

Buckner, R. L., Andrews-Hanna, J. R., & Schacter, D. L. (2008). The brain's default network: Anatomy, function and relevance to disease. In R. T. Johnson (Ed.), *Annals of the New York Academy of Sciences, The Year in Cognitive Science 2008* (pp. 1–38). New York: Wiley.

Cambray, J., & Carter, L. (2004). Analytic methods revisited. In J. Cambray & L. Carter (Eds.), *Analytical psychology: Contemporary perspectives in Jungian analysis* (Chapter 5). New York: Brunner-Routledge.

Carr, L., Iacoboni, M., Dubeau, M. C., Mazziotta, J. C., & Lenzi, G. L. (2003). Neural mechanisms of empathy in humans: A relay from neural systems for imitation to limbic areas. *Proceedings of the National Academy of Sciences, USA, 100,*(9), 5497–5502.

Castonguay, L., Goldfried, M., Wiser, S., Raue, P., & Hayes, A. (1996). Predicting the effect of cognitive therapy for depression: A study of unique and common factors. *Journal of Consulting and Clinical Psychology, 64,* 497–504.

Cohn, J. F., & Tronick, E. Z. (1988). Mother-infant face-to-face interaction: Influence is bi- directional and unrelated to periodic cycles in either partner's behaviour. *Developmental Psychology, 24,* 386–392.

Colman, W. (2006a). The analytic superego. *Journal of the British Association of Psychotherapists, 44*(2), 99–114.

Colman, W. (2006b). Imagination and the imaginary. *Journal of Analytical Psychology, 51*(1), 21–42.

Colman, W. (2006c). Is the analyst a good object? *British Journal of Psychotherapy, 22,* (3), 295–309.

Colman, W. (2008). On being, knowing and having a self. *Journal of Analytical Psychology, 53,* (3), 351–366.

Colman, W. (2010). Mourning and the symbolic process. *Journal of Analytical Psychology, 55,* 2, 275279.

Cozolino, L. (2002). *The neuroscience of psychotherapy.* New York: Norton.

Crowther, C. (2004). *Addictive states of mind.* Unpublished manuscript.

Csibra, G., & Gergely, G. (1998). The teleological origins of mentalistic action explanations: A developmental hypothesis. *Developmental Science, 1,* 255–259.

Csibra, G., & Gergely, G. (2007). "Obsessesed with goals": Functions and mechanisms of teleological interpretation of actions in humans. *Acta Psychologica, 124,* 60–78.

Damasio, A. (1999). *The feeling of what happens: Body, emotion and the making of consciousness.* London: William Heinemann.

Deacon, T. (1997). *The symbolic species: The co-evolution of language and the human brain.* New York: Norton.

Decety, J., & Chaminade, T. (2003). When the self represents the other: A new cognitive neuroscience view on psychological identification. *Consciousness and Cognition, 12,* 577–596.

Decety, J., & Meyer, M. (2009). Imitation as a stepping stone to empathy. In M. de Haan & M. Gunnar (Eds.), *Handbook of developmental social neuroscience.* New York: Guilford.

Decety, J., Michalska, K. J., Akitsuki, Y., & Lahey, B. (2009). Atypical empathic responses in adolescents with aggressive conduct disorder. *Biological Psychology, 80,* 203–211.

De M'Uzan, M. (1973). A case of masochistic perversion and an outline of a theory. *International Journal of Psychoanalysis, 54,* 455.

Dennett, D. (1995). *Darwin's dangerous idea: Evolution and the meanings of human life.* London: Allen Lane/Penguin.

Deutsch, H. (1942). Some forms of emotional disturbance and their relationship to schizophrenia. *Psychoanalytic Quarterly, 11,* 301–321.

Devinsky, O. (2000). Right cerebral hemispheric dominance for a sense of corporeal and emotional self. *Epilepsy and Behavior, 1,* 60–73.

Durkheim, E. (1951). *Suicide: A study in sociology* (J. A. Spaulding & G. Simpson, Trans.). New York: Free Press. (Original work published 1897)

Eagle, M., & Wakefield, J. (2004). How not to escape from the Grunbaum syndrome: A critique of the "new view" of psychoanalysis. In A. Casement (Ed.), *Who owns psychoanalysis* (Chapter 17). London: Karnac.

Eliot, T. S. (1936). Animula. In *Collected Poems 1909–1962.* London: Faber.

Eliott, R., Shapiro, D. A., Firth-Cozens, J., Stiles, W. B., Hardy, G. E., Llewelyn, S. P., et al. (1994). Comprehensive process analysis of insight events in cognitive-behavioral and psychodynamic-interpersonal psychotherapies. *Journal of Counselling Psychology, 41,* 449–463.

Elkin, I., Shea, T., Watkins, J. T., Imber, S. D., Sotsky, S. M., Collins, J. F., et al. (1989). National Institutes of Mental Health Treatment of Depression Collaborative Research Program. *Archives of General Psychiatry, 46,* 971–982.

Ellenberger, H. F. (1970). *The discovery of the unconscious: The history and evolution of dynamic psychiatry.* London: Allen Lane/Penguin.

Enfield, N. J., & Levinson, S. C. (2002). Introduction. In N. J. Enfield & S. C. Levinson (Eds.), *Roots of human sociality: Culture, cognition and interaction*. Oxford: Berg.

Fairbairn, W. (1952a). *Psychoanalytic studies of the personality*. London: Tavistock.

Fairbairn, W. (1952b). A revised psychopathology of the psychoses and psychoneuroses. In *Psychoanalytic studies of the personality*. London: Tavistock.

Fairbairn, W. (1952c). Schizoid factors in the personality. In *Psychoanalytic studies of the personality*. London: Tavistock.

Farrer, C., Frith, C. (2002) Experiencing oneself vs another person as being the cause of an action: The neural correlates of the experience of agency. *NeuroImage,15*, 596–603.Fodor, J. (2000). *The mind doesn't work that way: The scope and limits of computational psychology*. Cambridge, MA: MIT Press.

Fogassi, L., Ferrari, P. F., Geiserich, B., Rozzi, S., Chersi, F., & Rizzolatti, G. (2005). Parietal lobe: From action organization to intention understanding. *Science, 302*, 662–667.

Fonagy, P. (1991). Thinking about thinking: Some clinical and theoretical considerations in the treatment of the borderline patient. *International Journal of Psychoanalysis, 72*, (4),639–656.

Fonagy, P. (1999). Memory and therapeutic action. *International Journal of Psychoanalysis, 80*, (2),, 215–224.

Fonagy, P. (2007). Attachment here and now: An interview with Peter Fonagy. *Attachment: New Directions in Psychotherapy and Relational Psychoanalysis, 1*.

Fonagy, P., Gergely, G., Jurist, E., & Target, M. (2002). *Affect regulation, mentalization and the development of the self*. New York: Other Press.

Fonagy, P., & Luyten, P. (2009). A developmental, mentalization-based approach to the understanding and treatment of borderline personality disorder. *Development and Psychopathology, 21*, 1355–1381.

Fonagy, P., & Tallindini-Shallice, M. (1993). Problems of psychoanalytic research in practice. *Bulletin of the Anna Freud Centre, 16*(1), 5–22.

Ford, G. (2001). *The contented little baby book: The simple secrets of calm, confident parenting*. New York: New American Library.

Fordham, F. (1958). *Ruthless greed*. Unpublished paper presented at the Society of Analytical Psychology. (Shortened version published in *Harvest, 9*, 1963).

Fordham, M. (1985). Defences of the self. In *Explorations into the self.* Library of Analytical Psychology, Vol. 7. London: Academic Press.

Fordham, M. (1996a). Analyst-patient interaction. In S. Shamdasani (Ed.), *Analyst-patient interaction: Collected papers on technique*. London: Routledge.

Fordham, M. (1996b). Analytical psychology and countertransference. In S. Shamdasani (Ed.), *Analyst-patient interaction: Collected papers on technique* (Chapter 15). London: Routledge.

Fordham, M. (1996c). Notes on the transference. In S. Shamdasani (Ed.), *Analyst-patient interaction: Collected papers on technique*. London: Routledge.

Fosshage, J. (2002). A relational self psychological perspective. *Journal of Analytical Psychology*, 47, (1),, 83–90.

Fosshage, J. (2004). The explicit and implicit dance in psychoanalytic change. *Journal of Analytical Psychology*, 49, 49–66.

Fraiberg, S., Adelson, E., & Shapiro, V. (1975). Ghosts in the nursery: A psychoanalytic approach to the problem of impaired infant-mother relationships. *Journal of the American Academy of Child Psychiatry*, 14, 387–422.

Freud, S. (1918). From the history of an infantile neurosis. In *Collected papers, Vol. III*. London: Hogarth.

Frith, C. D., & Frith, U. (1999). Interacting minds—a biological basis. *Science, 286*, 1692–1695.

Gabbard, G. (2003). Miscarriages of psychoanalytic treatment with suicidal patients. *International Journal of Psychoanalysis, 84*, 249–261.

Gallagher, S. (2000). Philosophical conceptions of the self: Implications for cognitive science. *Trends in Cognitive Sciences, 4*(1), 14–21.

Gallagher, S. (2006). How the body shapes the mind: An interview with Shaun Gallagher by Thomas Z. Ramsoy. *Science and Consciousness Review, 1.*

Gallese, V. (2007). Before and below "theory of mind": Embodied simulation and the neural correlates of social cognition. *Philosophical Transactions of the Royal Society, 362*, 659–669.

Gallese, V. (2009). Motor abstraction: A neuroscientific account of how action goals and intentions are mapped and understood. *Psychological Research, 73*, (4), 486–498.

Gallese, V., & Lakoff, G. (2005). The brain's concepts: The role of the sensory-motor system in conceptual knowledge. *Cognitive Neuropsychology, 22*, 455–479.

Gallese, V., Rochat, M., Cossu, G., & Sinigaglia, G. (2009). Motor cognition and its role in the phylogeny and ontogeny of action understanding. *Developmental Psychology, 45*, (1), 103–113.

Gallese, V., & Sinigaglia, S. (2010). The bodily self as power for action. *Neuropsychologia, 48*, 746–755.

Gallese, V., & Umilta, M. (2002). From self-modelling to the self-model: Agency and the representation of the self. *Neuropsychoanalysis, 4*(2), 35–40.

Georgaca, E. (2001). Voices of the self in psychotherapy: A qualitative analysis. *British Journal of Medical Psychology, 74*, 223–236.

Gergely, G., & Watson, J. (1996). The social biofeedback model of parental affective mirroring. *International Journal of Psychoanalysis, 77*, 1181–1212.

Gerhardt, S. (2005). *Why love matters*. London: Brunner-Routledge.

Gerhardt, S. (2010). *The selfish society: How we all forgot to love one another and made money instead*. New York: Simon & Schuster.

Goldberg, S., Blokland, K., Cayetano, P., & Benoit, D. (1998). Across the transmission gap: Adult attachment and response to infant emotions. Paper presented at the Waterloo Conference on Child Development, University of Waterloo, Ontario.

Gordon, R. (1978). *Dying and creating: A search for meaning*. London: The Society of Analytical Psychology. Reprinted London: Karnac Books (2000).

Gotthold, J. J., & Sorter, D. (2006). Moments of meeting: An exploration of the implicit dimensions of empathic immersion in adult and child treatment. *International Journal of Psychoanalytic Self Psychology, 1*, 103–119.

Gould, S. J. (2001). *The lying stones of Marrakesh: Penultimate reflections in natural history*. New York: Vintage.

Green, A. (1986). The dead mother. In *On private madness*. London: Hogarth.

Greenberg, J. (1964). *I never promised you a rose garden*. New York: Penguin.

Greenberg, J. R., & Mitchell, S. (1983). *Object relations in psychoanalytic theory*. Cambridge, MA: Harvard University Press.

Greicius, M. D., Kiviniemi, V., Tervonen, O., Vainionpää, V., Alahuhta, S., Reiss, A. L., et al. (2008). Persistent default-mode network connectivity during light sedation. *Human Brain Mapping, 29*, (7), 839–847.

Grotstein, J. (1983). Review of Tustin's *Autistic States in Children.* *International Review of Psychoanalysis, 10,* 491–498.

Hamilton, V. (1996). *The analyst's preconscious.* Hillsdale, NJ: Analytic Press.

Hayes, A. M., Castonguay, L. G., & Goldfried, M. R. (1996). Effectiveness of targeting the vulnerability factors of depression in cognitive therapy. *Journal of Consulting and Clinical Psychology, 64,* 623–627.

Heimann, P. (1973). Certain functions of introjection and projection in early infancy. In M. Klein, P. Heimann, S. Isaacs, & J. Riviere (Eds.), *Developments in psychoanalysis.* London: Hogarth.

Hendriks-Jansen, H. (1996). *Catching ourselves in the act: Situated activity, interactive emergence, evolution and human thought.* Cambridge, MA: MIT Press.

Henry, J. P. (1993). Psychological and physiological responses to stress: The right hemisphere and the hypothalamo-pituitary-adrenal axis, an inquiry into problems of human bonding. *Integrative Physiological and Behavioral Science, 28,* 369–387.

Hermans, H., & Kempen, H. (1993). *The Dialogical Self: Meaning as Movement.* San Francisco: Academic Press.

Hermans, H., Rijks, T., & Kempen, H. (1993). Imaginal dialogues in the self: Theory and method. *Journal of Personality, 61,* 207–235.

Hesse, E. (1999). The Adult Attachment Interview: Historical and current perspectives. In J. Cassidy & P. Shaver (Eds.), *Handbook of attachment: Theory, research and clinical applications* (Chapter 19). New York: Guilford.

Hewison, D. (2005). Sex and the imagination in supervision and therapy. *Psychoanalytic Perspectives on Couple Work, 1,* 72–87.

Hinshelwood, R.D. (1989). *A dictionary of kleinian thought.* London: Free Association Books.

Hobson, R. (1985). *Forms of feeling: The heart of psychotherapy.* London: Tavistock.

Hoelzer, M., & Dahl, H. (1996). How to find FRAMES. *Psychotherapy Research, 6,* 177–197.

Hogenson, G. (2004). Archetypes, emergence and the psyche's deep structure. In J. Cambray & L. Carter (Eds.), *Analytical psychology: Contemporary perspectives in Jungian analysis* (Chapter 2). New York: Brunner-Routledge.

Hogenson, G. (2009). Synchronicity and moments of meeting. *Journal of Analytical Psychology, 54,* (2), 183–198.

Holmes, J. (2001). *The search for the secure base.* London: Brunner-Routledge.

Hopper, E. (1991). Encapsulation as a defence against the fear of annihilation. *International Journal of Psychoanalysis, 72*, (4), 607–624.

Isaacs, S. (1992). The nature and function of phantasy. In P. King & R. Steiner (Eds.), *The Freud/Klein controversies 1941–45* (pp. 264–321). London: Routledge. (Original work published 1952)

Jacobson, E. (1965). *The self and the object world.* London: Hogarth.

Jaffe, J., Beebe, B., Feldstein, S., Crown, C., & Jasnow, M. D. (2001). Rhythms of dialogue in infancy: Coordinated timing in development. *Monographs of the Society for Research in Child Development, 66*, (2), Serial No. 265).

James, H. (1957). The art of fiction. In *The House of Fiction: Essays On the Novel by Henry James,* Ed. Leon Edel. London: Rupert Hart-Davis.

James, W. (1983). *Principles of psychology._*Harvard University Press. (Original work published 1890)

Johnson, M. (1987). *The body in the mind: The bodily basis of meaning, imagination and reason.* Chicago: University of Chicago Press.

Johnson, M. H., & Morton, J. (1991). *Biology and cognitive development: The case of face recognition.* Oxford: Blackwell.

Jones, R. (2003). Between the analytic and the critical: Implications for theorizing the self. *Journal of Analytical Psychology, 48,* 355–370.

Joseph, B. (1982). Addiction to near-death. *International Journal of Psychoanalysis, 63,* 449–456.

Jung, C. G. (1966a). Principles of practical psychotherapy. In *Collected works of C. G. Jung: Vol. 16* (G. Adler & R. F. C. Hull, Ed. and Trans.). Princeton, NJ: Princeton University Press.

Jung, C. G. (1966b). Problems of modern psychotherapy. In *Collected works of C. G. Jung: Vol. 16* (G. Adler & R. F. C. Hull, Ed. and Trans.). Princeton, NJ: Princeton University Press.

Jung, C. G. (1966c). The psychology of the transference. In *Collected works of C. G. Jung: Vol. 16* (G. Adler & R. F. C. Hull, Ed. and Trans.). Princeton, NJ: Princeton University Press. The 1966 Edition was published by RKP in the UK and by the Bollingen Foundation in the U.S.

Jung, C. G. (1966d). The realities of practical psychotherapy. In *Collected works of C. G. Jung: Vol. 16* (G. Adler & R. F. C. Hull, Ed. and Trans.). Princeton, NJ: Princeton University Press. The 1966 Edition was published by RKP in the UK and by the Bollingen Foundation in the U.S.

Jung, C. G. (1967). The structure of the unconscious. In *Collected works of C. G. Jung: Vol. 7* (G. Adler & R. F. C. Hull, Ed. and Trans.). Princeton, NJ: Princeton University Press.

Jung, C. G. (1968). Psychology and alchemy. In *Collected works of C. G. Jung: Vol. 12* (G. Adler & R. F. C. Hull, Ed. and Trans.). Princeton, NJ: Princeton University Press.

Jung, C. G. (1969). Conscious, unconscious and individuation. In *Collected works of C. G. Jung: Vol. 9, part 1.* (G. Adler & R. F. C. Hull, Ed. and Trans.). Princeton, NJ: Princeton University Press.

Jung, C. G. (1970). The transcendent function. In_*Collected works of C. G. Jung: Vol. 8* (G. Adler & R. F. C. Hull, Ed. and Trans.). Princeton, NJ: Princeton University Press.

Jung, C. G. (1971). Definitions. In *Collected works of C. G. Jung: Vol. 6* (G. Adler & R. F. C. Hull, Ed. and Trans.). Princeton, NJ: Princeton University Press.

K. (2008). Report from borderland: An addendum to "What works?" *Journal of Analytical Psychology, 53*, (1), 19–30.

Kalsched, D. (1996). *The inner world of trauma: Archetypal defences of the personal spirit.* London: Routledge.

Kampe, K. K. W., Frith, C. D., & Frith, U. (2003). "Hey John": Signals conveying communicative intention toward the self activate brain regions associated with "mentalizing," regardless of modality. *Journal of Neuroscience, 23*, 5258–5263.

Karen, R. (1998). *Becoming attached: First relationships and how they shape our capacity to love.* New York: Oxford University Press.

Karmiloff-Smith, A. (1992). *Beyond modularity: A developmental perspective on cognitive science.* Cambridge, MA: MIT Press.

Kaye, K. (1982). Organism, apprentice and person. In E. Z. Tronick (Ed.), *Social Interchange in Infancy* (pp. 183–196). Baltimore: University Park Press.

Khan, M. (1974). The concept of cumulative trauma. In *The privacy of the self.* London: Hogarth.

Killingmo, B. (1989). Conflict and deficit: Implications for technique. *International Journal of Psychoanalysis, 70*, (1), 65–80.

Kinney, H. C., Brody, B. A., Kloman, A. S., & Gilles, F. H. (1988). Sequence of central nervous system myelination in human infancy. II. Patterns of myelination in autopsied infants. *Journal of Neuropathology and Experimental Neurology, 47*, 217–234.

Knox, J. (1995). Alcohol: A drug of dreams. *Journal of Analytical Psychology*, *40*, 161–175.

Knox, J. (2003). *Archetype, attachment, analysis: Jungian psychology and the emergent mind*. London: Routledge.

Knox, J. (2005). Sex, shame and the transcendent function: The function of fantasy in self-development. *Journal of Analytical Psychology*, *50*, (5), 617–640.

Knox, J. (2007a). The fear of love. *Journal of Analytical Psychology*, *52*, (5), 543–564.

Knox, J. (2007b). Who owns the unconscious? Or why psychoanalysts need to "own" Jung. In A. Casement (Ed.), *Who owns Jung?* London: Karnac.

Knox, J. (2009). When words do not mean what they say: Self-agency and the coercive use of language. *Journal of Analytical Psychology*, *54*, (1), 25–41.

Kohut, H. (1971). *The analysis of the self: A systematic approach to the psychoanalytic treatment of narcissistic personality disorders*. London: Hogarth.

Kohut, H. (1984). *How does analysis cure?* Chicago: University of Chicago Press.

Koos, O., & Gergely, G. (2001). A contingency-based approach to the etiology of "disorganized" attachment: The flickering switch hypothesis. *Bulletin of the Menninger Clinic*, *65*, 397–410.

Kundera, M. (1984). *The unbearable lightness of being*. London: Faber & Faber.

Lakoff, G., & Johnson, M. (1980). *Metaphors we live by*. Chicago: University of Chicago Press.

Lambert, M. J., Garfield, S. L., & Bergin, A. E. (2003). Overview, trends and future issues. In M. J. Lambert (Ed.), *Bergin and Garfield's handbook of psychotherapy and behaviour change* (5th ed.). New York: Wiley.

Ledermann, R. (1991). Regression and stagnation. *Journal of Analytical Psychology*, *36*, (4), 483–504.

Lepper, G. (2009a). The pragmatics of therapeutic interaction: An empirical study. *International Journal of Psychoanalysis*, *90*, (5), 1075–1094.

Lepper, G. (2009b). Response to "The future of the transference-based therapies." *British Journal of Psychotherapy*, *25*, (3), 352–355.

Lepper, G., & Riding, N. (2006). *Researching the psychotherapy process: A practical guide to transcript-based methods.* Basingstoke: Palgrave Macmillan.

Levinson, S. (2002). On the human interaction engine. in N. J. Enfield & S. C. Levinson (Eds.), *Roots of human sociality: Culture, cognition and interaction* (Chapter 1). Oxford: Berg.

Lewis, M., Allesandri, S. M., & Sullivan, M. W. (1990). Violation of expectancy, loss of control and anger expressions in young infants. *Developmental Psychology, 26,* (5), 745–751.

Lewontin, R. (2000). *It ain't necessarily so: The dream of the human genome and other illusions.* London: Granta Books.

Lichtenberg, J. D., Lachmann, F. M., & Fosshage, J. L. (2002). *A spirit of inquiry: Communication in psychoanalysis.* Hillsdale, NJ: Analytic Press.

Lieberman, A. (1999). Negative maternal attributions: Effects on toddlers' sense of self. *Psychoanalytic Inquiry, 19,* (5), 737–754.

Lipsey, M. W., & Wilson, D. B. (1993). The efficacy of psychological, educational, and behavioral treatment: Confirmation from meta-analysis. *American Psychologist, 48,* 1181–1209.

Lizkowski, U. (2006). Infant pointing at 12 months: Communicative goals, motives and social-cognitive abilities. In N. J. Enfield & S. Levinson (Eds.), *Roots of human sociality: Culture, cognition and interaction.* Oxford: Berg.

Lodge, D. (1997). Harold Pinter's last to go: A structuralist analysis. In *The practice of writing.* Penguin Books.

Lombardi, R. (2002). Primitive mental states and the body: A personal view of Armando B. Ferrari's concrete original object. *International Journal of Psychoanalysis, 83,* (2), 363–381.

Luborsky, L., Diguer, L., Seligman, D. A., Rosenthal, R., Krause, E. D., Johnson, S., et al. (1999). The researcher's own therapy allegiances: A "wild card" in comparisons of treatment efficacy. *Clinical Psychology: Science and Practice, 6,* 95–106.

Luborsky, L., Singer, B., & Luborsky, L. (1975). Comparative studies of psychotherapy: Is it true that "Everyone has won and all must have prizes?" *Archives of General Psychiatry, 32,* 995–1008.

Lyons-Ruth, K. (1999). The two-person unconscious: Intersubjective dialogue, enactive relational representation, and the emergence of new forms of relational organization. *Psychoanalytic Inquiry, 19,* 576–617.

Lyons-Ruth, K. (2008) Contributions of the mother-infant relationship to dissociative, borderline, and conduct symptoms in young adulthood. *Infant Mental Heqlth Journql, VOL.,* 203–218.

Lyins-Ruth, K., Bronfman, E., & Parsons, E. (1999) maternal disrupted affective communication, maternal frightened or frightening behavior, and disorganized infant attachment strategies. *Monographs of the Society for Research in Child Development*, 64, (3), Serial No. 258.

Maclean, P. D. (1990). *The triune brain in evolution: Role in paleocerebral functions*. New York: Plenum.

Mandler, J. (1992). How to build a baby: II. Conceptual primitives. *Psychological Review*, 99, ()587–604.

Martin-Vallas, F. (2005). Towards a theory of the integration of the other in representation. *Journal of Analytical Psychology*, 50, (3), 285–294.

Marvin, R., Cooper, G., Hoffman, K., & Powell, B. (2002). The Circle of Security project: Attachment-based interventions with caregiver-preschool dyads. *Attachment and Human Development*, 4, (1), 107–124.

McDougall, J. (1995). *The many faces of eros: A psychoanalytic exploration of human sexuality*. London: Free Association Books.

Meares, R. (2004). The conversational model: an outline. *American Journal of Psychotherapy*, 58, (1), 51–66.

Meares, R. (1998). The self in conversation: On narratives, chronicles and scripts. *Psychoanalytic Dialogues*, 8, 875–891.

Meltzer, D. (1995). Donald Meltzer in discussion. In S. Ruszczynski & J. Fisher (Eds.), *Intrusiveness and intimacy in the couple* (Chapter 6). London: Tavistock Institute of Marital Studies.

Meltzoff, A. N. (2005). Imitation and other minds: The "like me" hypothesis. In S. Hurley & N. Chater (Eds.), *Perspectives on imitation: From neuroscience to social science* (Vol. 2, pp. 55–77). Cambridge, MA: MIT Press.

Meltzoff, A. N., & Gopnik, A. (1993). The role of imitation in understanding persons and developing a theory of mind. In S. Baron-Cohen, H. Tager-Flusberg, & D. Cohen (Eds.), *Understanding other minds: Perspectives from autism* (pp. 335–366). New York: Oxford University Press.

Merchant, J. (2009). A reappraisal of classical archetypal theory and its implications for theory and practice. *Journal of Analytical Psychology*, 54, (3), 339–358.

Miller, A. (1988). *The drama of being a child*. New York: Virago.

Miller, B. L., Seeley, W. W., Mychack, P., Rosen, H. J., Mena, I., & Boone, K. (2001). Neuroanatomy of the self: Evidence from patients with frontotemporal dementia. *Neurology*, 57, 817–821.

Mitchell, S. (1988). *Relational concepts in psychoanalysis: An integration.* Cambridge, MA: Harvard University Press.

Mitchell, S. (2002). *Can love last? The fate of romance over time.* New York: Norton.

Modell, A. (1984). *Psychoanalysis in a new context.* New York: International Unversities Press.

Modinos, G., Ormel, J., & Aleman, A. (2009). Activation of anterior insula during self-reflection. *PLoS ONE, 4,* (2), e4618.

Mollon, P. (1996). *Multiple selves, multiple voices: Working with trauma, violation and dissociation.* Chichester: John Wiley.

Morgan, D. (2008). Enactments: Moving from deadly ways of relating to the beginnings of mental life. *British Journal of Psychotherapy, 24,* (2), 151–166.

Neimeyer, R. (2009). *Constructivist psychotherapy: Distinctive features.* Philadelphia: Taylor & Francis.

Northoff, G., & Panksepp, J. (2008). The trans-species concept of self and the subcortical-cortical midline system. *Trends in Cognitive Science, 12,* (7), 259–264.

Ogden, T. (1999). *Reverie and interpretation: Sensing something human.* London: Karnac.

Orwell, G. (1954). *Nineteen eighty-four.* New York: Penguin.

Oyama, S. (2000). *The ontogeny of information. Developmental systems and evolution.* Durham, NC: Duke University Press.

Palmer, G. B. (2007). Cognitive linguistics and anthropological linguistics. In D. Geeraerts & H. Cuyckens (Eds.), *The Oxford handbook of cognitive linguistics* (pp. 1045–1073). New York: Oxford University Press.

Panksepp, J. (1998). *Affective neuroscience: The foundations of human and animal emotion.* New York: Oxford University Press.

Panksepp, J. (2008). Carving "Natural" Emotions: "Kindly" from bottom-up but not top-down. *Journal of Theoretical and Philosophical Psychology, 28,* (2), 401–423.

Panksepp, J., & Northoff, G. (2009). The trans-species core SELF: The emergence of active cultural and neuro-ecological agents through self-related processing within subcortical midline networks. *Consciousness and Cognition, 18,* 193–215.

Panksepp, J., & Panksepp, J. B. (2000). The seven sins of evolutionary psychology. *Evolution and Cognition, 6,* (2), 108–131.

Papousek, H., & Papousek, M. (1974). Mirror-image and

self-recognition in young human infants: A new method of experimental analysis. *Developmental Psychobiology*, 7, 149–157.

Parsons, M. (2000). Sexuality and perversion a hundred years on: Discovering what Freud discovered. *International Journal of Psychoanalysis*, *81*, (1), 37–52.

Peck, S. D. (2003). Measuring sensitivity moment-by-moment: A microanalytic look at the transmission of attachment. *Attachment and Human Development*, *5*, 38–63.

Peirce, C. (1955). Logic as semiotic: The theory of signs. In J. Buchler (Ed.), *The Philosophical Writings of Peirce* (pp. 98–119). New York: Dover.

Perlow, M. (1995). *Understanding mental objects*. London: Routledge.

Petkova, V., & Ehrsson, H. (2008). If I were you: Perceptual illusion of body swapping. *PloS One*, *3*(12), e3832.

Pickering, J. (2006). Who's afraid of the Wolfe couple: The interlocking traumatic scene. *Journal of Analytical Psychology*, *51*, (2), 173–327.

Pinker, S. (1994). *The language instinct: The new science of language and mind*. London: Allen Lane/Penguin.

Pinker, S. (1997). *How the mind works*. London: Allen Lane/Penguin.

Pinter, H. (1991). *The caretaker*. London: Faber & Faber..

Pinter, H. (1999). *Various Voices: Sixty years of Prose, Poetry, Politics 1948–2008*. London: Faber & Faber.

Rachman, S., & Shafran, R. (1999). Cognitive distortions: Thought-action fusion. *Clinical Psychology and Psychotherapy*, *6*, 80–85.

Raichle, M., MacLeod, A. M., Snyder, A. Z., Powers, W. J., Gusnard, D. A., & Shulman, G. (2001). A default mode of brain function. *Proceedings of the National Academy of Sciences*, *98*, (2), 676–682.

Reis, B. (2005). The self is alive and well and living in relational psychoanalysis. *Psychoanalytic Psychology*, *22*, 86–95.

Reis, B. (2006). Even better than the real thing. *Contemporary. Psychoanalysis*, *42*, 177–196.

Reis, B. (2009). We: Commentary on papers by Trevarthen, Ammaniti and Trentini, and Gallese. *Psychoanalytic Dialogues*, *19*, 565–579.

Rinaman, L., Levitt, P., & Card, J. P. (2000). Progressive postnatal assembly of limbic-autonomic circuits revealed by central transneuronal transport of pseudorabies virus. *Journal of Neuroscience*, *20*, 2731–2741.

Rizzolatti, G., & Luppino, G. (2001). The cortical motor system. *Neuron*, *31*, 889–901.

Rizzolatti, G., & Sinigaglia, C. (2008). *Mirrors in the brain: How our minds share actions and emotions.* Oxford: Oxford University Press.

Rotmann, M. (2002). The alienness of the unconscious: On Laplanche's theory of seduction. *Journal of Analytical Psychology, 47,* (2), 265–278.

Salman, S. (1997). The creative psyche: Jung's major contributions. In P. Young-Eisendrath & T. Dawson (Eds.), *The Cambridge companion to Jung.* New York: Cambridge University Press.

Sander, L. (2002). Thinking differently: Principles of process in living systems and the specificity of being known. *Psychoanalytic Dialogues, 12,* 11–42.

Sandler, J. (1976). Countertransference and role responsiveness. *International Review of Psychoanalysis, 3,* 43–47.

Sandler, J., Holder, A., Dare, C., & Dreher, A.-U. (1997). *Freud's models of the mind: An introduction.* London: Karnac.

Sandler, J., & Joffe, W. G. (1967). The tendency to persistence in psychological function and development, with special reference to fixation and regression. *Bulletin of the Menninger Clinic, 31,* 257–271.

Savage-Rumbaugh, S., & Lewin, R. (1994). *Kanzi: The ape at the brink of the human mind.* New York: Wiley.

Schore, A. N. (1994). *Affect regulation and the origin of the self.* Mahwah, NJ: Erlbaum.

Schore, A. N. (2001). The effect of early relational trauma on right brain development, affect regulation and infant mental health. *Infant Mental Health Journal, 22*(1–2), 201–269.

Schore, A. N. (2003a). *Affect disregulation and disorders of the self.* New York: Norton.

Schore, A. N. (2003b). *Affect regulation and the repair of the self.* New York: Norton.

Schore, A. N. (2005). A neuropsychoanalytic viewpoint: Commentary on paper by Steven H. Knoblauch. *Psychoanalytic Dialogues, 15,* 829–853.

Schore, A. N. (2009). Relational trauma and the developing right brain: An interface of psychoanalytic self psychology and neuroscience. *Annals of the New York Academy of Sciences, 1159,* 189–203.

Schore, J. R., & Schore, A. N. (2008). Modern attachment theory: The central role of affect regulation in development and treatment. *Clinical Social Work Journal, 36,* 9–20.

Schwartz, J. (1999). *Cassandra's daughter: A history of psychoanalysis in Europe and America.* London: Allen Lane/Penguin.

Segal, H. (1986). *The work of Hanna Segal: A Kleinian approach to clinical practice*. London: Free Association Books/Maresfield Library.

Seligman, E. (1982). The half-alive ones. *Journal of Analytical Psychology, 27*, (1), 1–20.

Sell, R. (2007). Introduction: Literature as communication. *Nordic Journal of English Studies, 6*, (2), 1–16.

Shamdasani, S. (2003). *Jung and the making of modern psychology: The dream of a science*. New York: Cambridge University Press.

Shapiro, D., Barkham, M., Hardy, G. E., & Morrison, L. A. (1990). The second Sheffield Psychotherapy Project: Rationale, design and preliminary outcomes. *British Journal of Medical Psychology, 63*, (2), 97–108.

Shedler, J. (2010). The efficacy of psychodynamic psychotherapy. *American Psychologist, 65*, (2), 98–109.

Shweder, R. A. (1990). Cultural psychology—what is it? In J. W. Stigler, R. A. Shweder, & G. Herdt (Eds.), *Cultural psychology: Essays on comparative human development* (pp. 1–43). Cambridge: Cambridge University Press.

Sidoli, M. (1993). When meaning gets lost in the body: Psychosomatic disturbance as a failure of the transcendent function. *Journal of Analytical Psychology, 38*, (2), 175.

Siegel, D. (1998). The developing mind: Toward a neurobiology of interpersonal experience. *The Signal, 6*, 3–4, 1–11.

Siegel, D. J. (1999). *Developing mind: Toward a neurobiology of interpersonal experience*. New York: Guilford.

Siegel, D. (2003). An interpersonal neurobiology of psychotherapy. In M. Solomon & D. Siegel (Eds.), *Healing trauma: Attachment, mind, body, and brain*. New York: Norton.

Siegel, P., & Demorest, A. (2010). Affective scripts: A systematic case study of change in psychotherapy. *Psychotherapy Research*, March 23, 1–19 (Epub ahead of print).

Siegel, P., Sammons, M., & Dahl, H. (2002). FRAMES: The method in action and the assessment of its reliability. *Psychotherapy Research, 12*, 59–77.

Sinason, V. (2002). *Attachment, trauma and multiplicity: Working with dissociative identity disorder*. London: Brunner-Routledge.

Sinigaglia, C. (2008). Mirror neurons: This is the question. *Journal of Consciousness Studies, 15*, (10–11), 70–92.

Slade, A. (1999). Representation, symbolization and affect regulation in the concomitant treatment of a mother and child: Attachment theory and child psychotherapy. *Psychoanalytic Inquiry, 19,* (5), 797–830.

Smith, M. L., & Glass, G. V. (1977). Meta-analysis of psychotherapy outcome studies. *American Psychologist, 32,* 752–760.

Solomon, H. (2004). Self-creation and the limitless void of dissociation: The "as-if" personality. *Journal of Analytical Psychology, 49,* 635–656.

Spillius, E. (2001). Freud and Klein on the concept of phantasy. *International Journal of Psychoanalysis, 82,* (2), 361–373.

Steele, H., Steele, M., & Fonagy, P. (1996). Associations among attachment classifications of mothers, fathers and their infants. *Child Development, 67,* 541–555.

Stein, M. (2008). Divinity expresses the self: An investigation. *Journal of Analytical Psychology, 53,* (3), 305–328.

Steiner, J. (1993). *Psychic retreats: Pathological organization in psychotic, neurotic and borderline patients.* London: Routledge.

Stern, D. (1985). *The interpersonal world of the infant: A view from psychoanalysis and developmental psychology.* New York: Basic Books.

Stevens, A. (2002). *Archetype revisited: An updated natural history of the self.* London: Brunner-Routledge.

Stoller, R. (1977). *Perversion: The erotic form of hatred.* London: Quartet Books.

Sullivan, R. M., & Dufresne, M. M. (2006). Mesocortical dopamine and HPA axis regulation: Role of laterality and early environment. *Brain Research, 1076,* 49–59.

Talamini, L. M., Koch, T., Luiten, P. G. M., Koolhaas, J. M., & Korf, J. (1999). Interruptions of early cortical development affect limbic association areas and social behavior in rats: Possible relevance for neurodevelopmental disorders. *Brain Research, 847,* 105–120.

Taub, G. (2009). A confusion of tongues between psychoanalysis and philosophy: Is the controversy over drive versus relational theory a philosophical one? *International Journal of Psychoanalysis, 90,* (3), 507–527.

Taumoepeau, M., & Ruffman, T. (2008). Stepping stones to others' minds: Maternal talk relates to child mental state language and emotion understanding at 15, 24, and 33 months. *Child Development, 79,* (2), 284–302.

Tooby, J., & Cosmides, L. (2005). Conceptual foundations of evolutionary psychology. In D. M. Buss (Ed.), *The handbook of evolutionary psychology* (pp. 5–67). Hoboken, NJ: Wiley.

Trevarthen, C. (1993). The self born in intersubjectivity: An infant communicating. In U. Neisser (Ed.), *The perceived self.* New York: Cambridge University Press.

Tronick, E. (2007). *The neurobiological and social-emotional development of children.* New York: Norton.

Tuckett, D. (2005). Does anything go? Towards a framework for the more transparent assessment of psychoanalytic competence. *International Journal of Psycho-Analysis, 86,* 31–49.

Uddin, L. Q., Iacoboni, M., Lange, C., & Keenan, J. P. (2007). The self and social recognition: The role of cortical midline structures and mirror neurons. *Trends in Cognitive Sciences, 11,* (4), 153–157.

Van den Boom, D. (1994). The influence of temperament and mothering on attachment and exploration: An experimental manipulation of sensitive responsiveness among lower-class mothers with irritable infants. *Child Development, 65,* 1457–1477.

Van den Boom, D. (1995). Do first-year intervention effects endure? Follow-up during toddlerhood of a sample of Dutch irritable infants. *Child Development, 66,* 1798–1816.

van der Hart, O., Nijenhuis, E., & Steele, K. (2006). *The haunted self: Structural dissociation and the treatment of chronic traumatization.* New York: Norton.

Van der Kolk, B. A & Fisler, R. (1995). Dissociation and the fragmentary nature of traumatic memories: Overview and exploratory study. *Journal of Traumatic Stress, 8,* (4), 505–25.

Van der Kolk, B. A., & McFarlane, A. C. (1996). The Black Hole of Trauma. In B. A. Van der Kolk, A. C. McFarlane, & L. Weisaeth (Eds.), *Traumatic stress: The effects of overwhelming experience on mind, body and society.* New York: Guilford.

van Langenhove, L., & Harré, R. (1993). Positioning and autobiography: Telling your life. In N. Coupland & J. F. Nussbaum (Eds.), *Discourse and lifespan identity.* Newbury Park, NJ: Sage.

Vaughan, S., Spitzer, R., Davies, M., & Roose, S. (1997). The definition and assessment of analytic process: Can analysts agree? *International Journal of Psychoanalysis, 78,* 959–974.

Vygotsky, L. S. (1978). *Mind in society: The development of higher psychological processes.* Cambridge, MA: Harvard University Press.

Wallerstein, R. S. (1989). The psychotherapy research project of the Menninger Foundation: An overview. *Journal of Consulting and Clinical Psychology, 57,* 196–205.

Watson, J. S. (1994). Detection of self: The perfect algorithm. In S. Parker, R. Mitchell, & M. Boccia (Eds.), *Self-awareness in animals and humans: Developmental perspectives* (pp. 131–149). New York: Cambridge University Press.

Watson, J. S. (1995). Self-orientation in early infancy: The general role of contingency and the specific case of reaching to the mouth. In P. Rochat (Ed.), *The self in infancy: Theory and research* (pp. 375–393). Amsterdam: Elsevier.

West, M. (2007). *Feeling, being, and the sense of self: A new perspective on identity, affect and narcissistic disorders.* London: Karnac.

Whittle, P. (1999). Experimental psychology and psycho-analysis: What we can learn from a century of misunderstanding. *Neuropsychoanalysis, 1,* 233–245.

Wicker, B., Keysers, C., Plailly, J., Rovet, J. P., Gallese, V., & Rizzolatti, G. (2003). Both of us disgusted in my insula: The common neural basis of seeing and feeling disgust. In *Neuron, 40,* 655–664.

Wilkinson, M. (2003). Undoing trauma: Contemporary neuroscience. A Jungian clinical perspective. *Journal of Analytical Psychology, 48,* (2), 235–254.

Winnicott, D. (1965a). Ego distortions in terms of true and false self. In *The maturational process and the facilitating environment* (Chapter 12). London: Hogarth.

Winnicott, D. (1965b). The theory of the parent-infant relationship. In *The maturational process and the facilitating environment: Studies in the theory of emotional development* (Chapter 3). London: Hogarth.

Winnicott, D. (1971a). Interrelating in terms of cross-identifications. In *Playing and reality* (Chapter 10). London: Tavistock.

Winnicott, D. (1971b). The use of an object and relating through identifications. In *Playing and reality.* London: Tavistock.

Winnicott, D. (1975). Transitional objects and transitional phenomena. In *Through paediatrics to psychoanalysis.* London: Hogarth.

Index